P9-BIQ-245

PURE PORK AWESOMENESS

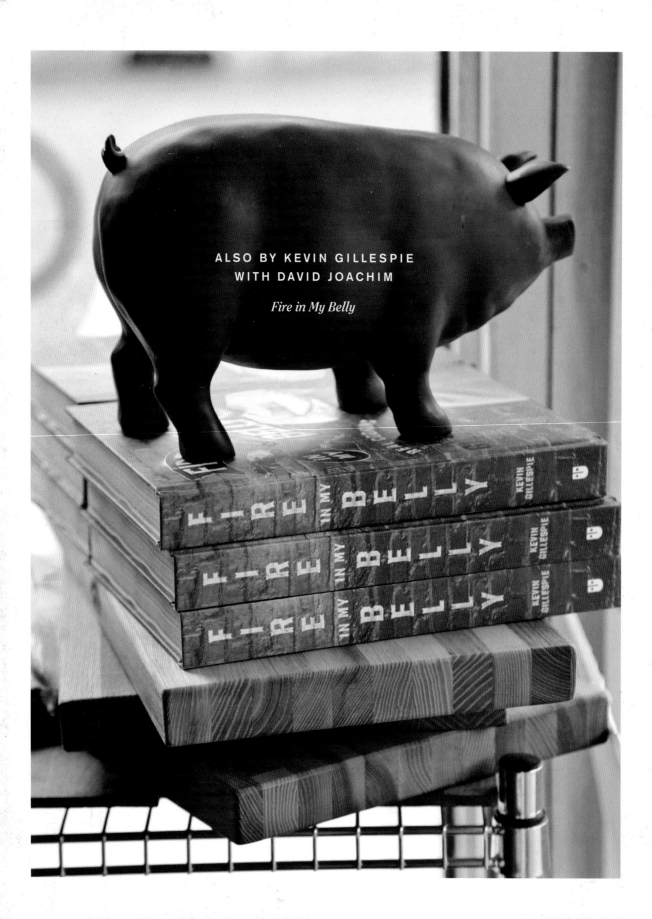

ALSO BY KEVIN GILLESPIE
WITH DAVID JOACHIM

Fire in My Belly

TOTALLY COOKABLE RECIPES FROM AROUND THE WORLD

PURE

Pork

AWESOMENESS

KEVIN GILLESPIE

With DAVID JOACHIM

PHOTOGRAPHY BY ANGIE MOSIER

Andrews McMeel
Publishing

Kansas City · Sydney · London

To all the pig farmers and ranchers
who meet the challenge of raising
great-tasting pork

CONTENTS

KISS A PIG

"KISS A PIG, HUG A SWINE
SOME OF THEM ARE GOOD FRIENDS OF MINE
I'M ESPECIALLY FOND OF THOSE
POLAND CHINA PORKERS
MORE FUN THAN A DOG AND
SMARTER THAN A HORSE
YOU MIGHT FIND THEM A LITTLE COARSE
BUT THEY AIN'T NEAR AS RUDE
AS SOME NEW YORKERS."

—RAY STEVENS, "KISS A PIG"

My Dad had a cassette tape of this Ray Stevens song in his little yellow pickup truck. When I was a kid, we'd ride around in the truck doing errands and he'd play the whole album, *I Have Returned*. It's all funny country songs with jokes that a kid can understand. "Kiss a Pig" is upbeat and easy to sing along with. Stevens sings about a pig that falls off the back of a truck, and he picks up the pig and they become friends. He takes the pig to a zoo and a ball game. The pig rides around in his car wearing a baseball cap. It's funny. But the line that really sticks with me is, "He was my buddy, he was my friend, he was my breakfast every now and then." That pretty much sums up my feeling toward pigs.

I love them as animals and I love them as meat. If I had only one animal to eat forevermore, I would eat pigs. Like Bubba Gump and his shrimp, I have a million ways to cook pork because I love it so much. I could eat a pork chop one day, pulled pork another, and bacon the next, and they'd all taste completely different. You can't do that with chicken. Chicken tastes like chicken no matter what part of the animal you eat. I love beef and lamb, but they don't have the amazing versatility of pork. Pork can be the star of the show or a background flavor.

This book is not a tome on mastering pigs and pork. It's a celebration of all the delicious forms that this food can take. The whole world is in love with this animal. They admire it and cook pork more than any other meat except goat. Everyone can find something delicious here. You'll find recipes for pork the way it's enjoyed in China, Germany, Mexico, Vietnam, Korea, Cuba, Thailand, Greece, Italy, Spain, France, Austria, Scotland, and the United States. From the United States, you'll see preparations that originated in places like

Kansas City, Chicago, Indianapolis, and Sheboygan, Wisconsin. I'm hoping this book opens some doors for people and gets them pumped about pork again. For a while there, only super-lean flavorless pork was available to consumers. But the quality and flavor just keep going up and up.

During recipe testing, I got excited all over again. There's just no end to what you can do with pork. Frying, roasting, braising, stir-frying, sausage-making . . . it's all here. And it's not hard. I developed these recipes specifically for everyday home cooks. A few dishes are more challenging, but mostly we're talking about things like A Really Good Cuban Sandwich (page 52), Sichuan Salt and Pepper Pork Chops (page 70), and Slow Cooker Country-Style Ribs (page 114). For special occasions or company, maybe you'll pull out the Celebration Pork Rack Stuffed with Dried Fruits (page 89), Vietnamese Spareribs with Chile and Lemongrass (page 112), or Banoffee Trifle with Candied Bacon (page 140). With dishes from Sunday morning Country Ham Breakfast Strata (page 171) to Friday night Serrano Ham Croquettes (page 165), I could eat pork every day of the week. Sometimes it's fancy; sometimes it's simple.

My hope is that this book becomes your go-to for cooking pork every which way. It's organized like the pig itself. The recipes start with cuts from the shoulder, then the loin of the pig, then the belly and hams (hind legs). Sausages, ground pork, and dishes using odds and ends like fatback and jowls come at the end.

Along the way, you'll come across tips on hog breeds and pork cooking methods, but if that's not your thing, this book is just a fun ride and a good read. Every day can be a reason to get on board and celebrate the incredible pig.

"I'VE ALWAYS LOVED PIGS: THE SHAPE OF THEM, THE LOOK OF THEM, AND THE FACT THAT THEY ARE SO INTELLIGENT."

—MAURICE SENDAK

№ 1

THIS LITTLE PIGGY

I always wanted a pet pig. I'm allergic to cats. Fish are boring. My mom is afraid of reptiles. And I don't think it's cool to cage birds. I wanted a pig. I'm not sure where the desire came from. None of my friends had a pig. But ever since I was a kid, I thought, "How cool would that be?" I had this vision of me walking with the pig on a leash. Me and Hamlet or whatever his name would be. My parents, of course, were not on board with this idea. They grew up witnessing firsthand the animals that ended up as food on their tables. They did not want Hamlet to end up as pork chops for dinner.

To give me a better understanding, they told me, "You should go play with some pigs." They took me to Noah's Ark, an animal rescue and wildlife preserve in Locust Grove, Georgia. Noah's Ark had horses, llamas, sheep, tigers, and bears, all of which had been neglected by their owners, kept illegally, or hurt in some way. You could pet the pigs—at least in theory. This is the day I learned that pigs are much smarter than I thought. I was determined to catch one. But they just ran and ran. An hour and a half later, I was completely ragged and still hadn't laid a hand on a single pig. I'm sure my parents thought it was hilarious, watching me chase piglets around this pen. That was a lesson. People have this impression that pigs are lumbering slobs, but nothing could be further from the truth. It turns out they're really fast. And smart.

Needless to say, my desire for having a pet pig was put to bed that day. We got a dog instead.

PIG FARMING

My interest in pigs, however, persisted throughout my life. After I became a chef, I went to Gum Creek Farms to see how they're raised. Gum Creek is in Roopville, Georgia, about an hour outside of Atlanta. The farmer, Tommy Searcy, raises Berkshire hogs. He also raises Hampshire hogs and a few Tamworth. Some cattle, too, just for themselves. It's a small mom-and-pop operation, but Gum Creek is focused on raising hogs the right way.

I was buying their pork for Woodfire Grill, and one day I thought, "We need to go see these pigs." In my mind, I had two visions: 1) me as a kid chasing a 25-pound piglet around a pen, and 2) a commercial pig factory farm in the middle of nowhere in the flatlands of Iowa. The reality was completely different. At Gum Creek, the pigs were all in the woods. Tommy fenced off a great deal of wooded area, and the pigs were free to roam. They move the fences now and then so the pigs can graze different areas, but the pigs find their way. Tommy and I talked for hours about how intelligent this animal is. If you watch them, you'll see pigs build these little spots where they sleep, their own little shelter. Of all the animals I've visited on farms—I'm talking about food animals like cattle, goats, and sheep that are destined to make their way to the dinner table— the only animals that seem to have a little more going on upstairs are pigs. Tommy's pigs were very curious and very gentle. They wanted to come up to you and almost chat because they were used to human contact. I even got to pick one up that day. In my mind, I thought a pig would feel sort of like one of those little stress balls—soft and squishy. But they're all muscle. It was more like picking up a boulder. And their hairs are coarse and wiry. I don't feel guilty about eating them. But there's something special about this animal.

I'd already developed quite a passion for eating pork, but visiting Gum Creek Farms gave me tremendous respect for pigs. It changed the way I viewed what I was cooking, serving, and eating. It drove me deeper into researching breeds and production methods.

Animal farming isn't all that different than anything else. When you scale up the project, you run the risk of the quality dropping precipitously. Crops are a little easier to scale up. But animals require your attendance day in and day out, 24/7. Just like human beings, animals also need space. If you try to pack too many in a confined area, they suffer. That's what we see nowadays when people talk about feedlots.

Tommy and Alicia Searcy have a lot of land—mostly wooded—so they contain the woods and let the animals go where they want to go. Their farming methods produce pork with a superior flavor and texture. Knowing that the animals were raised in the woods allows the person buying and cooking the pork to feel a little better about that choice. Despite what we'd like to believe, that all our food animals live a good life and drink up the sunshine outside, that image isn't always accurate. A farm is a farm. But we have the ability to judge right from wrong, and it seems right to provide animals with the space they need to thrive during their lives and to make sure they're not standing on concrete and wallowing in their own filth every day. Even if you don't care about the morality of it, and you say "Meat is meat—animals are for food," if you visited

WHY DO PIGS HAVE SNOUTS?

To sniff with! And to dig in the dirt for food. The bigger the snout, the better the sniffing and digging. A pig's sense of smell is so acute that the French use pigs to find wild truffles hidden among leaves and debris in the Périgord forests of southwest France. The Italians use dogs instead because Italian pigs just eat the truffles when they find them.

a feedlot facility and a pasture farm, I think you would still choose the animal coming off the farm. You would think the meat must be worth more and would taste better. And you'd be right.

I'm happy to lead the charge for better pork. At my restaurant and at home, I try every day to showcase this food's best qualities. I believe that pork, stacked side by side with all the other proteins we eat, is superior. Not just from a flavor perspective but also in terms of versatility and sustainability. Compared to beef, pork has dozens more uses and is far less impactful on the environment. My goal is to make sure we're raising, selling, and cooking with the best pork we can.

HOG BREEDING IN AMERICA

When looking for better pork, a lot of folks look to the heritage breeds of pigs. A little history helps explain why heritage pig breeds are all the rage these days. For many years, lard was the cooking fat of choice in the United States. Hog breeds like Berkshires and Tamworths were preferred because they were fatter and produced more available lard. It sounds crazy, but we didn't always cook with vegetable oils. The first hydrogenated oil was actually developed as a replacement for lard in 1911. It was made from cottonseed, and Procter & Gamble called it Crisco as an abbreviation of crystallized cottonseed oil. Up until then, we cooked in lard and raised big, fat pigs that produced lard first and meat second.

Through aggressive marketing, however, hydrogenated oil and margarine gradually replaced lard in the kitchen, and farmers had to cut their losses by finding breeds that produced more meat and grew faster. By the 1950s, Yorkshires became the breed of choice for those very reasons. Yorkshires are light-haired, pink-skinned pigs. Once this breed dominated the market, pink Yorkshire pigs became the quintessential image of all pigs. Just think of Porky Pig or Babe. But the reality is that different pig breeds have different looks (see Hog Breeds on pages 6–7).

The downside to this turn of events is that fast-growing pigs like Yorkshires don't develop as much flavor. They're too lean. In the 1960s and '70s, we were so hell-bent on producing lean meat that we forgot all about flavor. By 1987, to combat rising sales of lean, white-meat chicken, "Pork: The Other White Meat" became the famous calling card of lean commodity pork. Lo and behold, we now find ourselves in the situation where grocery store pork tastes pretty bland.

As it turns out, we've also discovered that hydrogenated oil and margarine are not any healthier for us than lard. Call it paleo or call it delicious: Consumers and farmers are now looking back to heritage breeds like Berkshires and Tamworths to bring back the meaty taste of pork. These breeds taste like pork should taste— porky, sweet, and with a satisfying chew. Do you need to ask your local farmers which breed they raise? Probably not. People will cite their favorite breeds, but buying a pastured product nearly guarantees you'll be eating some kind of heritage pork that will taste better than anything you can buy in a grocery store.

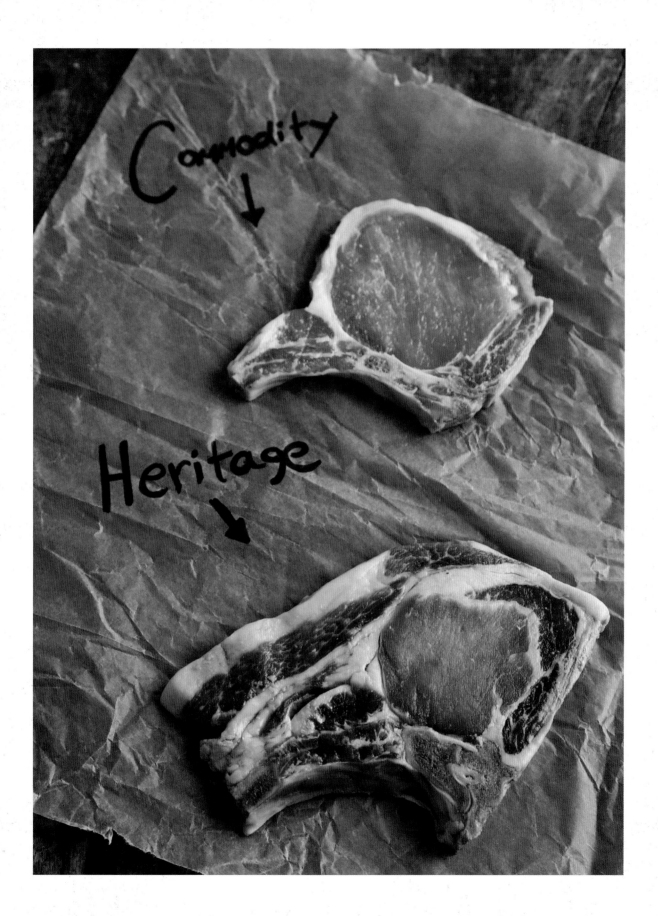

★ HOG BREEDS ★

YORKSHIRE AND POLAND CHINA WHITE: These are currently the predominant breeds for commodity pork production in the United States. These hogs have been bred for a consistently high proportion of lean meat with very little marbling and almost no back fat—something that the market demanded 50 years ago. Today, the demand is starting to shift back toward heritage breeds with more flavor. Here are some of the breeds you may have come across.

BERKSHIRE: One of the most popular heritage breeds, Berkshires are short, stocky pigs covered with dark hair. They have dense, sweet-tasting meat and a good balance of fat to lean. They're good all-around pigs for fresh meat and for curing into bacon and sausages. Farmers like them because they're docile. When bred in Japan, they're known as Kurobuta pigs.

DUROC: These broad, muscle-bound hogs have humongous hams and shoulders. They're like the offensive linemen of the pig world. They're slightly fattier than Berkshires. One downside is that they have downturned ears, which partially blocks their eyesight and makes them jumpy. They're one of the less docile breeds. Some pig farmers I know tried raising Durocs and would never do it again. These pigs are like meatheads that don't play well with others.

HAMPSHIRE: A black-and-white hog popular in Great Britain. Hampshires are among the leanest heritage breeds and fairly large in size, so they're valued for producing a great volume of meat.

HEREFORD: Just like Hereford cattle, this breed has a red body and a white face. It's a relatively new breed on the market and has an excellent meat-to-fat ratio. The meat is extremely sweet, tender, and flavorful, and the fat is dense and delicious.

Hampshire pigs

TAMWORTH: The limo of hog breeds, Tamworths look like stretched-out pigs. They're jokingly referred to as "bacon hogs" due to their humongous middles. They have a little less fat than Berkshires but take to curing very well. The flavor is good, but their major benefit is economic because of all the bacon you can sell off them. Breeders sometimes cross the Tamworth with other breeds to create a more stretched-out hog.

Tamworth pigs

MANGALITSA: This heritage breed from Austria only made it to the United States seven to ten years ago. Also known as wooly pigs, they're covered in curly, tan hair. These are funny-looking, cold-weather pigs bred to produce cured meat and lard. They have insane amounts of back fat—sometimes 12 inches thick. That's perfect for making lardo, but if you used this breed for barbecue, I'd laugh at you. It would be an inferno. The meat tastes delicious, but this is a true lard hog.

OSSABAW: Off the coast of Georgia, Ossabaw Island is considered one of the first places where hogs were raised. The Ossabaw is a flavorful and fattier form of feral or wild pig. This hog results from a domesticated herd returning to its feral nature. It's a little smaller in stature, with darker, gamier-tasting meat. They're a nightmare to raise and breed. When raised with other breeds, Ossabaws often fight and sometimes kill the other pigs. They're the wild and crazy cousins in the world of heritage pigs.

Berkshire pigs

PASTURED PORK VS. COMMODITY PORK

Gum Creek Farms produces what's known as pastured pork. Some people use the term *free-range*. All it means is that the animals are allowed to move from one spot to another and do what they want to do. The difference between that and commodity pork is the difference between milling about in your yard and living in a confined space on a concrete pad in a garage. The terms *free-range* and *pastured* say nothing about the breed of pig, what it eats, or how it's processed. It just implies that the animals were allowed to roam instead of being contained. The term *pastured* doesn't even specify how much they roam or for how long each day. So you have to ask questions. If you can talk to the farmer who raised the pigs, ask what the animal's living environment was like.

Ask about the animal's diet too. If you've ever grown plants, you may have put Miracle-Gro on your tomatoes at some point and then said: "Holy cow! Did you see those tomatoes? They're the size of basketballs!" Similar growth enhancers exist in animal feed. Some farmers use them, but they don't necessarily produce the best-tasting meat. Look for pork that's raised on high-quality vegetarian feed. For years, people fed pigs slop. And they'll eat it because these animals are omnivores. They're hungry. I understand the motivation. I've been known to wolf down two and a half bags of Funyuns if they're sitting in front of me. But feeding a hog better food creates better-tasting meat. Every farmer has his or her own proprietary mix in the feed. Smart farmers experiment with different ratios to find out what's best for their pigs. Ask the farmer what's in the feed. The good ones will be proud and say things like, "We use roasted soybeans with a touch of corn, some oats, and a little sorghum."

These aren't just meaningless decisions. Differences in feed and production methods produce different kinds of meat. If you break down whole hogs side by side, you can see the difference. Let's just say we cut two pork loins, one pastured and one commodity, and turn the cut sides out side by side (see page 5). On the commodity pork loin, you'll see a disproportionately large amount of lean meat compared to the fat. The "eye" of the loin dominates, with only very small pieces of fat where the loin joins the rib cage. The second thing you'll notice is the color. Commodity pork has a faint rosy color and often a peculiar iridescence reminiscent of fish. Plus, the meat is loose and floppy, like a water balloon. That's because it retains a great deal of water. The excess water makes a commodity pork loin flatten out at the top and bottom.

A pork loin from a heritage breed of pastured pork looks quite different. You'll notice the color right away. It will be darker pink—closer to red. That's because it's got more hemoglobin, a red protein that increases as a muscle is worked. That darker red color is what translates to better flavor in pastured pork. The more the pigs roam, the more their muscles are worked, and the redder, denser, and more flavorful the meat gets.

Now take a close look at the meat fibers. In the heritage breed of pastured pork, they are more tightly woven and less watery looking than in the commodity pork. That means the meat will have a more satisfying texture when you eat it. The "eye" of loin meat is also smaller and has more fat marbled throughout it. That section of the loin connecting the loin to the rib cage has thicker pieces of fat and a nice cap of fat facing up to the sky. In commodity pork, this cap of fat will be barely noticeable, but in heritage breeds of pastured pork, you can actually measure it. Berkshire hogs average about 2 inches of back fat, and Mangalitsas have upward of 10 inches.

I can hear the arguments now: Why would I want to pay for a pile of pork fat? To sum it up, fattier pork is juicier pork and more flavorful. Plus, the back fat can and should be removed so you can render it into lard for cooking (see page 211).

When you look at these cuts side by side, there really is very little room for debate. The meat speaks for itself. Cook up both and decide for yourself. Taste a pastured pork loin and a commodity pork loin side by side and tell me which one tastes better. That's really what it comes down to, isn't it? You'd be hard-pressed to argue that the meat coming from the commodity feedlots of the world tastes better than the meat coming from pasture farms.

Your one argument is price. But that is determined by demand. The reality is, the price of farm-raised pork will come down when demand goes up. You've seen it with poultry. People caught wind of the fact that commodity poultry farming can get pretty sketchy. They started demanding a higher-quality product. The same thing is happening with pork. People are demanding higher quality. If you think pastured pork tastes better, allocate your money toward it. The price will eventually come down.

HOG PROCESSING

I'm going to get on my high horse here for just a minute. I believe that all the work of raising a pig the right way—choosing the breed, finding the right location, dialing in the feed, and handling the animals gently—is completely in vain if you don't also concern yourself with how the animal is being killed. The responsibility for raising animals properly persists through the animal's life and its death. Why would a farmer pour his or her heart, soul, money, and time into raising a pig only to drop it off at a processor who kicks the animals, herds them through processing like car parts, and doesn't treat them with care and respect? Some commodity pork facilities process hundreds of hogs in the time it takes to process one hog the right way.

But let's dispense with morality for a moment. Processing matters purely from a taste perspective. When animals are stressed, the adrenaline and hormones released in their bodies create a lower-quality product. Adrenaline can cause blood spotting—little flecks of blood throughout the meat. That can lead to weeping, or draining, of water and juiciness right out of the meat. If the pigs are terrified or tortured during processing, stress hormones can transform what would have been delicious and succulent meat into something that tastes like nails. It can be foul.

For years, Tommy Searcy was forced to take his pigs to processors who didn't understand why he raised hogs the way he did. But he followed through on his principles and found meat processors who treated his pigs with the same care and respect he put into raising them. To this day, he drives his pigs from Roopville, Georgia, all the way down to Auburn, Alabama. There's a meat processor 10 minutes from his farm. But he knows that driving an hour south is the right thing to do.

★ PORK LABELS ★

You'll see all kinds of marketing lingo on packages of pork. Some terms are regulated by the USDA, and some aren't. Here's the lowdown.

ALL-NATURAL: This doesn't mean much of anything. It's more of a marketing buzzword. Almost all commodity pork carries this label. The legal definition is "contains no artificial ingredients or added colors and is minimally processed." But pork shouldn't have anything artificial in it anyway.

NO ANTIBIOTICS: Farmers tell me that they can administer antibiotics to their animals, but they have to cull the herd and document which animals have been given what and when. It doesn't mean that antibiotics are never used on that farm. It means that you can be assured that the meat you are eating does not contain antibiotics.

NO HORMONES: The Feds don't permit using added hormones in any type of pork production (or poultry production, for that matter). Whether or not you see this label, pork does not contain added hormones.

100 PERCENT ORGANIC: This refers to an entire method of production and processing. Organic pork comes from pigs raised in living conditions that accommodate their natural behaviors (such as the ability to graze on pasture), that are fed 100 percent organic feed and forage, and that have not been given antibiotics or hormones. If less than 100 percent organic feed is used, you might see the meat described as organic (95 percent organic feed) or made with organic (70 to 95 percent organic feed).

VEGETARIAN-FED: Pigs are omnivores. They eat everything. But it's better to feed them a vegetarian diet instead of slop. They're particularly fond of nuts, which also make better-tasting meat.

FREE-RANGE: The pigs had continuous access to pasture for at least 80 percent of their production cycle.

PASTURED: There's no USDA definition for this term, but many farmers prefer it. It means essentially the same thing as *free-range*. However, many producers of pastured pork go beyond the *free-range* requirements and give the pigs more time to roam and vegetarian feed in addition to their natural diet of forage.

HUMANELY RAISED: Again, the USDA doesn't have a definition. If you see a label with wording such as "Certified Humane" or "Animal Welfare Approved," it means that a third-party organization has inspected the farm operations and determined that the animals have been handled humanely throughout their growth cycle.

LOCALLY GROWN: There is zero consensus here. Some folks propose a 250-mile radius, others a 500-mile radius, and some say it has to be in the same state. It's really about economics and environmental impact. Buy locally if you want to support producers in your area and shorten the distance your food travels from farm to fork. Often, a local producer down the road from you will be selling great pork. Check around. Eatwild.com and localharvest.org are handy directories showing who is producing pork in your area.

WHY DO PIGS WALLOW IN MUD?

To cool off! Like other hairless mammals such as elephants, hippos and rhinos, pigs don't have sweat glands to help cool them down. And unlike dogs, panting doesn't help. Like hippos and rhinos, pigs get deeper into the earth to cool off because the temperature there is lower than it is in the open air.

BUYING PASTURED PORK

Higher-end stores like Whole Foods and Fresh Market are starting to carry higher-quality farm-raised pork. Yes, it costs more, but part of what you pay for is the convenience of having a great product in a national chain store. Truth be told, your best route is still your local farmers' market. Pop-up markets happen in different neighborhoods all over the country. I was driving recently from the Charleston Food and Wine Festival back to Atlanta in the middle of Nowhere, South Carolina: I'm pumping gas, and I see a sign across the street in the parking lot of a church that says, "Saturday Morning Farmers' Market—9 a.m. to Noon." I got so excited. I was not in a major metropolitan city, and this little town had its own farmers with their own market. The farmers inevitably live right down the road. They used to have to drive all the way to Atlanta or Charleston to sell their stuff, but now people everywhere are starting to embrace the principles of good farming and good food. Customers are lining up at local markets to buy better-quality, better-tasting products from their local farmers. Look for a market in your area. Ask around or check eatwild.com, localharvest.org, or buyfreshbuylocal.org. Show up at the market on a Saturday or Sunday morning, talk to the farmers, and make friends. The end result will be something on your dinner table that tastes ten times better than what you were eating before.

★ PRIMER ON PIG PARTS ★

This book is not a PhD class in porcine anatomy or science. But it helps to know what you're working with in the kitchen. The recipes are organized by retail cuts of pork. Here's a snapshot of where those cuts come from.

Head

Gives us the jowls and cheeks. Jowls are the haunchy part of meat sitting at the base of the neck running toward the shoulder. When cut from the pig, the jowl has a triangular shape. A pork cheek is the round pocket of meat sitting high on the cheekbone.

Shoulder

Includes the entirety of the front legs from top to bottom, down to what we would call the pig's knee. When you bisect the shoulder horizontally, the top part is the Boston butt; the bottom is the picnic ham. The shoulder is also cut into thin pork blade chops and thick pork blade steaks or ground into pork sausage.

Trotter

Below the knee on either the forelegs or hind legs, you have the shanks (shins) and trotters (feet). Osso buco is a slice across the shinbone that includes the meat. Ham hocks come from the lower part of the shank just shy of the feet.

Ham

These are the rear legs in their entirety. Fresh, cured, smoked, or baked, it's all called ham. Like the shoulder, the ham can be cut in half horizontally, and then it's called, logically, a half ham.

Loin

This is the top quarter of the center of the animal. Draw a line down the top of a pig, and you create two whole pork loins, each including sirloin and rib bones. All pork chops, loins, country-style ribs, and pork sirloin come from this loin section. Use your X-ray vision to see inside this area, and you'll see the tenderloin running along the underside of the backbone.

Belly

Also called side meat or middles, the belly falls below the loin. Fresh whole pork belly, trimmed-up belly for bacon, spareribs, St. Louis–style ribs, pork skirt steak, flank steak, and flap meat are all located here.

Ribs

Baby back ribs and spareribs are connected as a single side of the animal's rib cage. We have to manually separate them. When you cut one side of the rib cage in half crosswise, it becomes baby back ribs and spareribs.

Skin

Pork rinds and cracklings can be made from the skin on any part of the animal.

Fatback

This is the fat on the back of the pig that's connected to and above the pork loin facing northward toward the sky.

"HE WAS MY BUDDY.
HE WAS MY FRIEND.
HE WAS MY BREAKFAST
EVERY NOW AND THEN."

—RAY STEVENS, "KISS A PIG"

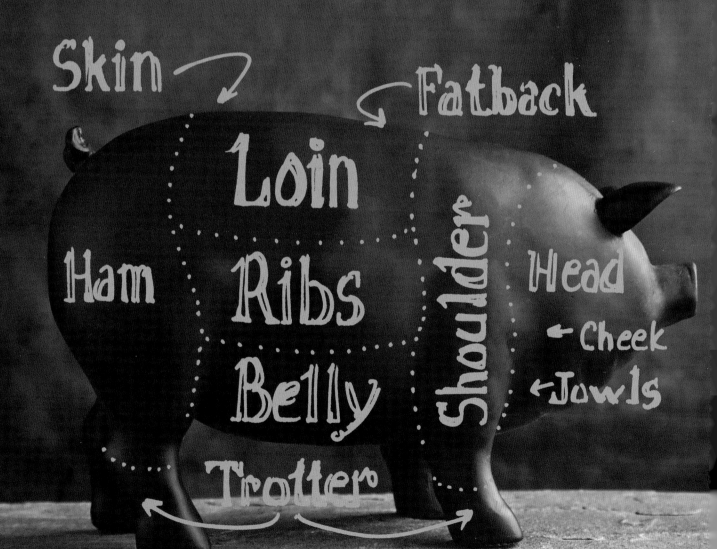

Skin

Fatback

Loin

Ham

Ribs

Shoulder

Head

Belly

Cheek

Jowls

Trotter

Cottage Bacon

Belly Bacon

Jowl Bacon

COOKING COMMODITY AND PASTURED PORK

Ever wonder why supermarket pork chops over-cook and dry out so easily? It's because the muscle structure is so weak that the water drains out during cooking. Pastured pork has a denser muscle structure, and that keeps the juices in. That muscle structure also means pastured pork cooks more slowly and evenly; as the marbling in the meat melts and bastes, that extra fat prevents overcooking and creates juicier-tasting meat.

Bottom line: Pastured pork is more forgiving and less likely to overcook. For that reason, the bigger cuts may also take a little longer. A pork minute steak won't take any longer, but a pork shoulder will. Trust your instincts. When you're cooking a roast or larger cut of pork, doneness is what you want to watch for—not time. If you're braising a pork shoulder that's supposed to be fork-tender in two hours, but when you stick a fork into it, it's still stiff, forget the timer and cook it until the meat is fork-tender.

Speaking of doneness, pastured pork cooked to well done may still be pink inside (remember the hemoglobin that makes the meat red?). Don't worry; pink pork is perfectly safe to eat. That's the biggest hurdle we all have to get over: years of conditioning that pork must be overcooked for it to be safe. Not anymore. After decades of research and study, the USDA has finally decreed that 145°F is a safe internal temperature for cooked pork. At that temperature, both commodity and pastured pork may still be pink inside, and that's just fine. Pink does not mean unsafe. Cook your pork to 145°F inside and it will be safe to eat—and delicious. But cook the lean cuts like loin to 155°F and the meat may not be worth eating at all because it will have totally dried out.

All of the recipes in this book were tested with both commodity and pastured pork. If you're just buying chops from the grocery store, you can be assured of success. When in doubt, pay closer attention to the internal doneness temperature than to the estimated times given in the recipes.

"ASKING A CRITIC TO NAME HIS FAVORITE BOOK IS LIKE ASKING A BUTCHER TO NAME HIS FAVORITE PIG."

—JOHN McCARTHY

№ 2

PANTRY RECIPES

The recipes in this chapter are step one for making great-tasting pork. Most cookbooks put these sorts of "basic" recipes at the back of the book, but I think they should be right up front. Chicken stock, ham broth, a good all-purpose pickling liquid . . . these essential items are always in my pantry. They're not simply components used in one or two other dishes; they're universal preparations. The first time you make Sweet and Smoky Barbecue Sauce (page 28), it might be for Deep-Fried Baby Back Ribs (page 128), Crispy Pork Meatballs (page 202), or My Version of Bacon Explosion (page 189). But you could also use this sauce anywhere you'd use another barbecue sauce or even in place of ketchup.

If you're not already in the habit, get in the habit of making stock. It's dead easy. Roast a chicken for dinner, and then freeze the bones. Whenever it's convenient, throw the bones in some water with a few onion pieces and vegetable scraps to make stock. Or make Chicken Stock (page 26) the way I like to—with a cut-up raw bird and nothing else in the water. Either way, keep that stock in the freezer. It's like liquid gold that you can pull out at a moment's notice to create delicious food. If you don't have that basic preparation on hand, you're already starting behind the eight ball.

Here's the upside to learning these recipes first: When you go beyond this book and experiment in the kitchen, these basic preparations will still be perfectly valid and useful. I use the Dry Brine (page 22) all the time in my professional kitchen and my home kitchen. Same goes for the Pepper Vinegar (page 24). Through trial and error, I've learned that these recipes work over and over again for multiple dishes in multiple cuisines around the globe. Start here, go anywhere.

INGREDIENTS AND TECHNIQUES

The recipes in this book are written with utter clarity. But I tend to go over the top with everything, so here's a little more detail on items you'll see throughout the book.

INGREDIENTS

ACCENT SEASONING: One of the main ingredients in Accent seasoning is monosodium glutamate (MSG). I know some people have issues with it, but let's be honest: The flavor of glutamate is the flavor of awesome. It's not some weird chemical created in a lab. Glutamate is found naturally in everything from meat and seaweed to soy sauce and mushrooms. It's what gives those foods their deep, savory, indescribably delicious taste. I use Accent seasoning in small amounts here and there to bring out those flavors and amplify the others flavors in a dish.

DUKE'S MAYONNAISE: If you have to use prepared mayonnaise, at least buy the best. Duke's is the best. It's the closest you can get to homemade mayonnaise from a store. If you read the label, you'll recognize everything listed there. That's what distinguishes it from other brands out there. It's just a simple, straightforward, usable mayonnaise. If you like your mayo sweet, add a little sugar to it. Or if you can't find Duke's, make your own: For 1 cup mayo, blend 2 egg yolks, 3 tablespoons fresh lemon juice or vinegar, 1 teaspoon Dijon mustard, and ½ teaspoon salt in a blender or food processor. Keep the machine running, then drizzle in 1 cup canola or other neutral-tasting oil until the mayo is thick.

ESPELETTE PEPPER: When I want a little more heat than paprika but not so much as cayenne, I use Espelette pepper from France. It has an aromatic floral quality to it. Look for authentic *piment d'Espelette* from France. If you can't find it, use hot paprika instead.

OILS: Grapeseed oil is my go-to oil for high-temperature cooking like stir-frying, sautéing, searing, and roasting. I use it the same way people use canola oil or "vegetable" oil. It has no flavor. A neutral flavor is critical when you start thinking diligently about all the flavors you are building in a dish. Grapeseed oil also has a high smoke point, which means it can stand up to the brutally high heat needed for proper stir-frying and searing. It's also high in omega-3 fatty acids. It's a good fat.

When I use olive oil, it's usually from Arbequina olives. I've done several olive oil tastings, and 100 percent Arbequina olive oil is never too spicy, too peppery, or too floral. It's the perfect, middle-of-the-road all-purpose olive oil for cooking. I'll use a few different extra-virgin olive oils made from different olives, but I generally reserve those for raw preparations because extra-virgin oil is more fragile.

I use canola oil regularly—primarily for deep-frying. Old Southern purists swear up and down that peanut oil is the best for frying. But canola oil has a more neutral flavor than peanut oil and a higher smoke point. So why not use grapeseed oil for frying? Economics. Filling up a fryer with grapeseed oil would get mighty expensive. If grapeseed oil is too expensive or you can't find it, you could use canola oil in place of grapeseed oil in any of the recipes here.

One other oil I use is dark toasted sesame oil. Think of it as a seasoning. It has a pronounced flavor, so it's best used sparingly. It also goes rancid quickly. Buy a small quantity and keep it in the fridge.

SALT: There are a bajillion salts out there, and I like to experiment, but mostly I stick with two: kosher salt and flake salt. I use Diamond Crystal kosher salt for 99.9 percent of all applications. It has the right texture for pinching, dissolves easily, and gets absorbed quickly. It also has a clean taste with no specific minerality. Just like canola and grapeseed in the oil world, Diamond Crystal kosher has a neutral taste in the salt world. Keep in mind that if you try to substitute another brand of kosher salt, it will measure differently. Morton kosher and Diamond Crystal kosher are not tit for tat. One teaspoon of Diamond Crystal = ¾ teaspoon of Morton. You might also see the term *Kevin pinch* in reference to salt. I use my whole hand to pinch up salt and 1 Kevin pinch = about 1 teaspoon.

VINEGAR: Red wine vinegar, sherry vinegar, rice vinegar . . . I use them all. But cider vinegar is my go-to. I like the taste. I'm talking about 100 percent unfiltered apple cider vinegar. A lot of what you find at the grocery store is actually distilled white vinegar with some portion of apple "flavoring" or apple cider vinegar added to it. It has a caustic acidity with only a tiny whiff of apple aroma. What I'm suggesting you use is vinegar made from 100 percent fresh apple juice that has been fermented. It has a more gentle acidity and stronger apple aroma. Bragg's is a good national brand.

WONDRA FLOUR: I use this flour for dusting meats before browning them in a hot pan. It gives you a very thin coating on the meat and produces a crunchy exterior that's barely visible. The flour is baby-powder fine and perfect for breading fish. You can dredge the skin side of a trout fillet in this flour, bang off the excess, and get a super-crispy skin. It's so finely ground that it doesn't cake up at all. Wondra is essentially low-protein flour that's moistened, cooked, dehydrated, and then ground like talcum powder. That process makes the flour take up water so fast, it doesn't form lumps. It was originally designed for thickening lump-free sauces, but it's a godsend for thin, crispy breading.

TECHNIQUES

BIAS SLICING: Picture your favorite Chinese take-out food. Most of the vegetables are sliced on an angle (on the bias) to give them more surface area. That extra surface area gives the food more contact with the hot wok so the food cooks faster. Bias slicing and high heat are essential to quick Chinese cooking. Bias cuts are also important for cutting through the grain of certain meats. Pork leg fillet, for instance, is cut on the bias to cut through muscle fibers in order to shorten the tough fibers and make the meat easier to chew or more "tender." Whenever a recipe tells you to bias-slice an ingredient, just cut it on an angle instead of cutting straight across it.

TOASTING NUTS AND SPICES: What tastes better, a slice of bread or a slice of toast? A slice of toast—it has more flavor! The same holds true for nuts and spices. When you toast them, you enhance their flavors. I like to toast nuts at a low temperature for a long time. That browns them all the way through instead of just on the surface. Put the nuts on a pan in a 225°F oven and you'll get awesome flavor and less of that tannic astringency peculiar to some nuts. For spices, high heat works better than low. You

want to toast them in a hot pan to draw out their oils. Put the spices in a skillet over medium to medium-high heat and toast them just until they send up a whiff of smoke. There's one exception: cumin seeds. Cumin tastes so strong to me that I prefer to mellow its flavor by toasting the seeds a little longer—get them super-dark. Then crush the toasted spices, and you're good to go. You can crush spices in a spice grinder, a mortar and pestle, or in a plastic bag with a hammer, rolling pin, or other heavy weight.

3-STEP BREADING METHOD: You've no doubt seen this before. You set up three bowls—one with flour, one with beaten egg, and one with bread crumbs—and then dip your food into the flour, the egg, and then the crumbs. The flour absorbs moisture and promotes crispness; the egg is the glue; and the crumbs stick to the egg, creating a thick crispy crust. That triple dip is the first thing you do for breaded and fried food. Use one hand for dipping in the dry ingredients and the other for wet ingredients to keep your fingers from getting caked up with breading. Or use tongs. To make sure the crust is set before you fry the food, let the breaded food sit on a cooling rack for 10 to 15 minutes first. Some folks use plain-Jane flour, but I prefer a seasoned flour. Whenever I mention the 3-step breading method, the flour I'm talking about is the Seasoned Breading Mix on page 23.

WASHING MACHINE METHOD: Ever watch a washing machine at work? The drum spins, but the center agitator stays in place. It's an efficient way of mixing the detergent and clothes together. The same holds true for mixing ingredients in a bowl or pan. Hold your spoon in the center and shake or rotate the pan vigorously to quickly mix everything together. It's like reverse whisking, and it's particularly useful for blending and emulsifying fats and liquids when making a pan sauce.

DRY BRINE

MAKES ABOUT 2½ TABLESPOONS

Brining adds moisture and flavor to foods. It's usually done by immersing the food in salt water and whatever seasonings you like. The salt softens up the food and, through osmosis, the water tries to equalize itself between the food and the brine solution. Result: The food takes on more water and whatever seasonings are in the water. Brining is a great method for making juicy meat. But wet brines are a pain, especially if you're brining something big like a suckling pig or even a pork loin. You need a bathtub, cooler, or giant bucket to get the job done. And it has to stay cold. Plus, more water in meat can dilute the taste of the meat itself. This can be an issue with mild-flavored cuts of pork like loin. I find that dry brines are easier. They flavor the meat without watering it down. I call this a dry brine and not a rub because it's used to impart flavor and soften the texture of meat—not to form a crust on the outside.

2 tablespoons kosher salt

1 teaspoon garlic powder

1 teaspoon ground black pepper

¼ teaspoon cayenne pepper

In a small bowl, combine all of the ingredients and mix well. Store in a tightly covered jar for up to 2 months.

Good to know

Dry brining is step one for several recipes like Indianapolis-Style Fried Pork Loin Sandwich (page 100), Pork Minute Steaks with Potato Pancakes and Pumpkin Butter (page 82), and Springfield-Style Cashew Pork (page 92). But don't stop there. Use this dry brine on any lean meat to improve its flavor and texture. The amount here is what you'll need for most of the recipes in this book, but if you want to make more and store it, you can easily double or quadruple the recipe.

SEASONED BREADING MIX

MAKES ABOUT 5 CUPS

Does this even merit being a recipe? It does because the exterior of fried food is often the most overlooked component. People usually season the food but neglect to season the breading. Fried food should be properly seasoned inside and out. Through years of trial and error, I've optimized the perfect seasoning level. The spices here are standard flavors like onion, garlic, and pepper that go with almost any fried food–pork or otherwise. Consider this a universal seasoned breading to use whenever you fry. It's the flour mixture I use whenever I do my 3-step breading method for frying.

4 cups all-purpose flour

5 tablespoons kosher salt

5 tablespoons ground black pepper

3 tablespoons onion powder

2 tablespoons garlic powder

5 teaspoons red pepper flakes

In a medium bowl, mix all of the ingredients together. Store in an airtight container for up to 6 months.

PEPPER VINEGAR

MAKES ABOUT 6 CUPS

Eastern Carolina barbecue sauce is thin, vinegary, sharp, and spicy. That's what I'm going for here—but with a little more kick. It's the sauce I use for my whole hog barbecue. I also use it to season greens and spike a Bloody Mary. This vinegar benefits any food that needs a little something-something, such as the Brunswick Stew (page 218). A little shot before serving pulls it all together.

5¼ cups apple cider vinegar

¼ cup sweet Hungarian paprika

¼ cup sugar

¼ cup kosher salt

2 tablespoons ground black pepper

2 tablespoons red pepper flakes

3 cloves garlic, crushed

Combine all of the ingredients in a Dutch oven and bring to a rolling boil over high heat. Boil for 3 minutes. Remove from the heat and cool to room temperature. Strain through a fine-mesh strainer, discarding the solids. Cover and store at room temperature for up to 6 months.

=== *Good to Know* ===

Use this vinegar as a basic barbecue mop for tough meats or as a lean, mean table sauce.

ALL-PURPOSE PICKLING LIQUID

MAKES 3 CUPS

There couldn't be a more straight-to-the-point recipe than this. You'll see slightly different recipes for everything that can possibly be pickled. That's all well and good if you're a pickling fanatic. But this is the One Ring to rule them all. It's a solid base recipe. I use it to pickle carrots and turnips that get served with Rustic Pork Terrine with Spicy Mustard and Vegetable Pickles (page 204) but also to pickle peaches for Mosaic Pork Terrine (page 206) and apples for Grilled Pork Belly with Pickled Apples and Smoked Peanut Butter (page 120). Just add spices and herbs to this liquid to flavor different pickles however you like.

2 cups apple cider vinegar

½ cup sugar

¼ cup pickling spice

2 tablespoons kosher salt

Combine all of the ingredients in a small saucepan and bring to a boil. Stir to dissolve the sugar and salt, and remove from the heat. Strain over the items you are pickling and cool to room temperature. Refrigerate the pickles and, for the best taste, let them pickle for about a week before eating. The longer you pickle them, the more intense the flavor will be.

=== *Good to know* ===

For my pickled apples, I add cinnamon sticks to this liquid. For cucumber pickles, you might want to add dill seeds or garlic. For carrots, add caraway seeds and bay leaves. Add whatever seasonings you think will taste good with the food you're pickling.

CHICKEN STOCK
MAKES ABOUT 2½ QUARTS

It always throws my cooks off when they see me making stock with only chicken and no vegetables. My argument is that you can always add vegetables later. But you can't take them out. I use this bare-bones chicken stock as a vehicle. It's like a blank canvas that I can fill with flavor later on. Using only cut-up chicken—skin, bones, and all—produces a more flavorful, pure-tasting chicken stock. It doesn't produce a stock that's clear, but I don't care about that. Will it have more fat? Yes. I just skim it off after the stock is refrigerated. The point of leaving the skin on is to extract the gelatin. That's what gives this stock a rich mouthfeel.

1 whole chicken, about 3 pounds

Break down the bird by cutting down along one side of the bird's breastbone. Then run the knife along the contour of the rib cage and around the wishbone to remove the breast meat; repeat on the other side and reserve the breast meat. Using kitchen shears, cut from the tail end up to the neck end on either side of the backbone to remove the backbone; place the backbone in an 8-quart stockpot. Cut the chicken wings from the body and put in the stockpot. Bend the leg away from the body, cut down to the joint, then bend the joint to break it; cut between the ball and socket and then down around the carcass to remove the entire leg/thigh portion. Separate the drumsticks and thighs into separate pieces and cut each in half to expose additional bone. Put all of the drumstick and thigh pieces into the stockpot. Cut the remaining carcass in half and put in the stockpot. Fill the pot with enough water to completely cover all the bones.

Set the pot over high heat and bring to a boil. Lower the heat so that the liquid simmers very gently; you only want a few bubbles coming up now and then. Using a ladle, skim and discard any foam and fat from the pot. Drop the chicken breasts into the water and poach just until no longer pink (165°F internal temperature), about 15 minutes. Remove the breasts and reserve for another use.

Simmer the stock very gently for 2 hours, skimming the surface now and then. Pull the pot from the heat and let cool for 1 hour. Using tongs, remove and discard the bones. Strain the stock through a fine-mesh strainer and then through a double layer of wet cheesecloth to remove any sediment. Cool to room temperature. Refrigerate for up to 1 week or freeze for up to 6 months.

=================== *Worth Knowing* ===================

If you think this stock would taste better with some mirepoix (chef-speak for minced onion, celery, and carrots), go ahead and chuck some in with the chicken. There you go, problem solved. Just remember that if you use this stock to cook a pot of beans, you've already put the mirepoix in there, so you might not want to double up on the flavoring in the beans.

HAM BROTH
MAKES 2 QUARTS

Years ago, it struck me walking through the grocery store that you can buy boxes of high-quality hermetically sealed stock for everything under the sun, like beef, chicken, vegetables, and mushrooms—but not pork. Why is there no pork stock? Well, here it is. Use this broth whenever you're cooking pork and need some porky liquid to go with it. Smoked ham hocks give it a smoky flavor and incredible mouthfeel due to the gelatin in the shin of a pig. To extract maximum gelatin and flavor, I score the hocks all the way down to the bone before adding them to the stock. That also allows you to easily pick the meat off the bone.

3½ pounds smoked ham hocks (see Worth Knowing)

3 tablespoons grapeseed oil or canola oil

1 large onion, sliced, about 2 cups

10 cloves garlic, root end trimmed

1 (3-inch) piece fresh ginger, sliced into coins, skin on

¼ cup apple cider vinegar

1 tablespoon black peppercorns

1 teaspoon red pepper flakes

2 quarts Chicken Stock (page 26)

Score the hocks all the way around and to the bone in 1-inch intervals. If the hocks are big enough, score them lengthwise down the bone too. This helps release flavor into the broth while tenderizing the meat.

Heat a large heavy-bottomed Dutch oven over high heat. Add the oil, and when it begins to smoke, add the onions, garlic, and ginger. This high heat will quickly caramelize the vegetables while leaving them firm. Stir occasionally and cook until all edges are nicely caramelized, about 4 minutes. Add the vinegar, peppercorns, red pepper flakes, chicken stock, and hocks, cover, and bring to a boil. Lower the heat and simmer, covered, until the meat on the ham hocks is fall-apart tender, about 2½ hours.

Remove from the heat. Remove and reserve the hocks. Strain the broth through a medium-mesh sieve and discard the solids. When the hocks are cool enough to handle, pick the meat from the bones. You'll end up with about ½ cup meat. The meat is great for flavoring beans and greens. Store the broth covered and refrigerated for up to 1 week or frozen for up to 6 months.

Worth Knowing

You want lots of surface area in your ham hocks here. If yours are big (1 pound or more), 3 hocks will work fine. If they're small (8 to 12 ounces), you'll need about 5 of them. Look for the biggest, plumpest hocks you can find. The skin and bones will release a lot of gelatin and umami/unctuousness, and the meat will be easier to pull from the bones.

SWEET AND SMOKY BARBECUE SAUCE

MAKES ABOUT 2 CUPS

People get weird when defending their intellectual property related to barbecue. As such, I have been sworn to secrecy with some of my family's barbecue sauces. But I wanted to give you a sauce you could rely on for everything from ribs to chicken. This is the style of sauce that most people associate with barbecue—thick, sweet, and smoky. It could be your new ketchup. It's thick enough to dunk a French fry into or spread on a burger. Use it to glaze barbecued ribs or serve at the table. I'm not a ketchup dude. This is my alternative.

1 cup ketchup

¾ cup finely minced shallot

½ cup sorghum
   (see Good to Know)

8 cloves garlic, minced, about
   2 tablespoons

2 tablespoons apple cider
   vinegar

2 tablespoons Worcestershire
   sauce

1 tablespoon Frank's RedHot
   sauce

1 tablespoon ground black
   pepper

1 tablespoon kosher salt

1 tablespoon yellow mustard

½ teaspoon liquid smoke

⅛ teaspoon ground allspice

⅛ teaspoon ground cinnamon

Combine all of the ingredients in a medium saucepan and bring to a boil. Decrease the heat to low and cook for 10 minutes. Remove from the heat and cool to room temperature. Cover and store, refrigerated, for up to 1 month.

 Good to Know

You can replace the sorghum with ⅓ cup honey and 2 tablespoons molasses.

BASIC CABBAGE SLAW

MAKES 4 CUPS

You need an all-purpose slaw for backyard barbecues, church suppers, picnics, and weeknight dinners? You're looking at it. Nothing fancy—just a good old Southern-style coleslaw. I use this for crunch and creaminess in A Really Good Ham Sandwich (page 161), alongside Chicken-Fried Pork Steak (page 158), and with Slow Cooker Country-Style Ribs (page 114). It could show up with almost anything on your table.

1 small head green cabbage, shredded, about 8 cups

¼ cup sugar

2 tablespoons salt

⅓ cup Duke's mayonnaise

1 tablespoon apple cider vinegar

In a large bowl, toss the cabbage with the sugar and salt. Set aside for 1 hour, or until the cabbage starts to wilt and there's some liquid in the bottom of the bowl. Pour out the liquid and, using paper towels, squeeze the cabbage dry. Stir in the mayonnaise and vinegar. Chill before serving. Store covered and refrigerated for up to 1 week.

"YOU CAN NEVER PUT TOO MUCH PORK IN YOUR MOUTH AS FAR AS I'M CONCERNED."

—LEWIS BLACK

№ 3

ON THE SHOULDER

I got my first sous-chef job opening TWO Urban Licks in Atlanta. This restaurant was the hottest shit in the city when it opened up. I'm not saying this because I worked there. I'm saying it because it's true. When I interviewed, they told me, "We'll be serving 1,000 people a night." I thought to myself, "Yeah, right." At my last job at the Ritz-Carlton, we served about 19 people a night. There was no way they could serve 1,000 people every night.

Lo and behold, when TWO Urban Licks opened, we did 1,100 covers a night. On some nights we did 1,200, and on Mother's Day, 1,600 people. We had eighteen line cooks, another ten for prep, and eight dishwashers. This restaurant served shocking volumes of food. It was enough to send you into a delirium.

My job was to open the restaurant first thing every day. I was in charge of the prep team. Low man on the totem pole in the chef world, but I still couldn't get out of there during service because there was so much to do. I started work at 5 a.m. and couldn't leave until we closed the place at 1 a.m. This went on seven days a week. Needless to say, I was a zombie and barely remember half of my time there. It's like when you get really wasted and say to your buddy the next day, "Yeah, I remember we were at that party. And I remember being on my roof. And then someone said we should hop over that electric fence." It's all a haze to me now.

But I do have one distinct memory: the day I suggested a new dish for the menu. We needed dishes that could be cooked in advance because of the huge volume we served. I said to my boss, chef Scott Serpas, "Why don't we do pork shoulder? We could cook it in advance, hold it hot, and put it right on the plate." Serpas said, "Make me what you're thinking." So I got a boneless pork butt and sliced it up into 5-inch wedges. They looked sort of like short ribs. Then I browned them off and braised them in a rich veal stock with cinnamon sticks, star anise, and dried hot chiles until the pork was nice and tender. When I served it to Serpas, he absolutely loved it. He said it had big bold flavor and was right in the restaurant's wheelhouse. Score one for Gillespie!

But that was the day I signed my own death warrant. My responsibilities had just gone from "organize the prep team and be here all day" to "oh yeah, and prep this entire dish for the menu every day." That wouldn't be such a big deal in a smaller restaurant, but TWO Urban Licks did a ton of volume.

The first time the delivery truck showed up with the pork shoulders, it was 5 a.m. on a Friday morning. It was late October, and I was standing outside the restaurant functioning, barely, on three hours sleep. The delivery guy unloaded a case of pork shoulders. Then he unloaded another, and then another. When we slid the tenth case of pork shoulders into the walk-in cooler, the stack went from floor to ceiling. I called my boss—way too early in the morning—and said, "What's the deal with all these pork shoulders?" He replied, "We're putting that dish on the menu tonight." "Yeah, but why so much?" He laughed and said, "That's how much we need." I was sitting on eighty goddamn pork shoulders that I had to cut down into 5-inch pieces all on my own—while making sure all the other jackanapes were getting all their stuff done.

I did it. I cut up all eighty shoulders. There were two boneless shoulders in each Cryovac pack. I cut apart the packs, trimmed away the fat and glands from each shoulder, and cut each piece of meat into 5 by 5-inch blocks about 2 inches thick. If you've ever cut into a pork shoulder, you know it's tough meat. You need a heavy knife—a freaking butcher's scimitar—to cut up that meat. And I wanted every piece to be perfect. By the end, my hands were covered in huge blisters. Score one for pork shoulder.

I browned off all the pork in this giant frying pan that held about three shoulders of meat at a time. I filled every hotel pan we had with the cooked pork. The whole time I'm laughing to myself, thinking, "There's no way this amount can be right." We had 400 portions.

That night, we started service with more than 900 reservations. With walk-ins, we did about 1,300 covers that night. The next morning, when I came in at 5 a.m., the delivery truck was waiting for me. The delivery guy offloaded ten more cases of pork shoulder. That's when I realized we had completely sold out of all 400 portions the night before. Then it really hit me. I was the only guy who knew how to make this dish. I would be trimming and cutting up eighty pork shoulders into little 5-inch blocks every day for the rest of my life.

I left the restaurant after six months. It's a miracle that I still cook pork shoulder at all. God and I made a deal the day that I left: If I could muster the sanity to write this recipe down for the next poor sap who had to make it, I was going to walk away from this particular protein forever.

Well, as it turns out, pork shoulder is just too good to walk away from. After shredding my hands for six months on this godforsaken meat, I still love it. I love it braised, I love it smoked, and I love it cut in chops and grilled. Seems I'm not alone. Different cultures and cuisines around the world love it too. The recipes in this chapter are evidence of that. I hope they give you a taste of what I'm talking about.

GOOD TO KNOW ABOUT
Pork Shoulder

IT'S ALMOST IMPOSSIBLE TO OVERCOOK:
A pork shoulder is the most forgiving cut on the
animal. Your chances for success are pretty high.
It's a great starting point if you're not used to cooking
pork. The intramuscular fat in a pork shoulder makes
the cut self-basting, so it's almost impossible to overcook it. I see home cooks preparing pork tenderloin
all the time, but that cut actually requires a little more
skill because it can dry out so easily. A pork shoulder,
by contrast, is relatively idiot-proof.

IT'S TOUGH MEAT: Full-grown hogs weigh about
250 pounds. The shoulders of the animal support
most of that weight. The shoulders are also
physically smaller than the hams (the hind legs),
so the shoulder muscles get worked even harder.
The more a muscle is worked, the tougher it gets.
Translation: Shoulder meat is tough meat. Since
pork shoulder is so tough, it's best for slow cooking
methods like braising, slow roasting, and smoking.

IT'S PERFECT FOR SAUSAGE: The shoulder of a
pig also has a higher concentration of marbling and
connective tissue than any other part of the animal. If
you took out the bone, an untrimmed pork shoulder
would have about a 75:25 ratio of lean protein to fat.
That's the exact ratio in a store-bought package of

ground pork. So pork shoulder is perfect for grinding
into ground meat and for making sausage.

TWO SHOULDERS IN ONE: In the grocery store,
pork shoulders are rarely sold whole. It's economics.
Who needs a huge shoulder? Butchers usually
separate it into two cuts. Pork butt (aka shoulder
butt, Boston butt, Boston roast, and shoulder roast)
is the top half of the shoulder. Don't ask me why it's
called the butt; it's the part closest to the head and
farthest from the feet of the animal. But I do know
that it's almost always sold without the skin and often
boneless. Pork butt is fairly inexpensive and the most
popular cut for smoked pork barbecue. When people
say, "I'm smokin' butts," this is the cut they're referring
to. The smaller, bottom half has a label that's even
more peculiar: picnic ham or picnic shoulder. The
ham of a pig is the leg, so "ham" makes no sense. The
word *picnic* sometimes refers to a smaller piece, and
this is the smaller, lower part of the shoulder, so at
least that makes a little sense. The picnic ham usually
has the skin on, and that's what you need for good
barbecue to help protect the meat (see photo page
35). For my Kansas City–Style Sliced BBQ Pork
Shoulder (page 49), I use skin-on Boston butt, but
you could use the same weight of skin-on picnic ham.
For most recipes in the book, either cut will work,

CUT IT YOURSELF: I highly encourage you to buy a whole shoulder from a farmer and break it down yourself. It's cheaper that way. You'll find pockets of glands on the side of the animal that faces the head. If you see any grayish, spongy, fatty bits, just trim those out and discard them. They're nasty. The rest can be cut into two big roasts (the Boston butt and the picnic ham) for dishes like Slow-Cooked Pork Barbacoa (page 50) and Pork Pastrami on Rye (page 54).

CUT ACROSS THE GRAIN: Even when cooked, a pork shoulder is not super-tender, but cutting across the muscle fibers will make it easier to chew. That also makes the meat tender enough to grill. To slice a whole pork shoulder into steaks, you cut across the grain in the thinnest slices possible. When cut thin, these shoulder cuts are called pork blade chops or shoulder chops. When cut thick, they're called pork blade steaks or shoulder steaks. If they're cut without the bone, some butchers call them pork flatiron steaks because it's the same cut as a beef flatiron steak. Either way, it's a little tricky to cut pork shoulder at home because of all the interconnected muscle groups in the shoulder. Let your butcher cut pork shoulder steaks and chops for you.

BUY IT AND COOK IT: It's important to keep in mind that a whole pork shoulder is not a single muscle. It's a bunch of different muscles all woven together. That gives it a tendency to spoil more quickly than other cuts because there are more pockets of air between each muscle. Pork shoulder only keeps for a few days in the fridge. Don't buy this cut one week and plan to cook it the next. Buy it, cook it, and eat it as soon as you can.

Pork Butt

Picnic Ham

PORK SHOULDER SALTIMBOCCA

FEEDS 4

For classic saltimbocca, you pound out tender pieces of veal, flour them, and panfry them. I always thought it tasted kind of bland. At Clarklewis restaurant in Portland, Oregon, we sliced pork shoulder instead, threaded the pieces with ham and sage, and then grilled them. We also skipped the traditional cheese. It tastes light-years better, in my opinion. The only difference here is that I pan-sear the pork and then deglaze the pan with some wine and a little butter to make a pan sauce. It tastes bolder and more rustic than your classic saltimbocca, and the whole thing comes together in less than 30 minutes. I like it with some crispy oven-roasted potatoes alongside.

4 slices boneless pork shoulder steaks, each about 3 ounces and ½ inch thick

4 very thin slices country ham or prosciutto

16 thin slices sweet salami

8 fresh sage leaves + more for garnish

4 tablespoons butter, cut into small chunks

⅓ cup Madeira or dry white wine

½ cup Chicken Stock (page 26)

1 lemon, halved

Kosher salt and ground black pepper

Arrange the steaks on your work surface with the widest side toward you; layer each with a slice of country ham, 6 slices salami, and 2 sage leaves on the center of the meat. Fold the ends toward the center of the meat, one on top of the other, basically folding it into 3 even layers, kind of like you're folding a letter, but sideways. Thread a skewer down the center of the meat, across the fold, so the layers will hold together while cooking.

Heat a heavy-bottomed skillet over medium heat, add 2 tablespoons of the butter, and melt until bubbly and just starting to brown. Add the pork skewers flat across the pan, increase the heat to medium-high, and cook for 2 minutes, just until the pork starts to brown. Flip the skewers over, arranging so the meat is flat on the pan, and cook for another 2 minutes, or until the pork starts to brown. Transfer the skewers to a platter, pour off the remaining butter, and return the pan to the heat. Add the wine and, stirring with a wooden spoon, deglaze the pan, scraping all the browned bits into the sauce. Add the chicken stock and stir to combine, scraping the browned bits into the sauce. Return the skewers to the pan and cook for another 2 minutes in the sauce. Transfer the skewers to a plate and tent with foil to keep warm. Increase the temperature to high and reduce the liquid by half, to a syrupy consistency, which will take about 2 minutes.

Remove the pan from the heat, add the remaining 2 tablespoons butter, and swirl until melted. Squeeze in 1 teaspoon lemon juice and swirl to combine. Taste and add salt and pepper as needed. Return the meat and any accumulated juices to the pan and stir the sauce to combine. Baste the meat with the sauce and transfer, one piece at a time, to a cutting board. Remove and discard the skewer, and slice the meat on the diagonal, across the grain.

Serve with a spoonful of sauce over the top of the meat and garnish with a lemon wedge and a fresh sage leaf.

MUSTARD-BRAISED PORK SHOULDER

FEEDS 6

I made this dish on *Top Chef Las Vegas* when we cooked for the Air Force. We were challenged to give members of the Air Force and their families a taste of home. Since many of the service people are from the Deep South, I chose this dish for its nostalgia. If you're in the mood for barbecue but are short on time, it's a great stovetop option. You just brown chunks of pork shoulder and then braise them for an hour or so. That gives you the richness and tenderness of slow-cooked shoulder meat along with a tangy Georgia-style barbecue sauce in a lot less time. Serve the shoulder meat with roasted root vegetables, crusty whole-grain bread, and your favorite beer.

2 pounds trimmed boneless pork shoulder, cut into 1-inch pieces

Kosher salt

½ teaspoon ground black pepper

3 tablespoons grapeseed oil or canola oil

1 large onion, sliced root to stem end, about 2 cups

2 cloves garlic, minced, about 1 tablespoon

½ cup whole-grain Dijon mustard

¼ cup apple cider vinegar

2 tablespoons Worcestershire sauce

¾ cup Chicken Stock (page 26)

1 tablespoon smooth Dijon mustard

1 tablespoon dark molasses

Pat the meat dry and season all over with the salt and pepper. Line a baking sheet with parchment paper and place a roasting rack on the pan.

Heat a heavy-bottomed Dutch oven over high heat, add the oil, and heat until smoking. Add one layer of meat to the pan, leaving space around the pieces so they are not crowded, and cook until the meat is browned, about 3 minutes. Decrease the heat to medium-high, flip, and cook until all sides are browned, about 10 more minutes. Work in batches until all the meat is browned, probably 3 batches. When the last batch is browned, add the rest of the cooked meat back to the pan, stir in the onion, and toss to coat. Stir in the garlic and mustard until combined. Cook for another 2 minutes; the mustard seeds will start popping and the onion will start to brown. Add the vinegar, Worcestershire, and chicken stock, bring to a rapid boil, and lower the heat to a simmer. Cover and braise for 1 hour.

Remove from the heat and stir in the Dijon and molasses. Taste and add a little more salt and pepper as needed.

COCA-COLA GLAZED PORK SHOULDER

FEEDS 4 TO 6

When I lived in Portland, Oregon, there was a Malaysian restaurant near me called Malay Satay Hut. I was pretty unfamiliar with Malaysian food at the time, and the menu was daunting. But it was full of pork dishes, so I ordered the sweet and spicy glazed pork chops. When they came to the table, they smelled like Coca-Cola. I'm certain the chops were not cooked in Coke. But I could smell the vanilla, citrus, and cinnamon. To this day, I can't find a recipe that remotely resembles what they served. So I created one using pork shoulder. Even though this is a roast, it has the same sticky caramel coating on the outside and bold spice notes throughout the meat like at Malay Satay Hut. If you've never cooked with Coke, it makes a fantastic marinade because it's high in acid, which tenderizes tough muscle fibers. And the flavor . . . well, Coke has been a winner since the late 1800s. Serve this with mashed or roasted potatoes and pan-seared brussels sprouts.

1 cup Coca-Cola

2 teaspoons kosher salt

1 teaspoon lemon vinegar

½ teaspoon ground black pepper

¼ teaspoon vanilla extract

⅛ teaspoon ground cinnamon

2½ pounds boneless pork shoulder roast

2 teaspoons grapeseed oil or canola oil

In a large zip-top bag, combine the Coca-Cola, salt, vinegar, pepper, vanilla, and cinnamon, squishing to mix. Add the roast, squeeze out excess air, zip closed, and marinate for 1 hour at room temperature.

Preheat the oven to 450°F.

Remove the roast from the marinade and pour the marinade into a small saucepan. Bring to a boil over high heat, then remove from the heat.

Spray a roasting pan and rack with nonstick spray. Pat the roast dry, brush lightly with the oil, and place on the rack, fat side up.

Roast for 15 minutes, then brush with the boiled glaze, flip, and roast for another 10 minutes. Turn the oven down to 300°F and continue flipping and basting the meat every 15 minutes until it reaches 160°F, about 1¼ hours.

Remove the roast from the oven and let it rest for at least 20 minutes before carving.

=========================== Good to know ===========================

Look for lemon vinegar in gourmet stores. If you can't find it, use 1 teaspoon lemon juice + 1 drop lemon extract.

For this recipe, look for a fattier roast rather than a lean one. The fat will keep the meat nice and juicy.

Be sure to let the roast cool down before you carve it. It roasts pretty quickly, and you have to give the meat time to reabsorb the juices. If you carve it right away, the meat will be dry and the glaze won't be set. Just be patient. You be rewarded with juicy meat and a nice, thick glaze.

MILK-BRAISED PORK SHOULDER

FEEDS 6 TO 8

In high school, watching chefs cook on TV helped me decide that I wanted to become a chef myself. My favorite was—and still is—Mario Batali. It's not just because he's fat and redheaded like me. He clearly has a scientific mind, yet he cooks from his soul—two qualities I deeply appreciate. My grandmother bought me Batali's book *Simple Italian Food*, and I read it cover to cover. As a high-school kid, I couldn't get all of the ingredients the book called for or execute all the techniques, but his recipe for milk-braised pork seemed approachable. I've cooked several versions since then, and this recipe is an homage to Batali's. I use pork coppa here (he used pork loin), and I aggressively season the sauce with sage and lemon. What makes the dish successful is the method. When you braise meat in milk, the milk curdles, caramelizes, and deepens in flavor. Just blend up the pan contents, and you get a rich and creamy sauce to ladle over the meat.

3-pound boneless pork coppa, trimmed (see Good to Know)

Kosher salt and coarsely ground black pepper

1 tablespoon olive oil

1 tablespoon butter

8 sprigs sage + more for garnish

2 cups heavy cream

3 cups whole milk

½ sprig rosemary + more for garnish

4 fresh bay leaves

2 lemons

Preheat the oven to 350°F.

Trim and pat the coppa dry. Season it on all sides with salt and pepper and truss with butcher's twine (see page 81). Heat a low, straight-sided pan with a lid over medium heat. (You can also use a Dutch oven.) Add the oil, swirl, add the butter, and swirl until the foam subsides. Add the meat and cook until nicely browned, about 4 minutes, then turn and cook until all sides are browned, about 12 minutes total. Add the sage sprigs; they will immediately crackle. Add the cream; it will bubble up and cool the pan. Add the milk, rosemary sprig, and bay leaves.

Cover and braise in the oven for 1¼ hours. Carefully remove from the oven; remember the top and handle are crazy hot.

Transfer the roast to a plate and tent with aluminum foil to keep warm. The sauce will look curdled, which is okay. Discard the bay leaves and herb stems, and then blend the sauce with a blender—either a stand blender or immersion blender will do. Strain the blended sauce through a medium-mesh sieve and discard the solids. Return the sauce to the pan and bring to a boil over medium-high heat. Boil for 2 to 3 minutes to thicken slightly.

Finely grate the zest from 1 lemon into the sauce and stir in 2 tablespoons of lemon juice. Remove from the heat and season to taste with salt and pepper.

Slice the coppa and serve with a little sauce, a sage and a rosemary sprig, and lemon wedges.

Good to know

Coppa is a specific muscle in the shoulder. Ask your butcher for it. Or use any boneless cut of pork shoulder. Coppa is the Rolls-Royce of pork shoulder cuts because it's located near the loin and it's both flavorful and tender. Only problem is, you don't see this cut too often—just like a Rolls-Royce. But it's unbelievably simple to carve this muscle from the shoulder. My advice is to ask a good butcher to cut out the coppa for you; or buy a whole uncut bone-in pork shoulder and cut out the coppa yourself. Position the shoulder on a work surface with the narrow shank end facing you (hanging off the work surface) and the wider shoulder end away from you. At the wider shoulder end, the coppa is the muscle at the very top. With the whole shoulder in that position, the muscle runs from east to west and looks like a pork loin 3 to 4 inches in diameter. Use your knife to trim the surface fat 3 to 4 inches from the top of the shoulder, and find the spot under the fat where this muscle ends and the rest of the shoulder begins. Then simply make a horizontal cut below this muscle to remove it. The cut should start 3 to 4 inches from the top of the shoulder. As you cut, pull the coppa muscle away from the featherbones, fat, and connective tissue, cutting those as necessary but leaving the muscle intact. It will look like a miniature pork loin but will be well marbled.

SOUR ORANGE CARNITAS

FEEDS 4

When I was growing up, my dad and I would get lunch at Los Avinas, a little hole-in-the-wall a couple miles from where he worked. I loved the carnitas and always wondered how they got the meat crunchy on the outside but tender inside. With braising, I was always taught to brown the meat first, then add liquid and cook it. But it's the exact opposite for carnitas. That's the secret. You simmer the meat in liquid first, then after the pan goes dry, you brown the meat. That blew my mind, but it works great. Some of the fat renders out of the pork, which thickens up the liquid. You often see the meat served with tomatillo salsa, but it's so juicy, it doesn't really need it. Rice and beans are plenty. Serve any leftovers in tacos, burritos, or casseroles. It's super-versatile.

2 pounds boneless pork shoulder, trimmed, cut into 1-inch cubes

8 cloves garlic, crushed

2 teaspoons kosher salt

¼ teaspoon red pepper flakes

¼ cup lard, melted

3 oranges

3 cups Chicken Stock (page 26)

¼ cup freshly squeezed lemon juice

½ cup thinly sliced onion

¼ cup fresh cilantro leaves

Place the pork in a Dutch oven. Toss with the garlic, 1 teaspoon of the salt, the red pepper flakes, and the melted lard. Juice the oranges and reserve the juice for later. Quarter the orange rinds and add the rinds to the pork. Add just enough stock to cover the meat and orange rinds. Bring to a boil over high heat, then lower to a simmer, cover, and cook for 1 hour.

Remove the lid, return to a boil, and cook down for 30 minutes; almost all of the liquid will be cooked out and the mixture should start frying.

Using tongs, remove and discard the orange rinds. Lower the heat to medium, turn the meat, and continue browning it for another 5 minutes. A nice film, or *fond*, will build in the bottom of the pan. Add the reserved orange juice and the lemon juice and stir all the *fond* into the sauce. Bring to a rapid boil; the sauce should reduce quickly. Remove from the heat and stir in the remaining 1 teaspoon salt, the onion and cilantro.

BRAISED PORK SHOULDER WITH SAUERKRAUT

FEEDS 8 TO 10

My mom worked multiple jobs when I was a kid and didn't have much time to cook. This was one of her slow cooker standbys that I always loved. The most important step is to brown the meat first. I can't stress that enough. Browning the meat is what creates deep flavor in any braise—whether it's done in a slow cooker, on the stovetop, or in the oven. After you brown the meat, then you can walk away from the pot. For this dish, you add a couple bags or jars of sauerkraut to the pot (I like homemade sauerkraut best), and some onion and beer (that meant Budweiser in the Gillespie household), and then just let the pork braise away. Some folks add a little brown sugar, molasses, or diced apple at the end for sweetness. I prefer it tangy and tart. Sometimes I stir in a little coarse, grainy German-style mustard.

3 pounds boneless pork butt

Kosher salt and ground black pepper

2 tablespoons grapeseed oil or canola oil

1 (12-ounce) bottle German-style lager

1 large onion, peeled, root and stem ends trimmed

1 (32-ounce) bag sauerkraut

2 tablespoons apple cider vinegar

1 Fuji apple (optional)

1 tablespoon sorghum or molasses

Aggressively season all sides of the pork with large Kevin pinches of both salt and pepper (see page 20 for a definition of a Kevin pinch). Heat a 10-inch heavy-bottomed skillet over high heat, add the oil, and swirl to coat the pan. When the oil starts to smoke, add the pork butt. Sear until deep golden brown, about 3 minutes per side. You want it very brown; that's what creates flavor here. Use tongs to flip the meat so that all sides are browned, even the two ends. Transfer the meat to a plate and set aside. Pour half of the beer into the pan to deglaze, scraping all the browned bits into the sauce. Reserve.

Cut the onion, stem to root end, into eighths. Drain the sauerkraut in a colander, discarding the juices. Pour the remaining beer into a large slow cooker. Add the onion, sauerkraut, vinegar, pork and any accumulated juices, and the pan sauce. Cover and cook on low until the meat shreds apart easily and the sauerkraut is broken down and almost dissolved, about 7 hours. Check after 6 hours and, if you like, slice the apple thinly and add the slices on top; cover and continue cooking until tender, about another hour. Serve drizzled with the sorghum.

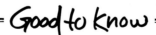

Good to Know

If you're buying sauerkraut instead of making it, I like Boar's Head best.

Get a good sear on all sides of the meat. That's the most important part of this recipe and a step many folks leave out of slow cooker cooking. But that's what takes the dish from ho-hum to something special.

This is great served with oven-roasted potatoes. If you have leftovers, serve them as hot sandwiches on a crisp roll with a smear of whole-grain mustard.

KOREAN BARBECUED PORK BULGOGI

FEEDS 4

If you've never eaten at a Korean barbecue restaurant, you gotta go. It's fun. You grill your own strips of marinated meat, then add whatever spicy, sharp, and crunchy accompaniments you like. The requisite spread usually includes kimchi, pickles, chiles, and lettuce leaves to wrap it all up. Beef is most common but there are pork versions too, which I like better. To simplify the dish, I pan-sear thin slices of pork shoulder and turn the accompaniments into a sort of slaw that you wrap up in the lettuce. You could brush a little hoisin in there before you roll it up, or squirt on some sriracha. Use whatever condiments you have or none.

1 cup reduced-sodium soy
   sauce

½ cup sugar

1 teaspoon sesame oil

1 teaspoon Korean red chili
   powder (or Espelette pepper)

1 teaspoon mashed garlic

12 ounces paper-thin sliced
   boneless pork shoulder

¼ cup Duke's mayonnaise

1 tablespoon sweet chili sauce

1-inch piece fresh ginger, grated,
   about 2 teaspoons

2 limes

¼ teaspoon kosher salt

½ teaspoon sambal oelek, or
   more as desired

1 carrot

¼ small head cabbage, finely
   shredded, about 2 cups

4 scallions, root end trimmed,
   thinly sliced on the bias

8 butter or Bibb lettuce leaves,
   for serving

In a gallon-size zip-top bag, combine the soy, sugar, sesame oil, chili powder, and garlic and smush to combine. Add the meat and smush around so all pieces are well coated. Squeeze out the air, zip the top shut, and marinate for 15 minutes at room temperature. The meat is so thin and the marinade so strong that a quick marinade is all this needs.

In a large bowl, whisk together the mayonnaise, chili sauce, ginger, 1 tablespoon lime juice, the salt, and the sambal oelek. Taste and add more sambal oelek if you like it spicy.

Grate the carrot on the largest hole of the box grater; you'll get about 1 cup. Squeeze dry in a paper towel, then toss the carrot, cabbage, and half the scallions with the dressing to combine.

Heat a grill pan over high heat. Remove the meat from the marinade and discard the marinade. Working in batches, grill the meat in a single layer for 30 seconds, then flip and grill for another 30 seconds; it will shrink and get some good color and grill marks. The meat is so thin that it should cook through in this short amount of time. Transfer the meat to a plate and stack. Slice the meat crosswise into 1-inch slices.

Layer the meat and slaw on the lettuce leaves and garnish with the remaining scallions.

Good to know

Look for thinly sliced pork shoulder at Korean markets. It's pretty common. Or just ask your butcher to thinly slice some boneless pork shoulder for you. Call ahead, because they usually freeze the meat for a little while to make it easier to slice paper-thin. You could also do the same thing at home.

RED CHILE POSOLE

MAKES 3 QUARTS: FEEDS 6 TO 8

If it's cold and dreary out, here's your dish. It's a classic Mexican stew that comes together in less than an hour and a half. I like the pork to be tender but not blown apart into shreds. I also prefer extra-small hominy here—not those gargantuan pellets that look like horses' teeth. The small ones have a more delicate texture. Traditionally, the stew has a soupy consistency, but I like it better with more heft, so I add pureed chiles to give it a more velvety mouthfeel. But the most important step is to panfry the pureed chiles and onion. That one simple step amplifies and concentrates all the flavors. Traditionally, you top the stew with cabbage, radishes, cheese, and a squeeze of lime. To simplify things, I make a slaw out of those ingredients. That way, you get a bright pop of flavor in every spoonful.

4 dried ancho chiles

4 dried pasilla chiles

3 dried guajillo chiles

1 tablespoon light brown sugar

2 pounds boneless pork shoulder, cut into 1-inch cubes

Kosher salt

3 tablespoons grapeseed oil or canola oil

2 sweet onions, peeled and cut into rough chunks, about 3 cups

½ cup cloves garlic, peeled

2 teaspoons dried oregano

4 cups Chicken Stock (page 26)

2 (15.5-ounce) cans hominy, rinsed and drained

3 limes

4½ cups Posole Slaw (recipe follows)

Crispy tortilla strips, for serving

Tear open the chiles, remove the stems and seeds, and place the chiles in a 2-quart pot. Add the brown sugar and just enough water to cover the peppers, about 6 cups. Bring to a boil over high heat. Cover the pot, decrease the heat to low, and simmer for 15 minutes. Remove from the heat.

Pat the pork dry and aggressively season all over with salt. Heat a Dutch oven over high heat and add the oil, making sure to generously cover the bottom. Add the cubed pork to the Dutch oven. It will be crowded, but that's all right. Stir the pork a couple times until it is browned and crispy, making sure a good amount of the fat has rendered out, about 15 minutes.

Add the onions, garlic, and oregano to a blender and blend to a chunky paste. Using tongs, transfer all the peppers to the blender, add 1½ cups of the chile broth from the pot, and blend everything to a smooth, thick paste. Carefully add the paste to the sizzling-hot pork. You're basically frying the sauce in the rendered pork fat to develop flavor. It will sizzle and pop, so step back and be careful. Once it's good and fried all over, add the chicken stock, stirring to release the browned bits of pork and fat from the bottom of the pot. Add the hominy, return to a boil, decrease the heat to low, cover, and simmer until the pork is tender, about 1 hour.

Stir in 1 teaspoon salt (maybe a little more if you think it needs it) and 3 tablespoons lime juice.

Serve in large soup bowls topped with a generous mound of slaw, some tortilla strips, and a large wedge or two of lime for squeezing.

Continued

Posole Slaw MAKES ABOUT 4½ CUPS

½ small head green cabbage, finely shredded, about 2 cups

1 bunch cilantro, leaves coarsely chopped, about 1 cup

1 small sweet onion, cut into small dice, about 1 cup

4 radishes, thinly sliced

½ cup crumbled cotija cheese

1 lime

½ teaspoon kosher salt

In a medium bowl, toss together the cabbage, cilantro, onion, radishes, and cheese. Squeeze the lime juice into the mixture, add the salt, and toss. The other ingredients can be prepped ahead but should be tossed with the lime and salt just before serving.

Good to know

You can buy the crispy tortilla strips from the grocery store. Or, if you want to make them yourself, cut corn tortillas into strips, then coat them with nonstick spray and some salt and chili powder and bake them at 375°F in single layers on baking sheets until nice and crisp.

If you're not familiar with hominy, it's field corn that has been soaked in an alkaline liquid to remove the tough hull. Most grocery stores carry it in cans. Be sure to look for small hominy for the best texture. La Preferida is a good brand.

Cotija cheese (*queso añejo*) is aged Mexican cheese with a sharp flavor. If you can't find it, use another aged cheese such as dry Jack or aged Asiago.

KANSAS CITY-STYLE SLICED BBQ PORK SHOULDER
MAKES 1 BIG BUTT

I have a gripe with overcooked, oversmoked pork shoulder. I prefer the texture of Kansas City–style pork barbecue. It's sliceable but not fall-apart tender. That's how they serve it at famous KC barbecue places like Arthur Bryant's. You could come up with a million different rubs to flavor the meat, but at the end of the day, salt and smoke are what you're really after here. It's so incredibly flavorful that you don't even need sauce. But you do need a bone-in pork butt with the skin on. The bone adds flavor to the meat, and the skin helps to protect the fat layer underneath so the fat slowly melts and keeps the meat nice and juicy. The skin also absorbs some smoke and keeps the meat from oversmoking and tasting like an ashtray.

1 bone-in, skin-on Boston butt, about 9 pounds

Kosher salt

Heat a smoker to 280°F.

Pat the meat dry and rub aggressively with salt. Place the meat directly on the rack in the smoker and smoke, with full smoke, for 8 hours, maintaining the temperature at 280°F.

Stop feeding smoke into the smoker (or transfer to a 280°F oven) and continue cooking at 280°F for an additional 7 hours. Turn the heat off and leave the meat in the cooker to rest for another 2 hours, or until cool enough to handle.

Carefully remove the top layer of "bark" (smoked skin) and reserve for another use. Scrape off the soft layer of fat and any visible chunks of fat and place in a medium saucepan. Place over medium-low heat to render the fat. The mixture will start out looking milky and then turn into clear fat and solids. Strain and discard the solids, reserving the smoked fat for another use.

Traditionally, KC–style BBQ is sliced. This butt will pull just fine, but slicing is the way to go for a really great piece of meat.

SLOW-COOKED PORK BARBACOA
FEEDS 12

When I worked at TWO Urban Licks in Atlanta, most of the crew was Hispanic. Every Saturday, one of the cooks would bring in barbacoa tacos he bought from a guy named Manuel out on Buford Highway. Manuel sold these barbecued goat tacos right out of his apartment with a soccer game on in the background and his family milling about. This kind of Mexican barbecue isn't smoky. It tastes more steamed because the meat is cooked in a pit in the ground. Everyone knows Mexican tacos can be dry, but Manuel's were moist and juicy, with spices like clove, allspice, and cinnamon along with hot peppers. I loved them. I've stayed true to Manuel's flavors here, but I use pork instead of goat, wrap it up in foil, and then bake it until it's tender enough to shred. If you have a pit in your backyard, have at it. But the foil-and-oven method works great. The meat is delicious in tacos. I also use it as the base meat for Nachos de Puerco (page 60), Breakfast Burritos (page 51), and A Really Good Cuban Sandwich (page 52).

2 tablespoons kosher salt

1 tablespoon ancho chili powder (or other single chili powder, not a blend)

½ teaspoon ground cinnamon

¼ teaspoon ground cloves

5 pounds bone-in pork shoulder

1 onion, quartered

10 cloves garlic, peeled

3 dried bay leaves

Adjust the rack in the oven to a lower level so the roast will easily slide in. Heat the oven to 350°F.

In a small bowl, combine the salt, chili powder, cinnamon, and cloves. Pat the pork dry and generously season all over with the salt mixture. Cut a large piece (about 24 inches) of heavy-duty foil and place in a roasting pan. Add the roast, onions, garlic, and bay leaves and wrap everything up tightly in the foil. Roast for 3½ hours.

Remove from the oven and let rest, still wrapped in the foil, for 30 minutes. The foil will keep all the moisture and flavors in the packet and the shoulder will braise as it cools, creating very tender and juicy meat. Discard the onion, garlic, and bay leaves before shredding the meat.

=== Good to Know ===

Instead of Boston butt, you could use the picnic part of the shoulder. Or use the whole shoulder if you have one. Just trim the fat down to ⅛ inch or so.

For a simple family meal, just serve the shredded meat in corn tortillas with rice and beans and whatever toppings you like—chopped onion, grated cheese, a squeeze of lime.

BREAKFAST BURRITOS

MAKES 4 BURRITOS

How hard is it to make a decent breakfast burrito? Pretty hard, apparently, because most of them suck. They're dry and taste like a pile of dry meat with just a tiny bit of everything else. Is it really that difficult to make sure you get a taste of every ingredient in every bite? And they're supposed to be portable. You shouldn't need a big tub of salsa to dunk them in to keep the burritos from tasting like shoe leather. Sorry to get on the high horse, but c'mon. In this recipe, I keep the meat juicy with Slow-Cooked Pork Barbacoa (page 50). If you don't have that, fry up some bacon. Step two is to bake a potato, or use leftover spuds. Then you chop up the potatoes and fry them with onions, peppers, and the pork. That's your base. You could make the whole base the night before and keep it in the fridge. In the morning, just crack a couple eggs into a hot pan, add some cheese, and fry the whole thing into a hash with the meat and potato base. Chuck the hash into a hot tortilla and you're good to go.

1 large russet potato

2 teaspoons grapeseed oil or canola oil

1 Anaheim or poblano chile, stem and seeds removed, cut into ¼-inch rings

½ red onion, split lengthwise, then cut crosswise into ¼-inch rings

6 ounces Slow-Cooked Pork Barbacoa (page 50), pulled or cut into bite-size pieces

2 tablespoons butter

8 eggs

4 ounces sharp cheddar cheese, coarsely grated

Kosher salt and ground black pepper

4 (10-inch) flour tortillas

½ cup Salsa Verde (page 115) or Cantina Salsa (page 61)

¼ cup sour cream

Prick the potato and bake or microwave until fork-tender (425°F oven for 45 to 60 minutes, or on high for 8 to 10 minutes, turning once). Let cool to the touch. Peel and cut into 2-inch pieces.

Heat a large cast-iron skillet over medium heat. Add the oil and swirl to coat the pan. Add the potatoes and cook until they start to brown, about 4 minutes. Using a metal spatula, flip the potatoes and break into smaller chunks. Cook until nicely browned, another 3 minutes. Add the peppers and onions and continue cooking until the vegetables are softened, about 4 more minutes. Add the pork, the salt and pepper, toss again and heat through. Spread the mixture evenly in the pan and turn the heat to the lowest setting.

In a nonstick skillet, heat 1 tablespoon of the butter over medium-high heat until the foam subsides. Fry 4 of the eggs in the pan over easy, sliding onto the pork mixture and topping with the cheese. Add the remaining 1 tablespoon butter, fry the rest of the eggs over easy, and slide onto the cheese. Use the spatula to break the yolks and chop the eggs into the pork mixture. You want runny yolks here for flavor and moisture in the burritos.

Heat the tortillas in the microwave or over a gas burner to soften them, and then divide the egg mixture among the tortillas. Fold the sides in and roll to close. Serve with salsa and a dollop of sour cream.

Good to know

If you're feeding a crowd, double or triple the recipe and make the meat-and-potato base ahead of time.

A REALLY GOOD CUBAN SANDWICH

MAKES 4 SANDWICHES

After years of trying them, I have had very few excellent Cuban sandwiches. They always seem dry. My version here may not be traditional, but everyone likes it. I use soft, sweet challah bread rather than the traditional baguette-style bread. When you toast it, the sandwich still gets crispy on the outside, but the bread stays soft and moist inside. For a group of friends, split the whole loaf in half lengthwise and make 1 big sandwich on a large griddle or extra-large panini press (see photo). I'll take those melters, Gruyère and Gouda, over dry Swiss cheese any day. And for the ham, I have no idea why people use the least flavorful deli ham available. A good Virginia-style pit ham—a little sweet and a little smoky—will never steer you wrong. Just don't slice it paper-thin. It should have some chew when you bite into it. And for the roast pork, I use moist and juicy Slow-Cooked Pork Barbacoa (page 50). The signature flavor of mojo, Cuba's orange and olive oil sauce, comes in the form of mojo mayonnaise. The mayo helps to carry those citrus flavors through the entire sandwich.

1¼ cups Duke's mayonnaise

1 large orange, for juicing

1 lime, for juicing

5 cloves garlic, mashed to a paste, about 4 teaspoons

1 tablespoon toasted and finely ground cumin seeds

2 teaspoons kosher salt

1 bunch cilantro, leaves only, about 1 cup

4 Cuban-style sandwich loaves, or 1 loaf brioche or challah bread, cut into eight ¾-inch-thick slices (see headnote)

2 teaspoons yellow mustard

1 cup grated Gouda cheese (could be any kind of rich, easy-melting cow's milk cheese)

1 cup grated Gruyère cheese

4 ounces thick-sliced deli ham

10 ounces Slow-Cooked Pork Barbacoa (page 50), sliced

Dill pickle slices, preferably flat, thinly sliced cucumber dill pickles

In a blender, combine the mayonnaise, ½ cup orange juice, 1 tablespoon lime juice, garlic, cumin, and salt until smooth. Add the cilantro and blend until smooth and creamy, about 30 seconds.

The order of assembly is important here! Spread the bottom slice of bread with mustard and sprinkle with the Gouda. Build the rest of the sandwich on the top slice of bread, starting with the Gruyère, followed by a slice of ham and the Barbacoa. Place a liberal layer of pickles over the pork, and top that with a full-on slathering of the cilantro mayonnaise. Flip the bottom up onto the top and press down firmly to compact.

Heat a panini press to medium and coat lightly with nonstick spray or a brush of grapeseed or canola oil. You really want a nice, slow melt and toast. Place the sandwiches on the press, top side down, and close the top. Cook for 3 minutes, or until the bread is toasty and golden brown and the cheese starts melting. Alternatively, if you're using a griddle, heat to medium and coat the pan lightly with nonstick spray or a brush of oil. You do not want a smoking-hot griddle here, or it will char the bread. Place the sandwiches on the griddle, top side down, and place a baking sheet on top of the sandwiches and then place some heavy weights on top to compress the sandwiches. Cook for 3 minutes, or until the bottom surface of the bread is golden brown and you start to see the cheese melting. Remove the baking sheet from the sandwiches, brush the top of the bread lightly with oil, then flip. Replace the baking sheet and weights on top and continue cooking until the sandwiches are golden brown and crispy and you can see the rest of the cheese melting, another 2 to 3 minutes. Remove the sandwiches, flip over, and cut in half on the diagonal. Serve the sandwiches with the remaining cilantro mayonnaise for dipping.

Worth Knowing

These sandwiches are rich and chock-full of meat, so half a sandwich may be all you need.

PORK PASTRAMI ON RYE

MAKES 4 SANDWICHES

Yes, I know, Jews don't eat pork. I'm prepared for the hate mail. But hear me out. Pork pastrami has a beautiful sweet flavor that's more delicate than beef pastrami. It makes a helluva good sandwich on buttered and toasted rye bread with melted cheese, sauerkraut, and a smear of mustard. It's even better with some Pork Fat Pommes Frites (page 223) on the plate. The pork pastrami itself requires little more than time to brine the pork and a smoker to cook it—just like beef pastrami. The brine keeps the meat moist and gives it a rosy pink color. The smoke flavors the meat, as does the black pepper, coriander, and caraway crust.

1 loaf seeded rye bread, sliced into 8 (¾-inch thick) slices

3 tablespoons butter, softened

8 thin slices Swiss cheese

1 cup sauerkraut

¼ cup finely minced Vidalia onion

1 tablespoon Dijon mustard

12 ounces Pork Pastrami (recipe follows), sliced about ¼ inch thick

Heat a griddle to medium or 325°F.

Spread both sides of the 8 slices of bread with the butter. Griddle the bread just until starting to brown, about 2 minutes. Flip the bread, add a slice of cheese, and grill until toasted and the cheese is melted, another 1 to 2 minutes.

Drain the sauerkraut and squeeze dry. Mix the sauerkraut, onion, and mustard and spread on the griddle, chopping and turning with a metal spatula just until heated through, about 3 minutes.

Build each sandwich with the pastrami and the sauerkraut-onion mixture and press to compress. Slice and serve hot.

Pork Pastrami MAKES ABOUT 2 POUNDS

3 pounds boneless pork butt

½ cup kosher salt

¼ cup packed light brown sugar

¼ cup pickling spice mix
(see Good to Know)

1 teaspoon curing/pink salt (see
Good to Know)

1 tablespoon ground black pepper

1 Vidalia onion, root and stem ends
trimmed, cut into 6 wedges

12 cloves garlic, smashed

3 cups ice cubes

2 tablespoons black peppercorns

1 tablespoon coriander seeds

1½ teaspoons caraway seeds

Trim the pork butt to remove any loose connective tissue or small pieces of meat.

Combine 6 cups water, the salt, sugar, pickling spice, curing salt, ground pepper, onion, and garlic in a large saucepan over high heat. Stir and, just when bubbles start forming at the edge, remove from the heat. You just want to heat the liquid enough to dissolve the sugar and salt and, most important, release the essential oils from the onions and garlic into the brine.

Stir the ice cubes into the brine to cool it, then pour the brine into an extra-large (2-gallon) zip-top bag and add the pork. Squeeze the air out of the bag, zip shut, place in a second zip-top bag, and refrigerate for 7 to 14 days, turning and checking every 2 days to make sure the bag isn't leaking and all sides are immersed in brine. It's always good to label and date the bag. The pork needs to cure for a minimum of 7 days, but you can leave it in the cure for up to 14 days. The longer it cures, the stronger the flavor. Once the pork has cured in the refrigerator for at least 7 days, remove the pastrami from the brine, rinse, and pat dry.

Combine the peppercorns, coriander, and caraway seeds in a spice grinder or a mortar and pestle and grind to a coarse mix. Pour the spice mixture onto a baking sheet and roll the pork in it to coat with spices on all sides.

Heat a smoker to 200°F and feed with hickory wood. Place the pork directly on the rack of the smoker and smoke for 3 to 4 hours, until the meat is tender and has reached an internal temperature of 160°F. Slice while still warm.

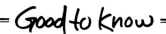

Good to Know

Most grocery stores carry premixed pickling spice in the spice aisle.

Curing/pink salt (aka curing salt #1) helps to prevent bacterial growth in cured meats and sausages. You can get it from online sausage supply houses such as butcherpacker.com.

You can keep the smoked meat refrigerated for about a week or up to several months if you vacuum-seal it. For hot sandwiches, I like to slice off pieces and heat them in a skillet. To carve it right off the hot roast like they do at Katz's, Carnegie, and other New York Jewish delis, wrap the whole pastrami in plastic wrap and microwave it for a few minutes, just until it's warmed through. Then carve away.

GRILLED PORK BÁNH MÌ

MAKES 4 SANDWICHES

Quoc Houng is a Vietnamese take-out place in Atlanta known for its bánh mì sandwiches. I modeled this version on Quoc Houng's but took a few liberties. The traditional bread is like a baguette but with some rice flour in the dough, which makes the bread light and airy. That bread is hard to get, so I just use a soft baguette or hoagie bun. Don't worry about going artisan here—you want the bread to be soft and fluffy inside. The pork shoulder is marinated in Asian herbs and spices, and then quickly grilled for a smoky-sweet-savory flavor. And here's the redneckification of the sandwich: I slather it with Duke's mayonnaise. Instead of pickled chiles, I top it with prepared chili-garlic sauce like sambal oelek. And in place of the traditional pickled daikon and carrots, I use raw carrots and sweet bread-and-butter pickles. All in all, you get the signature bánh mì flavors with a lot less work. When we tested this recipe, my kitchen crew was just coming into the restaurant for the day. They're all big fans of traditional bánh mì, and they absolutely loved these sandwiches.

1 pound boneless pork shoulder, very thinly sliced

⅓ cup fish sauce

¼ cup sugar

1 tablespoon oyster sauce

1 lemongrass stalk, crushed and very thinly sliced, about ⅓ cup

1-inch piece fresh ginger, finely grated, about 1 tablespoon

1 clove garlic, minced

4 soft hoagie buns

¼ cup Duke's mayonnaise

2 teaspoons sambal oelek

1 large carrot, peeled and finely julienned, about 1 cup

¾ cup bread-and-butter or sweet pickle slices

One by one, sandwich the pork slices between plastic wrap and pound very thin, the thinnest you can get without tearing. Combine the fish sauce, sugar, oyster sauce, lemongrass, ginger, and garlic in a gallon-size zip-top bag and squish to combine and dissolve the sugar. Add the meat, squeeze out all the air, and zip the top closed. Marinate for 1 hour at room temperature.

Heat a grill pan over high heat and spray with nonstick spray.

Slice the rolls in half lengthwise. Using your fingers, remove the bulk of the soft insides and discard. Spread both cut sides of the buns with mayonnaise and a thin smear of sambal. Sprinkle the bottom with a layer of carrots and pickles.

Remove the meat from the marinade and discard the marinade. Pat the meat dry. Grill the meat in a single layer for about 1 minute, then using tongs, flip and cook for another 2 to 3 minutes. Ultimately, you want to render the chewy fat from the meat.

Add the meat straight from the grill to the sandwiches. Press to compact, and serve.

COTTAGE BACON CROQUE MONSIEUR

MAKES 4 SANDWICHES

If you like lean, thick-cut bacon, you'll love this sandwich. It's made with shoulder bacon, aka cottage bacon. You cook the bacon, layer it between thick slices of toasted challah bread, spoon a creamy cheddar sauce over the top, and broil the whole thing. It's a knife-and-fork kind of sandwich and completely delicious. Pretty classic, too, although I swap in super-sharp cheddar cheese for the traditional Gruyère. To make it a croque madame, add a fried egg to the top of the sandwich.

12 thin slices Cottage Bacon (page 132)

2 tablespoons + 2 teaspoons butter

1 loaf brioche or challah bread, cut int eight ¾-inch-thick slices

2 teaspoons all-purpose flour

1 cup half-and-half

3 ounces Fiscalini or other super-sharp cheddar cheese, grated

4 teaspoons Dijon mustard

2 tablespoons freshly grated pecorino or Parmesan cheese

Arrange the bacon in a single layer in a large sauté pan and place over medium heat, working in batches as needed. Cook for 2 minutes, then flip and cook until the edges are crispy, the bacon is pinkish in color, and the fat starts turning translucent, about 2 more minutes. Transfer to a paper towel–lined plate and repeat the process until all of the bacon is cooked. Remove the pan from the heat, add 2 tablespoons of the butter, and swirl to melt into the drippings.

Adjust the rack in the oven to the highest setting and preheat the broiler to high.

Brush a baking sheet with the buttery bacon drippings and brush one side of each slice of bread with the drippings. Place the bread, brushed side up, on the baking sheet. Broil until the edges start to brown, about 2 minutes. Remove from the oven, flip the bread, and brush the other side with the buttery bacon drippings. Return to the oven and toast until the edges start to brown, another 2 minutes or so.

Decrease the broiler temperature to low and move the oven rack down one notch.

In a small saucepan over medium heat, melt the remaining 2 teaspoons butter. Stir in the flour and, stirring constantly, cook for 2 minutes. Slowly stir in the half-and-half and bring to a boil; cook for another 2 minutes, or until thick. Stir in the cheddar until melted and smooth.

Spread each toast with Dijon and a light sprinkling of pecorino. Build each sandwich with 3 slices cottage bacon and a toast on top. Place on a parchment paper–lined baking sheet and spoon a generous amount of sauce over each sandwich, making sure all of the edges are covered completely with sauce so they won't burn. Evenly sprinkle the remaining pecorino over the tops of the sandwiches and broil until browned and bubbly, about 4 minutes.

TACOS AL PASTOR
FEEDS 4

When I was 20, my Mexican friend Vincente took me to Mexico City for *tacos al pastor*. We walked up to this super-busy stall that had spits of marinated, sliced, and stacked pork rotating near a fire—almost like the meat for gyros. Pineapples rotated near the fire right next to the pork. The tacos are called *al pastor* because missionaries came from Jerusalem to Mexico and brought their Middle Eastern foodways with them. Over time, *tacos al pastor* became one of the most popular Mexican tacos. Go figure. Anyway, here's my veiled attempt to nail down the spicy-sweet-savory flavors. The texture is nearly impossible to get right without 200 pounds of sliced pork rotating on a spit. Instead, I use trim and scraps of pork shoulder, cut them small, and then sear the pork in a smoking-hot pan. Garnish the meat with spicy salsa and some chopped onion and cilantro, and it makes a damn fine taco.

1 pineapple, peeled, cored, cut into 1-inch cubes, about 2 cups, or 1 (20-ounce) can unsweetened pineapple chunks, drained

1 medium Vidalia onion, cut into rough chunks

10 cloves garlic, peeled

2 tablespoons ancho chili powder

1 tablespoon cumin seeds

1 tablespoon dried oregano

1 tablespoon kosher salt

1 teaspoon red pepper flakes

1 pound lean pork shoulder, cut into ¾-inch chunks (see Worth Knowing)

3 teaspoons grapeseed oil or canola oil

8 fresh corn tortillas

½ cup sour cream

1 lime

1 bunch cilantro

Reserve ½ cup pineapple chunks and onion and refrigerate for later use. Combine the remaining pineapple, onion, garlic, chili powder, cumin, oregano, salt, and red pepper flakes in a blender and blend to a paste. Place the meat and marinade in a gallon-size zip-top bag, squeeze out excess air, and zip closed. Refrigerate overnight.

Strain the pork and discard the marinade.

Heat a sauté pan over high heat. Add just enough of the oil to the pan for a thin coating and heat until the oil just starts to smoke. Working in batches, add the tortillas in a single layer and heat just until starting to char, about 1 minute per side, then flip and cook for another minute. Wrap in aluminum foil to keep warm.

Add just enough of the oil to cover the pan, swirl to coat, and heat until smoking. Add the pork and reserved pineapple and cook for 1 minute, or until browned. Shake the pan to flip the meat and cook until the pork is cooked through and the pan juices have cooked dry, about 7 minutes, shaking the pan frequently.

In a small bowl, combine the sour cream with the juice of ½ lime and whisk until smooth. Cut the remaining ½ lime into 4 wedges.

Coarsely chop ½ cup cilantro leaves. Reserve 4 sprigs.

Serve the tortillas topped with the meat and pineapple mixture, reserved pineapple and onion, chopped cilantro, a drizzle of the lime sour cream, a lime wedge, and whole sprig of cilantro.

Worth Knowing

Look for a lean shoulder roast for this recipe. It will be a piece of a boneless Boston butt. Get the smallest and leanest roast you can find, which will probably be 2 to 3 pounds. If you get a piece with excess fat, just trim it away before cutting the meat into chunks.

NACHOS DE PUERCO

FEEDS 8 TO 10

As a huge fan of nachos, I'm often disappointed. They come out gloppy, soggy, and impossible to eat. But there's a dive bar in Atlanta called Elmyr that serves good nachos. They keep the chips crisp, and that's the key. I like to build nachos with a layer of chips, then the cheese, then the meat, then a few more layers of chips, cheese, and meat. That's all you need. Save the wet stuff like salsa and sour cream for the top or on the side. The meat here is Slow-Cooked Pork Barbacoa (page 50). At the very end, I top the nachos with some lime crema and avocado salsa. At Gunshow, all the cooks just happened to show up for work while we were testing this recipe. The entire tray of nachos was gone in less than 4 minutes.

2 avocados

2 cups Cantina Salsa (recipe follows)

¼ cup sour cream

1 lime

1 (1-pound) bag crispy corn tortilla chips

8 ounces Monterey Jack cheese, finely grated

6 ounces Slow-Cooked Pork Barbacoa (page 50), shredded and warmed

Slice the avocados in half, remove the pits and peel, and dice the avocado flesh into ½-inch cubes. Fold into the salsa and refrigerate.

In a small bowl, whisk the sour cream with the juice of the lime.

Heat the oven to 350°F.

Spread one-third of the chips in a single layer on a baking sheet lined with nonstick foil or parchment paper. Sprinkle with one-third of the cheese and pork, add another layer of chips, cheese, and pork, and then build a final layer of chips and cheese. Reserve the remaining one-third of the pork. Bake for 5 minutes, or until all the cheese melts.

Remove from the oven and sprinkle with the remaining pork. Spoon the salsa over the top and drizzle with the lime sour cream.

Cantina Salsa MAKES ABOUT 3 CUPS

1 Vidalia onion

6 cloves garlic, root ends trimmed

1 small jalapeño pepper

1 teaspoon grapeseed oil or
    canola oil

3 tomatoes, cored and quartered

1 lime

1 teaspoon kosher salt

½ teaspoon ancho chili powder

½ cup fresh cilantro leaves

Peel the onion; trim and discard the root and stem ends. Cut the onion in half north to south. Lay the cut sides down on the cutting board and slice into ½-inch rings.

Heat a large cast-iron skillet until smoking hot; add the onions, garlic, and jalapeño to the skillet and quickly char them, turning once and then drizzling with the oil. You're not looking to cook the vegetables all the way through, just give them some nice deep color on the surface. As the vegetables char, transfer them to a blender, leaving the jalapeño in the pan until charred on all sides, about 5 minutes. Add the tomato to the blender, along with the juice from the lime, the salt, and chili powder, and pulse to combine. Add the cilantro and blend on low speed until blended but still coarse, about 30 seconds. Store covered and refrigerated for up to 4 days.

"PORK—
NO ANIMAL IS
MORE USED FOR
NOURISHMENT,
AND NONE MORE
INDISPENSABLE
IN THE
KITCHEN."

—ALEXIS SOYER

№ 4

LOINS

In middle school, I went camping with two friends, Chris Brown and Joseph Crumbley. We were on spring break, and Chris's dad drove us to North Carolina up some dirt road to a completely remote log cabin in the woods halfway up the side of a mountain. The cabin was not the kind with an air hockey table. It was a dusty old one-room cabin made of rough-hewn lumber. It had four walls and a cast-iron wood stove, and the outhouse was fifty yards away. I remember thinking, "Where the hell are we? Is this where Abe Lincoln was born?"

We slept on the floor in our sleeping bags. We spent our days playing in the streams, catching fish, shooting bottles with a .22, shooting other stuff with a shotgun, and generally hanging out doing old-school camping stuff. Now, when I went camping with my dad, we didn't bring much food. We usually ate what we found, caught, or killed. But Chris's dad brought all sorts of things to eat, and we had awesome breakfasts and lunches.

One morning, Chris's dad digs this big hole in the ground. "What's your dad doing, Chris?" I asked. "I have no idea," he said. So we asked him. "I'm going to cook this pork loin in the ground," he announced. Meat cooked in the ground? This was big news to a middle-schooler. I remember he built a fire and once it burned down, he pushed all the coals into this hole. Then he wrapped the pork loin in foil with vegetables and seasonings and put the foil pack in the ground and buried it in the coals. You can imagine the skepticism. Thirteen-year-olds are skeptical of everything. We're going to eat this stuff out of the ground? Riiiiight. I guess I'll be having toothpaste for dinner tonight.

We played all day long. When it got dark, Chris's dad fished the blackened foil pack out of the ground. I thought it was all fucked up because it was black. Then he opened it up. Inside was this perfectly cooked whole pork loin. This big chunk of meat was golden brown all the way around. The onions and potatoes were soft and soaked in the juices. It had something almost like a gravy. He just ripped open the package, sliced up the meat, and plunked it down on a low table. We sat around and ate the pork right out of this big burnt foil package. The seasonings were pretty basic—salt and pepper mostly—but that pork loin was one of the best things I have ever eaten.

I have such a fond memory of that trip: It makes my mouth water just telling the story. The taste of that pork loin has stayed with me my whole life. I now hold every pork loin up to that standard. I figure if Chris's dad, who is not a professional cook, could make this piece of meat taste moist and delicious in the middle of the woods with some coals and a hole in the ground while 13-year-old kids were bothering him all day, anybody with a kitchen should be able to make a decent-tasting pork loin.

Maybe it's just because we were camping, but for some reason, everything seems to taste better outside. And I love camping; it's one of my all-time favorite things. My dream job is park ranger. If someone asked me, "If you could do anything you wanted?" I would say, "park ranger." That basically means you're a professional camper. And if I could eat that pork loin every day in the mountains, I'd be in heaven.

★ GOOD TO KNOW ABOUT ★
Pork Loin

DON'T FREEZE IT: Always buy fresh cuts from the loin area. Pork loin doesn't freeze well. Water expands as it freezes and tears apart the muscle fibers. When the meat defrosts, those tears in the muscles let the water and juices leak out. Before you even start cooking, you lose a lot of moisture from a cut of meat that's already prone to dryness. That's why thawed and cooked pork chops taste so dry. Buy fresh loin.

COOK IT TO 145°F: More than any other cut on the animal, pork loin suffers the most from overcooking and dryness. Overcooked pork loin is pretty much unsalvageable. Treat this cut like you would a filet mignon. Doneness is critical. For perfect doneness, you should cook and rest pork loin to an internal temperature of 145°F. At that temperature, the pork will be slightly pink in the center, juicy, and delicious. It's a common misconception that pink pork is unsafe to eat. According to the National Pork Board and the USDA, pork cooked to 145°F and slightly pink in the center is perfectly safe to eat.

PORK LOIN IS LEAN AND HEALTHY: This is the leanest part of the animal. Lean pork has less fat than beef and even some cuts of chicken. Pork gets a bad rap for being unhealthy, but truth be told, if you're watching your weight, pork loin cuts make a very healthy choice.

PORK LOIN LABELS: A pork loin stretches across the entire length of the animal from the shoulder to the ham (leg). That means different loin cuts vary in toughness, tenderness, and density. That's also why pork loin has the most confusing labels in the grocery store. The USDA recently launched new names for pork cuts to align the names with similar cuts of beef. Here's a quick label decoder.

Pork chops just means that the loin was cut crosswise, across the backbone of the animal.

Boneless center-cut chops or top loin chops (aka New York chops) come from directly over the rib cage.

Rib chops come from the same place but include the bone. Bone-in rib chops or "rib eye" chops are the deluxe cut. They're the Mercedes-Benz of pork chops and the most expensive.

Sirloin chops are narrower and come from directly above the hind leg, include a part of the hip bone, and have slightly tougher meat than rib chops.

Pork T-bone or porterhouse is equivalent to a T-bone of beef. It's a bigger center cut from across the backbone of the animal, with the loin on one side and the tenderloin on the other side of a T-shaped bone (the backbone) in the middle.

Pork minute steaks come from any point on the loin; they're usually ¼ inch thick and sometimes labeled as breakfast chops.

Pork blade chops and steaks are actually cut from the shoulder (see page 35).

Loin roasts consist of some portion of the large-diameter muscle known as the loin. The narrower and longer muscle on the inside of the rib cage is the tenderloin; it's shaped more like a baseball bat. The loin and the tenderloin are not the same cut and don't always work in place of one another in recipes.

Rack of pork is the whole bone-in center section of the loin. It's equivalent to a bone-in prime rib of beef and one of my all-time favorite cuts of pork. It's not always sitting in the butcher's case, so you might have to request it for dishes like Celebration Pork Rack Stuffed with Dried Fruits (page 89).

Keep in mind that something labeled as whole pork loin does not necessarily refer to the entire loin. It could just be a 1½-pound roast cut from anywhere on the loin. To know what you're getting, you're better off buying the entire pork loin and cutting it yourself.

A true whole pork loin is about the size of beef tenderloin—about 10 pounds boneless or 20 pounds bone in—and is usually packaged in Cryovac. If it's sold boneless, the whole loin roast could be called a New York roast.

COOK IT QUICK: For all cuts of pork loin, quick cooking works best. Unless you're roasting a whole loin, the cuts here—chops, steaks, and tenderloin—cook in a matter of minutes. Like prime beef steaks, the quicker you brown pork loin cuts and get them off the heat, the better off you'll be. Unlike pork shoulder, pork loin doesn't have pockets of fat to baste the meat and keep it moist during cooking. High-heat methods like roasting, grilling, frying, panfrying, stir-frying, and sautéing work best here. For the same reason, loin is not the best choice for braising, stewing, or slow cooking.

BOURBON STREET
RIB EYE OF PORK

FEEDS 4

I grew up in Locust Grove, Georgia, south of Atlanta. It's a small town with only a few restaurants, but there was one really good one called the Bank. The place used to be the main bank in town, and after it closed, a chef from Atlanta bought it. It was easily the nicest restaurant in Henry County—the kind of place where you celebrated birthdays and anniversaries. I always chose the Bank when I got to pick what restaurant we went to. And I always ordered the Bourbon Street steak, a grilled beef rib eye marinated in pineapple juice and bourbon. It had all my favorite flavors—a little sweet, a little caramelized, and a lot of juicy meat. As delicious as those flavors are with beef, they're even better on a nice thick rib eye of pork. I like a few grilled or oven-roasted sweet potatoes on the side here.

½ cup soy sauce

⅓ cup bourbon + some for drinking

⅓ cup firmly packed dark brown sugar

1 tablespoon Dijon mustard

2 teaspoons Espelette pepper or hot paprika

1 teaspoon smoked paprika

4 bone-in, center-cut pork chops, each about 14 ounces and 1½ inches thick

2 teaspoons kosher salt

1 teaspoon ground black pepper

1 tablespoon grapeseed oil or canola oil

Combine the soy sauce, bourbon, brown sugar, Dijon, Espelette pepper, and smoked paprika in a gallon-size zip-top bag and squish to combine. Add the chops and marinate at room temperature for 1 hour. Have a drink of bourbon.

Prepare a medium-hot grill, or heat a grill pan over high heat.

Remove the chops from the marinade and reserve the marinade. Pat the chops dry, sprinkle both sides with salt and pepper, and brush with the oil.

Transfer the marinade to a saucepan and bring to a boil over high heat. Decrease the heat to low and simmer until syrupy, about 5 minutes.

Grill the chops uncovered for 6 minutes, then rotate 45 degrees and continue cooking for another 4 minutes (this creates great grill marks). Flip the chops, brush with the cooked marinade, and close the grill cover (if using a grill pan indoors, place a domed lid over the chops). Cook the chops to an internal temperature of 140°F, another 8 to 10 minutes.

Flip the chops, brush again with the marinade, and immediately transfer to a plate to rest. The chops need to rest for 10 minutes before serving so the juices can be reabsorbed into the meat. Serve with any additional glaze on the side.

MY MOM'S PANFRIED PORK CHOPS WITH SAWMILL GRAVY

FEEDS 4

I would've eaten this twice a week growing up if I could have. It's that good. My mom probably had it on a monthly rotation, and it's one of the very first dishes I learned to cook. I made the gravy when I was 7 or 8 and started frying the chops a little later. It's good for breakfast with hash browns, biscuits, and eggs; and for dinner with collards or green beans and mashed potatoes. The key is a well-trimmed chop that's between ½ inch and 1 inch thick. That size chop will fry up pretty quickly but not so fast that it dries out. If you do overcook it, there's plenty of gravy or pan sauce simply built from the drippings, some flour, cream, and chicken stock. Sawmill means the gravy has a sort of sawdusty look to it from the specks of pepper. I use this same gravy as the base for Zigeunerschnitzel (page 96).

4 boneless pork loin chops, cut from strip end, each about ¾ inch thick and 5 to 6 ounces

Kosher salt

¾ teaspoon ground black pepper

½ cup all-purpose flour

½ teaspoon cayenne pepper

½ teaspoon garlic powder

¾ cup lard

¼ cup heavy cream

1½ cups Chicken Stock (page 26)

Season both sides of the pork with salt and the pepper and let them sit so they are nice and wet, about 15 minutes.

Place the flour, cayenne, garlic powder, and 2 teaspoons salt in a shallow bowl and whisk to combine. Dip the pork chops, one at a time, into the flour mixture and shake off any excess. The chops should be completely but lightly coated. Reserve the flour mixture.

Add ¼-inch depth of melted lard to a 12-inch cast-iron skillet and place over high heat. When the lard begins to smoke, add a pinch of flour to the hot oil; it should "pop" and turn brown when the oil is hot enough. Add the chops to the skillet in a single layer, leaving a little space between them, and lower the heat to medium. Cook until the sides start browning, about 3 minutes. Adjust the chops to make sure they are cooking evenly and when they are deep golden brown, after another minute or so, flip them and continue to fry until light golden brown on the second side, about 3 more minutes. The internal temperature should be 140° to 145°F (the temperature will rise a few degrees as the meat rests).

Remove the chops from the pan, place on a plate, and tent with aluminum foil to keep warm. Take the pan off the heat and, using a large spoon, carefully tilt the skillet and spoon out the excess fat and discard. Leave enough fat in the skillet to completely cover the bottom, about ¼ cup. With the skillet still off the heat, whisk the reserved flour into the fat, making sure all the flour is completely absorbed and dissolved into the fat. Return the pan to medium-low heat and whisk constantly until the mixture is golden, about 3 minutes. Continue whisking and add the cream and chicken stock until thick and bubbling, about 2 minutes. Stir any juices that have collected from the chops into the gravy and add the chops back to the skillet, turning to completely coat with gravy.

Good to know

Four steps to perfect pan gravy: 1) Scrape all the brown bits from the bottom of the pan; that's your flavor base right there. 2) Stir enough flour into the hot fat for the mixture to look like wet sand, and whisk the flour constantly to completely dissolve it and prevent lumps. 3) Cook this mixture, the roux, long enough to cook out the flour taste, but not so long that the fat separates back out from the flour. About 5 minutes will do it here. 4) Add cold or room temperature liquid to the hot roux, stirring constantly to prevent lumps.

SICHUAN SALT AND PEPPER PORK CHOPS

FEEDS 4

Hong Kong Harbor is a Chinese restaurant just down the street from Woodfire Grill, where I used to work in Atlanta. Salt and pepper pork chops is one of their best dishes. The chops are flash fried, so bone-in, thin chops work better than thick ones and will give you the best flavor. The breading is two parts all-purpose flour, one part cornstarch, and one part rice flour. That gives you a light, crisp crust. I retested this a few times to get it just right, and I can tell you that the dish won't be the same without the Sichuan peppercorns. They add that tongue-numbing buzz to the spice rub. The stir-fried vegetables add crunch. The chiles bring the heat. And all these elements combine to make the dish work as a whole. Serve it with cooked white rice.

½ ounce Facing Heaven dried chiles or chiles de árbol, about ½ cup (see Worth Knowing)

2 tablespoons Sichuan peppercorns

1 tablespoon + 1½ teaspoons kosher salt

1 teaspoon Chinese five-spice powder

About ½ cup grapeseed oil or canola oil

½ cup all-purpose flour

¼ cup cornstarch

¼ cup rice flour

4 bone-in pork rib chops, each about 2 ounces and ¼ inch thick

1½ cups julienned white onion, 1 large onion

1 bunch cilantro, leaves picked, about 20 (3-inch) stems reserved

3 large jalapeño peppers, thinly sliced into rings, about ¼ cup

6 cloves garlic, thinly sliced, about 3 tablespoons

3-inch piece fresh ginger, peeled and finely julienned, about 3 tablespoons

6 scallions, root and tough ends removed, very bias sliced, about 1 cup

In a spice grinder or using a mortar and pestle, coarsely grind the chiles and peppercorns. Add the salt and Chinese five-spice and grind to a powder.

Heat a 1-inch depth of oil in a wok or deep, heavy skillet to 350°F.

In a shallow bowl, whisk the all-purpose flour, cornstarch, and rice flour to combine. Pat the pork chops dry and cut in 1-inch intervals around the chop, through the outer layer of fat just down to the meat. (This helps keep the meat from curling up.) One by one, dredge the chops in the flour mixture, shaking off any excess, and fry for 1 minute. Transfer the chops to a paper towel–lined plate and lightly sprinkle with the spice mix.

Carefully pour the oil from the wok or skillet, reserving and returning ¼ cup back to the wok. Heat over high heat just until smoking. Have your vegetables ready to go; the cooking time here is very quick. Add the onion and cilantro stems to the wok and aggressively stir, using the washing machine method (see page 21), about 20 seconds. Continue stirring and cooking for 20 seconds after each addition, adding the jalapeño, garlic, and ginger, then the scallions and reserved cilantro leaves, then the pork chops and 2 teaspoons of the spice blend. Serve immediately.

Worth Knowing

Facing Heaven chiles are common in Sichuan home cooking. When they grow on the plant, the peppers point toward the sky and look similar to red jalapeño peppers but are a bit longer. If you can't find them, the same amount of chiles de árbol makes a good substitute.

This spice blend is very versatile and can be used to dust anything from okra to shrimp.

PORK VINDALOO

FEEDS 4

Most Indian dishes don't include vinegar. Vindaloo is one of the few that does. The vin in vindaloo actually refers to the technique of marinating meat in vinegar. Aloo refers to the potatoes in the dish. After you marinate the meat, you toast a bunch of spices in a dry pan, one of the hallmark techniques of Indian cooking. It gives sauces deep, complex flavor. From there, it's a matter of browning some finely chopped aromatics like ginger, garlic, shallots, and chiles; adding the pork and spices along with some stock and potatoes; and then simmering the whole thing until it's nice and saucy. You can tell it's done when the oil separates out and rises to the top. At that point, the flavor will be good and deep. I like a quick mix of yogurt, lemon juice, and honey dolloped over the top. Serve this with some naan or other flatbread on the side. It's great with basmati rice, too.

12 ounces boneless pork loin, cut into 1-inch pieces

½ cup malt vinegar

2-inch piece Ceylon stick cinnamon (see Good to Know)

2 tablespoons black peppercorns

1 tablespoon cumin seeds

1 tablespoon coriander seeds

1 tablespoon fennel seeds

3 tablespoons ancho or other ground chili powder

1 tablespoon red pepper flakes

1 teaspoon ground turmeric

¼ teaspoon ground cardamom

⅛ teaspoon ground cloves

1 jalapeño pepper, stem removed

3-inch piece fresh ginger, peeled and diced, about ⅓ cup

½ cup garlic cloves, peeled

3 shallots, diced, about ½ cup

½ cup grapeseed oil or canola oil

1½ cups Chicken Stock (page 26)

1 medium Yukon gold potato, peeled and cut into ½-inch dice, about 1 cup

2 teaspoons kosher salt

1 lemon

1 tablespoon + 1 teaspoon honey

½ cup plain Greek yogurt or other strained yogurt

½ cup fresh cilantro leaves, finely chopped + more for garnish

In a large bowl, toss the pork with the vinegar.

Break the cinnamon stick into pieces in a heavy skillet and then add the peppercorns, cumin seeds, coriander seeds, and fennel seeds. Toast over medium heat until fragrant and deep golden brown, shaking the pan occasionally, about 4 minutes. The spices will start popping and dancing in the pan, and you should dry-roast the spices a little longer than you might think is right; you want to develop some color on them, which adds more flavor. Once they start smoking, dump them from the skillet onto a piece of parchment or wax paper. Reserve the skillet. When the spices have cooled a bit, grind them to a powder in a spice grinder or using a mortar and pestle.

Transfer the ground spices to a bowl and whisk in the chili powder, red pepper flakes, turmeric, cardamom, and cloves.

In a food processor fitted with the metal blade, combine the jalapeño, ginger, garlic, and shallot and process to a fine chop.

Return the skillet to medium heat and add the oil. When the oil is shimmering, add the chopped ginger mixture. Stir frequently, and if the mixture starts to brown, remove the pan from the heat to cool it a bit, then return to a lower heat setting; you want to slowly fry and brown the shallots without burning them. Scrape and stir the browned bits until the ingredients are evenly golden, 8 to 10 minutes. Add the spice blend and cook for another 30 seconds. Stir in the pork and vinegar until the pork is completely coated with the spice mixture. Add the chicken stock, potatoes, and salt and increase the heat to medium-high. Cover and bring to a boil, and then decrease the heat to low and simmer for 30 minutes.

Remove the lid and simmer just until the sauce breaks or starts to separate, about 3 minutes. Basically, you'll get an oil slick on top of your sauce. Remove the pan from the heat.

Squeeze the lemon into a small bowl to make a little more than ¼ cup juice. Whisk in the honey, yogurt, and cilantro. Serve the pork topped with a dollop of the yogurt and some additional chopped cilantro.

Good to Know

This is a pretty spicy dish. For less heat, remove the ribs and seeds from the jalapeño or just use a little less.

Ceylon cinnamon sticks have a shaggy look similar to thin tree bark. Look for them in Latin American markets or specialty food shops (Walmart stocks them too). If you can't find Ceylon cinnamon, substitute ¼ teaspoon ground cinnamon. But don't be tempted to use thick, hard cinnamon sticks (cassia). They won't grind easily.

GRILLED PORK TENDERLOIN WITH SPANISH-STYLE GARLIC SHRIMP

FEEDS 4

Here's another one for the backyard barbecue. It's like Spanish surf and turf with shrimp and pork. The idea came from a Brazilian steakhouse in Atlanta, Fogo de Chao. They roast whole pork loins and carve them for you tableside. It's good, but I always thought it would be better with some surf to go with the turf. Classic Spanish garlic shrimp is just the thing. The dish is pretty lean overall, but there's nothing lacking in the flavor department. Garlic, olive oil, sherry, sherry vinegar, and smoked paprika pack tons of flavor into the grilled tenderloin and shrimp. It's pretty quick too. Once everything's marinated, it cooks in less than 15 minutes.

1 pork tenderloin, about 12 ounces

12 cloves garlic, peeled

½ cup extra-virgin olive oil + more for garnish

¼ cup sherry

4 teaspoons kosher salt

1 teaspoon ground black pepper

¼ cup sherry vinegar

2 tablespoons smoked paprika

16 jumbo shrimp (21–25 count), tails on, peeled and deveined, about 12 ounces

Fresh basil leaves, for garnish

Remove and discard the silver skin from the tenderloin. Thinly slice 8 cloves of the garlic and combine with ¼ cup of the olive oil, the sherry, 2 teaspoons of the salt, and ½ teaspoon of the pepper in a quart-size zip-top bag. Add the tenderloin and marinate in the refrigerator overnight.

Finely chop the remaining 4 cloves garlic and combine in a small bowl with the remaining ¼ cup olive oil, remaining 2 teaspoons salt, remaining ½ teaspoon pepper, sherry vinegar, and smoked paprika. Refrigerate overnight.

Heat a grill over medium-high heat or a grill pan over high heat. Divide the garlic-paprika sauce in half.

Arrange 8 shrimp in a line, all facing the same direction and, using 2 skewers, skewer through the shrimp on each end so they will stay flat and are easy to flip on the grill. Repeat with the remaining shrimp. Slather both sides of the shrimp with one-half of the garlic-paprika sauce and let marinate while the pork is cooking.

Remove the tenderloin from the marinade, and discard the marinade. Pat the pork dry and grill until nicely charred, about 3 minutes per side, for a total of 12 minutes. The pork should reach 145°F for medium rare. If your tenderloin is larger than the 12 ounces, you may need to finish cooking it on a cooler part of the grill for about 5 minutes. Place on a plate and tent with aluminum foil to keep warm; the carryover cooking will bring it to just the right temperature.

Continued

Arrange the shrimp so there's a little space between them on the skewers. Add the shrimp to the grill and cook for about 45 seconds, then flip and grill for another 45 seconds. Continue flipping and grilling for a total of 3 minutes cooking time. You don't want to char the shrimp, hence the flip-and-grill method. When the shrimp are done, they'll be opaque; they cook fast, so watch carefully. When they come off the grill, slather them with some of the other half of the garlic-paprika sauce.

Transfer the tenderloin to a cutting board, reserve the juices, and slice on the bias. Pour the reserved juices into the remaining garlic-paprika sauce and stir to combine. Arrange the tenderloin on plates, top with the shrimp, and drizzle with the sauce and some additional olive oil; sprinkle on some torn basil leaves.

PORK LOIN FORESTIERE
FEEDS 4

Sauce Forestiere is a classic mushroom sauce derived from the French mother sauce known as *espagnole* or brown sauce. I update and simplify the sauce here by deeply pan-roasting the mushrooms. That's what creates flavor. You want to draw out the water from the mushrooms so you can brown them. Then you stir in some wine, cream, and chicken stock to build up the sauce. Use cremini (baby bella) or oyster mushrooms if you like, but for the best flavor toss in a couple truly wild mushrooms like chanterelles, hen of the woods, or porcini. The pork part is easy. Just slice a pork loin into cutlets, toss them in flour, and brown them in a pan. I use instant flour like Wondra for a super-thin, super-crisp crust. The dish is traditionally served with rice pilaf, but I like some roasted root vegetables as well.

12 ounces pork loin, trimmed, cut into 8 slices (cutlets)

Kosher salt and ground black pepper

2 teaspoons Wondra flour

2 tablespoons grapeseed oil or canola oil

1 tablespoon butter

6 ounces wild mushrooms, trimmed

¼ cup dry white wine

½ cup heavy cream

¾ cup Chicken Stock (page 26)

⅛ teaspoon freshly grated nutmeg

½ teaspoon freshly squeezed lemon juice

Pat the pork dry and season with salt and pepper. Sprinkle a light dusting of Wondra on both sides of the cutlets.

Place the grapeseed oil and butter in a very large skillet over high heat until the butter is melted and just starting to brown. Add the cutlets to the pan and cook until browned around the edge, about 1 minute. These cutlets tend to curl up, so push them down lightly with a spatula if needed to keep them flat. Flip the cutlets and cook for a few seconds, just until you get a bit of color on the other side. The cutlets cook very quickly—you do not want to overcook these since there will be carryover cooking. Transfer them to a plate and tent with aluminum foil.

Return the skillet to high heat and add the mushrooms. When the smallest of the mushrooms starts to wilt, toss and flip, continuing to cook until all of the mushrooms have caramelized and turned a nice dark brown, about 4 minutes. Add the wine; it will evaporate almost immediately. Add the cream, bring to a boil, then add the chicken stock, stirring continuously and scraping the pan bottom to get the browned bits into the sauce. Cook until the sauce bubbles around the sides of the pan and is thick enough to coat the back of a spoon, about 2 minutes. Remove the pan from the heat, and add ½ teaspoon salt, ¼ teaspoon pepper, the nutmeg, and the lemon juice. Add the cutlets back to the pan and spoon the sauce over the top.

GRILLED PORK KABOBS WITH PINEAPPLE AND SOY

MAKES 8 KABOBS

I struggled with whether to include this dish because it's so cliché. But it's so good! It's a pork tenderloin marinated in homemade teriyaki (soy sauce, sesame oil, sugar, ginger, and garlic), and then grilled on skewers with pineapple and mushrooms. It's ultra-simple backyard barbecue food, but there are a couple keys to success. First, cut the meat into same-size pieces for even cooking. I like cubes about ¾ inch square. Second, skewer the food in the order listed and push it tightly together. You want a solid strip of food on each skewer to prevent overcooking and so that the pineapple is near the meat. That way, the pineapple bastes the pork, helps it brown, and keeps it juicy.

1 pork tenderloin, silverskin removed, cut into ¾-inch cubes

1 teaspoon sesame oil

4 tablespoons soy sauce

2 teaspoons sugar

1-inch piece fresh ginger

¼ cup garlic cloves, peeled

½ cup (1 stick) butter

8 ounces baby bella mushrooms, stems removed

1 pineapple, peeled, cored, and cut into 1-inch pieces, about 2 cups

Kosher salt

Place the pork in a zip-top bag and add the sesame oil, 2 tablespoons of the soy sauce, and the sugar. Peel and grate the ginger and mince 1 clove garlic and add to the bag. Squish to combine and coat the meat with the marinade. Squeeze the air out, zip the top closed, and place in the refrigerator overnight. If you don't have time to marinate overnight, marinate at room temperature while the mushrooms are braising. The longer the marinade time, the more flavorful the pork will be.

With the wide side of a chef's knife, crush the remaining garlic cloves, leaving them intact. You're crushing just to release the flavorful oils. In a 1-quart saucepan, melt the butter with the garlic over medium heat until foamy. Add the remaining 2 tablespoons soy sauce and mushroom caps to the pan and toss to combine. Cover and braise over medium heat until tender, about 20 minutes.

Remove the mushrooms from the braising liquid and reserve the liquid in the saucepan. Remove the meat from the marinade and pat dry. Discard the marinade. Skewer a piece of meat followed by a braised mushroom and then a piece of pineapple. Be sure to start and end with the meat. Keep the braising liquid warm over low heat.

Heat the grill to medium or a grill pan over medium-high heat. Grill the skewers for 2 minutes, basting with the braising liquid. Turn, baste, and turn again until all sides are charred, a total of about 8 minutes. When poked, the pork should spring back instead of holding an indentation. Brush the skewers one last time and sprinkle with salt to taste.

— Worth Knowing —

In Hawaii, they serve kabobs like this over steamed white rice and always with a side of cold macaroni salad. Yep, the same cold macaroni salad you find at church socials.

ROAST PORK LOIN WITH SOUR CHERRIES

FEEDS 10 TO 12

This recipe feeds a crowd, looks good, and isn't hard to make. It takes about 20 minutes of work and the oven does the rest. I tested it with a Sam's Club pork loin to illustrate that commodity pork—even though not my first choice—can be tender and delicious if cooked properly. Letting the roast rest out of the oven is one of the most important steps for juiciness. If you don't let it rest, the juices run all over the plate when you cut the roast, and you get dry meat. I also like to truss the roast. It's sort of like throwing a ratchet strap over your haul in a pickup truck. Is it absolutely necessary? No. But the extra insurance is worth the minute and a half it takes to tie it up.

4 pounds rib end pork loin

2 tablespoons + ½ teaspoon kosher salt

1½ teaspoons ground black pepper

½ cup Chicken Stock (page 26)

1¼ cups dried sour cherries + more for garnish

1 cup dry sherry

2 tablespoons sherry vinegar

1 tablespoon amaretto (or ⅛ teaspoon almond extract)

Center the rack in the oven and heat to 375°F (with convection turned on) or 400°F (without convection), making sure there's plenty of space above the rack for the pan and roast. A convection oven circulates the air and perfectly roasts the meat. Spray a roasting rack and roasting pan with nonstick spray. Alternatively, spray a baking sheet fitted with a cooling rack with nonstick spray; you need more air circulation here than a broiler pan will allow. Truss the pork for even roasting (see Good to Know), and then season all sides and ends with 2 tablespoons of the salt and 1 teaspoon of the pepper. This is an aggressive seasoning, which is needed to create a nice crust on the finished roast. Place the pork on the rack and roast to 135°F, about 1 hour.

Remove from the oven and carefully remove the roasting rack and roast. Add the chicken stock to the hot roasting pan and stir with a wooden spoon, scraping up all the browned bits. Add the cherries and replace the rack and roast. Cover the roast and pan tightly with foil and let rest for 1 hour (yes, 1 full hour). The pork will continue to cook to medium, and you'll have a really juicy pork roast from the steam released by the sauce.

Remove the rack and pork from the roasting pan. Cut and discard the trussing strings. Spoon out ½ cup of the cherries and reserve. Transfer the pan of sauce to a large skillet and bring to a boil over high heat. Remove the pan from the heat, add the sherry, and carefully tilt the pan away from you and back over the flame (if you have a gas stove) to ignite the sherry. You can also ignite the sherry with a long match. Once the flames subside, stir in the sherry vinegar and amaretto and return to a boil. Remove from the heat, add the remaining ½ teaspoon each salt and pepper, and blend the sauce with an immersion blender until smooth.

Return the sauce to the skillet, return to a boil to thicken the sauce a bit, and remove from the heat. Fold the whole cherries into the sauce and serve with the sliced pork roast.

Good to know

Trussing a roast creates a uniform shape so that the roast cooks evenly. To truss a whole pork loin, cut 1 foot of kitchen string for every 2 inches of roast (for example, for an 8-inch-long roast, cut 4 feet of string). Shimmy the string under the roast until it rests about 1 ½ inches from one end. Tie the string tight around the top, leaving only a few inches of excess string on one end of the string; knot the string on the top of the roast very tightly. Make a large loop with the remaining string and lasso the loop around the roast, then pull it tight about 1 ½ inches from the first knot. Continue looping and lassoing the roast at 1 ½-inch intervals. When you reach the opposite end of the roast, you should have a series of tight loops and a line of string across the top of the roast. Flip the roast over and pull the remaining string over and under every other loop of string along the roast. When you reach the opposite end, flip the roast right side up again. Tie the excess string around the first knot, pulling it tight and tying a final tight knot. Cut off the excess string.

PORK MINUTE STEAKS WITH POTATO PANCAKES AND PUMPKIN BUTTER

FEEDS 4

Give this recipe a shot any day of the week. The pork steaks are thin, so they cook super quick. I like to pan-sear them on one side only so they get deeply browned but don't overcook. The potato cakes are made with just grated potatoes and onions pressed into cakes that cook in the same pan as the pork steaks. In the hot pan, the potatoes steam and release their starch, binding the cakes together. As long as you use a starchy potato, the potato cake doesn't need any other starch. I like pumpkin butter here to fill out the flavors, but if applesauce is your thing, that works too.

2 tablespoons Dry Brine (page 22)

20 ounces center-cut boneless pork loin, cut into 8 chops, each about ½ inch thick

½ cup Pumpkin Butter (recipe follows)

2 russet potatoes, about 1 pound total

1 Vidalia onion, peeled, stem and root ends trimmed

Olive oil or canola oil, for brushing

¼ cup lard

Set aside and reserve 2 teaspoons of the dry brine. Sprinkle all sides of the pork with the remaining dry brine, stack them up, and wrap tightly in plastic wrap. Refrigerate for 4 hours or overnight. The chops really need some time in the dry brine so they'll be tender and juicy. The closer you can get to 8 hours, the more tender and juicy they'll be.

Bring the pumpkin butter to room temperature.

Peel the potatoes and, without rinsing, grate on the large holes of a box grater into a large bowl. You should get about 3 cups of grated potato. Grate the onion into the bowl. You should get a little more than 1 cup. Fold the onions and potatoes together. The potatoes will start oxidizing (turning pink) as soon as you mix in the onions; that's OK, but you want to work pretty quickly. Place the mixture into a large square of cheesecloth and squeeze the liquid into the bowl. Let the liquid settle; the starch will sink to the bottom. Carefully pour the pink, watery liquid from the top of the bowl, but allow the starchy residue to remain in the bottom of the bowl. This starch will ultimately bind the potato pancake together. Unwrap the potato mixture and dump back into the starch. Add 1½ teaspoons of the reserved dry brine and toss with your hands to mix.

Pat the pork dry with paper towels and brush a few drops of oil on each chop.

Place a 10-inch cast-iron skillet over high heat. Add the lard and heat until just starting to smoke. Don't worry; the lard and the hot pan will perfectly crisp and brown the potato pancake. Carefully, dump the entire potato mixture into the skillet and, using a metal spatula, press and spread evenly all the way to the edges. Press it down good to help bind it all together and create a pancake. Lower the heat to medium and cook until the potatoes look translucent, the sides of the pancake become brown and pull away from the edges, and the fat begins to bubble up, about 8 minutes. Carefully flip the entire pancake and cook for another 4 minutes. Transfer the pancake from the skillet to a plate and tent with aluminum foil to keep warm.

Return the skillet to high heat, again until it is smoking hot. Add the chops, in batches if the skillet gets too crowded. Cook until the edges of the pork are starting to brown and curl, about 2 minutes. Using tongs, flip and cook for another 30 seconds. Transfer the steaks to a plate and allow to rest for a few minutes, then sprinkle each steak lightly with a pinch of the remaining ½ teaspoon dry brine mix.

To serve, spread 1 tablespoon of the pumpkin butter on each plate, and top with a wedge of potato pancake, 2 pork steaks, and another dollop of pumpkin butter.

Pumpkin Butter MAKES 2 CUPS

⅔ cup packed light brown sugar

1 (15-ounce) can unsweetened 100% pumpkin puree, or 2 cups roasted and mashed

1 teaspoon ground cinnamon

¼ teaspoon ground cloves

¼ teaspoon ground ginger

1 teaspoon apple cider vinegar

½ teaspoon kosher salt

In a medium saucepan, combine the brown sugar with 2 tablespoons water and stir to dissolve. Bring to a boil and boil until foamy, about 2 minutes. Stir in the pumpkin, cinnamon, cloves, and ginger and cook out the raw pumpkin taste, about 2 minutes, stirring occasionally. Remove from the heat and stir in the vinegar and salt. Cool to room temperature and then store, tightly covered in the refrigerator, for up to 1 month.

Good to know

This recipe only works with russet potatoes. You need all the starch in a russet to bind together the pancake because there is nothing else holding it together—no flour, no egg . . . nothing.

You want a heavy skillet here, like cast iron. That thick metal helps hold the heat, which creates a nice brown crust on the potato pancake.

If you're not a fan of pumpkin butter, make applesauce instead. Mix thinly sliced apples and a little sugar in a microwaveable bowl, cover tightly with plastic wrap, nuke it until the apples fall apart, and then buzz the whole thing in the food processor.

GRILLED PORK TENDERLOIN WITH GREEN PEPPERCORN SAUCE

FEEDS 4

Classic steak Diane is served with a sauce of sautéed and cooked-down onions, garlic, whiskey, stock, cream, and crushed green peppercorns. Unlike black peppercorns, the green ones have a bright fruitiness to them. I love the same sauce on pork. I brine the tenderloin first to keep it juicy and then grill it whole. The grilling only takes about 10 minutes, and while the meat's resting, you make the sauce.

¼ cup packed light brown sugar

¼ cup kosher salt

Ice cubes

1 pork tenderloin, about 1¼ pounds

1 tablespoon + 1 teaspoon grapeseed oil or canola oil

Ground black pepper

1 carrot, peeled, cut into ¼-inch dice, about ½ cup

2 stalks celery, cut into ¼-inch dice, about ½ cup

1 small onion, cut into ¼-inch dice, about 1 cup

¼ cup bourbon or rye whiskey

1½ cups Chicken Stock (page 26)

¼ cup heavy cream

2 teaspoons Dijon mustard

1 teaspoon jarred green peppercorns, crushed

1 tablespoon minced fresh parsley

In a small saucepan, combine the brown sugar, salt, and 2 cups water. Bring to a boil over high heat, stirring to completely dissolve the sugar and salt. Remove from the heat and pour into a large metal bowl. Stir in ice cubes until the mixture is cooled. It should take about a quart of ice cubes. Pour the brine into a gallon-size zip-top bag and add the pork. Squeeze out excess air and brine the meat for 1 hour.

Remove the pork from the brine and pat completely dry. Brush the tenderloin with 1 tablespoon oil and season on all sides with pepper.

Heat a grill to medium heat. Grill the pork, with the grill top closed, for 5 minutes, then flip and grill for 5 minutes more, and repeat on the final side until the interior temperature reaches 145°F. If using a grill pan, heat over high heat, and grill the pork covered with a domed lid for the same times. Transfer the pork from the grill to a plate and tent with aluminum foil to keep warm. The pork will cook a little more as it rests. The pork needs to rest for about 15 minutes before slicing. Make the sauce during that time.

Heat a skillet over high heat, add the remaining 1 teaspoon oil to coat the bottom of the pan, and swirl until shimmering. Add the carrots, celery, and onion, lower the heat to medium, and cook, tossing occasionally until the onions are translucent and soft, about 3 minutes. Remove the pan from the heat, add the whiskey, and carefully tilt the pan away from you, toward the flame (if you have a gas stove), to ignite the whiskey. You can also use a long match to ignite the whiskey. Toss the vegetables and agitate the pan until the flames burn out. Add the stock and cream, bring to a boil, and continue to cook until the liquid is reduced in volume by half, about 5 minutes.

Continued

Strain the sauce into a bowl and discard the vegetables. Return the sauce to the skillet, and stir in the mustard and peppercorns. Return the sauce to high heat and bring to a simmer. Remove from the heat, swirl in the parsley, and add salt and pepper to taste. Serve a spoonful of sauce over each slice of pork.

Worth Knowing

Try making this recipe with pork leg fillet too. The back leg of a pig has a cluster of muscles and connective tissue holding the meat to the bone. You can use your hands to separate all the muscles, using a knife only when necessary. Just take out any of the whole muscles from the leg; for this recipe, you want a piece that weighs about 1¼ pounds. Trim off the silverskin, tendons, and ligaments, because these cause toughness. Trim off any excess fat too. You'll be left with a long, beautiful, boneless, lean piece of meat.

THAI RED CURRY PORK

FEEDS 4

If you gave me a box of Hamburger Helper, I would make it differently than it says to on the box. I'd approach it from the angle of "How do I make this delicious?" not "How do I make this quick?" That said, Thai curry paste is a pain in the ass to make. Even my Thai friends buy curry paste instead of making it. So I use curry paste here. But I don't follow the package directions. Instead of browning the meat first, I add it at the end. I sauté the vegetables first, and fry the curry paste in the pan to open up the curry flavors. Then I add stock and finally the pork. That way, the meat poaches in the liquid, stays juicy, and flavors the sauce. This order of operations gives you the maximum flavor and makes the dish taste more like it would in a Thai restaurant. Jasmine or white rice is the perfect go-with.

8 ounces pork loin, thinly sliced

2 teaspoons grapeseed oil or canola oil

1 small sweet onion, sliced ¼ inch thick from stem to root end, about 1 cup

1 red bell pepper, seeds and ribs removed, sliced ¼ inch thick, about 1 cup

1 tablespoon + 1 teaspoon red curry paste

1 lime

2 teaspoons light brown sugar

2 tablespoons fish sauce

1 (13.5-ounce) can unsweetened coconut milk

2 tablespoons toasted sunflower seeds

12 sprigs Thai basil, leaves cut into thin strips (chiffonade), about ½ cup

Pat the pork dry with a paper towel and arrange in a single layer between two sheets of plastic wrap. Gently and evenly pound until very thin but not falling apart. Stack the meat and slice into 1½-inch strips.

Heat a large skillet over high heat, add the oil, and swirl to coat the pan. Heat just until the oil starts to smoke. Add the onion and pepper and vigorously shake the pan, tossing the vegetables for 30 seconds. Stir and smush the curry paste into the vegetables so the vegetables are coated with the paste. Squeeze the lime (about 2 tablespoons of juice) into the vegetables, and stir in the brown sugar and fish sauce. Add the coconut milk and bring to a boil. Lower the heat and simmer for 3 minutes, to reduce to about 1 cup. Add the pork to the sauce one piece at a time, making sure to submerge each piece completely and separately in the sauce. Cook for another 3 minutes, just until the pork is cooked through. Serve topped with the sunflower seeds and basil.

Worth Knowing

If you don't have sunflower seeds, you can use crushed peanuts.

CELEBRATION PORK RACK STUFFED WITH DRIED FRUITS

FEEDS 6

The Heirloom Book Company in Charleston, South Carolina, sells rare antiquarian cookbooks like first editions of Escoffier. I was there flipping through a book on royal court cuisine for lords and barons, reading recipes for the most extravagant dishes you can imagine. One of these was a bone-in frenched whole pork loin stuffed with apples, dates, and duck liver. That sounded pretty awesome to me. I adapted the idea here but replaced the duck liver with bacon fat and threw in a few more dried fruits. If you have duck liver, by all means use it, but it's not a requisite. Serve this roast with your favorite mead, honey cakes, and frosted lemons. It's perfect for Christmas, Easter, or any other royal feast.

1 loaf sliced white bread, crusts removed

1 large onion

2 tablespoons bacon fat

4 teaspoons kosher salt

½ teaspoon ground ginger

¼ teaspoon ground cinnamon

¼ teaspoon ground mace

1 (6-bone) center-cut frenched pork rack, about 4 pounds

2 egg whites

⅓ cup heavy cream

1 tablespoon finely chopped fresh sage leaves

1 cup packed mixed, diced dried fruit (apricots, Craisins, currants, golden raisins)

½ cup Ham Broth (page 27) or Chicken Stock (page 26)

Heat the oven to 325°F. Cut the bread into ½-inch cubes; you should have about 2½ cups cubes. Toast the bread cubes on a baking sheet until crispy, about 8 minutes. Leave the oven on.

Finely dice ½ cup of onion and sauté with 2 teaspoons of the bacon fat in a skillet over medium heat until softened and translucent, about 3 minutes. You should have about ¼ cup sautéed onions. (You'll use the remaining onion later.)

Combine 2 teaspoons of the salt, the ginger, cinnamon, and mace in a small bowl.

Lay the pork rack bone side down on your cutting board and carefully slice down, across the bones toward the meat, leaving the meat intact in one piece; you're basically unrolling and slicing the meat to a 1-inch thickness (see photos). When you get to the eye, continue slicing about an inch in until the eye is about 2 inches in diameter, and then cut it out. Remove the pork eye and finely chop it.

In a food processor fitted with the metal blade, combine the chopped pork eye, egg whites, cream, and the remaining 2 teaspoons salt, and process to a smooth, sticky paste, about 2 minutes. Add the sautéed onions and sage and pulse just to combine. Transfer to a bowl and fold in the toasted cubed bread and dried fruit. Melt the remaining 1 tablespoon + 1 teaspoon bacon fat in the skillet for later use.

Spray a roasting pan and roasting rack with nonstick spray.

Continued

Sprinkle the pork rack and meat with the seasoning mix, coating both sides. Starting just where the meat starts on the bones and using about half the stuffing mix, spread a thin but complete layer of the stuffing over the rack and meat. Lightly brush with some of the melted bacon fat. Starting at the meat end of the rack, gently and lightly roll the meat back onto the bones, being careful not to squish the stuffing out the ends. Using butcher's twine, tie the rack, wrapping between the bones and around the end. Brush the rack on all sides with some of the melted bacon fat.

Brush a deep 2-cup baking dish with some of the melted bacon fat; place the remaining stuffing in the dish and brush the top with bacon fat; bake until cooked to an internal temperature of 150°F, about 30 minutes.

Coarsely chop the remaining onion, spread in the center of the prepared roasting pan under the roasting rack, and place the pork roast bone side down on the roasting rack, over the onions. Roast to an internal temperature of 145°F, about 1 hour. Remove the roasting rack from the pan and place over a plate to catch any juices that run off the pork as it cools.

Place the roasting pan over medium-high heat, add the ham broth, and, using a wooden spoon, stir the pan drippings and onion to deglaze the pan. Taste and add salt and pepper as needed. Strain the sauce and discard the solids.

Let the pork rest for at least 20 minutes before slicing. Stir any accumulated juices into the sauce. Slice the rack into 1-bone chops and serve with the pan sauce and a scoop of the baked stuffing on the side.

SWEET AND SOUR PORK

FEEDS 4

In culinary school, I met a guy whose parents owned a Chinese restaurant in North Carolina. He confirmed for me that most Chinese restaurants in America do not serve traditional Chinese dishes. What they serve are Americanized versions of Chinese dishes. Except for one: sweet and sour pork. His parents prepare sweet and sour pork the way it's prepared in Cantonese restaurants in China. Which includes ketchup in the sauce. Crazy, right? Apparently, ketchup is traditional in this dish. What's not traditional is a cloyingly sweet, neon red sauce that completely drowns the pork. When it's well prepared, the hallmarks of sweet and sour pork are a good balance of sweetness and sourness in the sauce, just enough sauce to glaze the pork, and a super-crisp breading on the meat. Serve with steamed white rice and steamed broccoli.

12 ounces boneless tail end pork loin, trimmed, cut into 1-inch cubes

2 teaspoons reduced-sodium soy sauce

1 teaspoon sweet white wine, such as mirin or Riesling

3 tablespoons ketchup

1 tablespoon oyster sauce

1 tablespoon grape jelly

2 teaspoons malt vinegar

1 teaspoon Worcestershire sauce

2 teaspoons cornstarch

Canola oil for frying

¼ cup all-purpose flour

1 red bell pepper, seeds and ribs removed, cut into ½-inch chunks, about 1 cup

1 small onion, cut into ½-inch chunks, about ½ cup

1 cup ½-inch pineapple chunks

4 scallions, white ends removed, green ends bias sliced

In a medium bowl, toss the pork with the soy sauce and wine. Allow to marinate for 30 minutes at room temperature.

Whisk together the ketchup, oyster sauce, grape jelly, vinegar, Worcestershire sauce, and 3 tablespoons water in a small bowl. Add the cornstarch and whisk until smooth.

Line a baking sheet with paper towels and place a rack on the pan. Pour a 1½-inch depth of oil into a wok and heat to 350°F.

Drain the marinade from the pork, pat dry with a paper towel, and dust with the flour, tossing to coat each piece. Working in batches if needed, add pork pieces to the hot oil and fry until dark golden brown, about 3 minutes. Using a slotted spoon, transfer the pork to the prepared rack.

Carefully pour the excess oil from the wok and discard. Wipe the wok with a paper towel to remove any browned flour, add 2 more tablespoons oil, and heat over the highest possible heat until smoking. Add the peppers, onions, and 2 tablespoons water to the wok, stirring vigorously. The water will steam to help quickly cook the vegetables. Stir vigorously until the vegetables are translucent, about 2 minutes. Again, stirring vigorously, add the fried pork, pineapple, and sauce mixture. Continue stirring and tossing until the sauce thickens slightly and takes on a shiny glaze, about 30 seconds. Remove from the heat and toss in the scallions.

SPRINGFIELD-STYLE CASHEW PORK

FEEDS 4

Cashew chicken is a culinary claim to fame for Springfield, Missouri. The story I heard is that a Chinese gentlemen name David Leong opened a Chinese restaurant in Springfield shortly after World War II. Midwesterners didn't take to his traditional Chinese food, so he adapted his recipes to their preference for deep-fried food with gravy on it. For cashew chicken, instead of stir-frying the meat, he deep-fried it, and he changed the sauce to more closely resemble brown gravy. I based this recipe off the original one from Leong's Tea Room in Springfield, but I use pork instead of chicken. My wife, Valerie, is from Springfield, and she tells me that this version—even with pork—is better than what you can currently buy in Springfield. She admits that Leong's was better, but his restaurant closed in 1997.

12 ounces boneless tail end pork loin, trimmed

1 teaspoon Dry Brine (page 22)

⅓ cup all-purpose flour

1 cup Chicken Stock (page 26)

2 tablespoons hoisin sauce

2 tablespoons oyster sauce (Panda brand is good)

2 tablespoons reduced-sodium soy sauce

1 tablespoon light brown sugar

¼ teaspoon Accent seasoning

¼ teaspoon ground black pepper

⅛ teaspoon ground white pepper

2 cloves garlic, crushed but still intact

¼ teaspoon sesame oil

Canola oil for frying

1 tablespoon cornstarch

¾ cup cooked long-grain white rice

⅓ cup roasted salted cashews, coarsely chopped

4 scallions, whites and tough green ends removed and discarded, thinly bias sliced

Pat the pork dry and cut into 1-inch pieces. Sprinkle with the dry brine and wrap tightly in plastic wrap. Refrigerate for at least 4 hours or overnight.

Place the dry-brined pork in a medium bowl and toss lightly to separate. Add the flour and toss again to coat thoroughly and evenly, making sure every piece is coated on all sides. There should be some excess dry flour in the bottom of the bowl; you'll need it later. Press a piece of plastic wrap into the bowl on top of the pork and set aside. The pork will weep a little and get sticky, which is what you want.

In a 2-quart saucepan, whisk the chicken stock, hoisin, oyster sauce, soy sauce, brown sugar, Accent seasoning, and the black and white peppers to combine. Place over high heat and bring to a rolling boil. Cut the heat to the lowest setting, add the garlic and sesame oil, and leave on the heat while you prepare the pork.

Line a baking sheet with paper towels and place a cooling rack in the pan.

Pour a 1½-inch depth of oil into a wok and heat to 375°F. Remove the plastic wrap from the pork. Using your hands, break up the sticky clumps and toss with the remaining flour from the bottom of the bowl; each piece should be separate and have a light, even coating of flour. Working in batches, add the pork pieces to the hot oil and fry until golden brown, about 3 minutes. The pork will look similar to chicken nuggets when it's done. Transfer to the prepared rack.

Place the cornstarch in a small bowl and, using a fork, stir in 1 tablespoon water until the cornstarch is dissolved.

Using a slotted spoon, remove the garlic cloves from the sauce and discard. Increase the temperature to medium-high and gently whisk in 1½ tablespoons of the cornstarch mixture. Cook, stirring occasionally, until bubbling and thickened, about 3 minutes. The mixture should coat the back of a spoon and be the consistency of syrup. If you want it a little thicker, stir in a little more of the cornstarch mixture.

To serve, divide the rice among plates and top with the fried pork, sauce, cashews, and scallions.

Worth Knowing

For this dish, I use the thinner tail end of the pork loin. The meat on that side is less dense. You can use the other end, but the meat will be slightly tougher.

You don't need a lot of sauce here. It's rich and salty, so use it sparingly.

PORK STROGANOFF WITH FINGER NOODLES

FEEDS 4

Most people are familiar with creamy beef stroganoff served over egg noodles. I modeled this version on what I learned from chef Alexander Wolf at the Ritz-Carlton in Atlanta. He's a German chef from Baden-Baden, and finger noodles are specific to that region. Finger noodles are almost like the love child of spaetzle and gnocchi. You make a dough from mashed potatoes, knead it real good, then cut off chunks and roll them into little ropes the size of your finger. They're panfried in butter, which gives the noodles a delicious crunchy surface. Then you toss the noodles with strips of pork loin sautéed with onions and mushrooms in a brandy and sour cream sauce. What's not to love?

4 tablespoons butter, or as needed

40 Finger Noodles (recipe follows)

¼ cup finely minced onion

8 ounces maitake/hen-of-the-wood mushrooms, trimmed

8 ounces boneless pork loin, well trimmed, cut into ¼-inch slices, then into ¼-inch strips

2 tablespoons brandy

½ cup Chicken Stock (page 26)

2 teaspoons whole-grain mustard

½ cup sour cream

4 tablespoons finely chopped fresh parsley

1 tablespoon freshly squeezed lemon juice

½ teaspoon kosher salt

¼ teaspoon ground black pepper

In a large heavy sauté pan over medium heat, melt 2 tablespoons of the butter until the foam subsides and it starts to smell nutty and get golden brown. Working in batches, add the finger noodles so they are not crowded and sauté until all sides are browned. Add more butter to the pan as needed between batches. Transfer the noodles to a paper towel–lined plate.

If all of the butter is gone from the pan, add just enough extra to cover the bottom. Increase the heat to medium-high and sauté the onions and mushrooms, breaking up any large clusters of the mushrooms, until just starting to brown on the edges, about 1 minute. Add the pork and stir, cooking for another 2 minutes, just until the pork starts browning. Remove from the heat, add the brandy, and carefully tilt the pan away from you, toward the flame (if you have a gas stove), to ignite the brandy. You can also ignite the brandy with a long match. Let the brandy burn off, and then add the stock and cook until most of the liquid evaporates, about 3 minutes. Lower the heat to medium and stir in the mustard and ⅓ cup of the sour cream. Stir in 2 tablespoons of the parsley, the lemon juice, and the salt and pepper.

Remove from the heat and fold in the finger noodles. Serve garnished with the remaining sour cream and the remaining parsley.

Finger Noodles MAKES ABOUT 80 NOODLES

Kosher salt

1¼ pounds russet potatoes, about 2 medium

1 egg

1 bunch chives, finely chopped, about ¼ cup

½ cup all-purpose flour + more for dusting

Bring a pot of water to a boil and salt the water. Boil the potatoes whole, with skins on, until fork-tender, 35 to 40 minutes. When cool enough to handle, peel the potatoes and pass through a ricer or food mill into a large bowl. You want to have 3½ cups of riced potatoes.

In a small bowl, whisk the egg and stir in the chives. Stir the egg mixture into the potatoes, sprinkle in the flour and 1 teaspoon salt, and mix to form a dough. Turn the dough onto a floured work surface and knead for about 1 minute to develop the gluten. It will feel fairly soft.

Divide the dough into 4 even pieces, cut each piece into eighths, and then pinch each piece in half. Flour your hands and roll each piece into a 4-inch noodle, kind of like rolling Play-Doh. Each one will look sort of like a slug, a little fatter in the middle than on the ends. You'll get about 80 noodles. Any noodles you don't use, you can spread out on a baking sheet, freeze, and transfer to a zip-top freezer bag and store in the freezer for up to 2 months.

ZIGEUNERSCHNITZEL

FEEDS 4

When I worked at the Ritz-Carlton, I asked the chef, Alexander Wolf, if Germans like spicy food. He said no, except for one dish: zigeunerschnitzel. Schnitzel is a breaded and fried cutlet and the *zigeuner* here means "gypsy-style schnitzel." It's served with a thick, spicy sauce punched up with Hungarian paprika and black pepper. The sauce reminds me of classic Southern tomato gravy mixed with sawmill gravy. So I use the Sawmill Gravy from My Mom's Panfried Pork Chops (page 68) as a base. Germans can't get enough of this dish from take-out menus. It seems no one makes it at home there. I have no idea why, because it's easy to make and delicious.

Canola oil for frying, about 1½ cups

6 ounces pork loin, trimmed, cut into 4 even slices, about 1½ ounces each

1 cup Seasoned Breading Mix (page 23)

2 eggs

1 teaspoon kosher salt

1¼ cups finely ground panko bread crumbs

1 red bell pepper, seeds and ribs removed, cut into thin strips

1 onion, stem and root ends trimmed, cut end to end into thin strips

1 tablespoon sweet Hungarian paprika

1 teaspoon Espelette pepper or hot paprika

1 tablespoon tomato paste

½ cup Chicken Stock (page 26)

1 cup Sawmill Gravy (page 68)

2 tablespoons freshly squeezed lemon juice

Pour ⅛ inch of oil into a deep cast-iron skillet and heat to 375°F. Line a baking sheet with a double layer of paper towels.

Place each pork loin slice between two sheets of plastic wrap and gently and evenly pound to a ¼-inch thickness. Pat the pork dry with a paper towel.

Spread the breading mix in a shallow bowl. Lightly beat the eggs with the salt in a second shallow bowl. Spread the panko in a third shallow bowl.

Using the 3-step breading method (see page 21), dust the pork with the flour, dip in the egg, and coat with the panko. Fry the pork until golden brown, about 2 minutes on the first side. Flip and cook until golden brown on the second side, another minute or so. Transfer the pork schnitzel to the prepared baking sheet to drain.

Carefully pour out the oil from the pan and discard. Add 1 tablespoon of new oil to the pan and heat until smoking. Add the peppers and onions; stand back because the pan should flash-ignite and smoke. Lower the heat to medium and, when the onions are translucent with a just a little color on them, add the paprika and Espelette, and toss to coat. Stir in the tomato paste to coat the vegetables, and then add the chicken stock. Stir and reduce until thickened a little, about 2 minutes; you'll have about ¼ cup. Remove the pan from the heat and stir in the gravy and lemon juice. Taste and add salt if needed. Return to medium-high heat and bring just to a simmer. Serve over the schnitzel.

SAUTÉED PORK WITH LONG GREEN HOT PEPPERS

FEEDS 4

I first tried this dish at a restaurant on Buford Highway called Chef Liu, and theirs is still the best. There are two keys to any great stir-fry. One: Have everything prepped ahead of time. Your vegetables and meat should be cut and your sauce ready to go. That's because the actual cooking is superfast. Two: Crank your stovetop burner as high as it can possibly go. The fact is, you can't get it hot enough. Most residential cooktops put out about 20,000 BTUs. A professional wok pit spits out at least 100,000 BTUs. That high heat is what creates flavor in wok cooking. So preheat your wok on full bore until it's extremely hot. Open a window in the house too. You'll get a little smoke when the ingredients hit the pan, which is exactly what you want. Serve the stir-fry over cooked white rice.

8 ounces strip end pork loin

¼ cup soy sauce

1 tablespoon sugar

1 teaspoon red pepper flakes

1 clove garlic, mashed, about 1 teaspoon

1 teaspoon cornstarch

1 teaspoon grapeseed oil or canola oil

2 long hot peppers, cut into ¼-inch rings, about 1 cup

1 small sweet onion, cut into ¼-inch slices, about 1 cup

3 scallions, root and tough green parts trimmed, thinly bias sliced

Cut the pork across the grain into ½-inch chops and slice each chop across the grain into ¼-inch strips.

In a small bowl, stir together the soy sauce, sugar, red pepper flakes, and garlic. Add the cornstarch and stir until dissolved.

Heat a wok over high heat for several minutes, until it's extremely hot. Add the oil and quickly swirl to coat. It should smoke immediately; add the pork, peppers, and onions and quickly and continuously stir, using the washing machine method (see page 21), until the onions are just starting to brown, about 1½ minutes. Stir in the soy sauce mixture, stirring until slightly thickened, another 30 seconds or so. Toss to coat all the ingredients. Top with the scallions.

SLOW-SMOKED PORK LOIN WITH BITTER GREENS

FEEDS 4

Think of this as an American take on classic steak carpaccio. But the meat is pork and it's cooked with smoke. You thinly slice the smoked pork loin, lay it on a plate, and then top it with greens dressed with a simple anchovy vinaigrette. The smoked pork tastes almost like Canadian bacon but without the curing. To get a jump on things, you can smoke the loin up to a week ahead of time and keep it in the fridge. For that matter, you can make the vinaigrette ahead too. Keep those elements in the fridge, and this dish is the perfect last-minute lunch or light supper.

12 ounces Slow-Smoked Pork Loin (recipe follows)

¼ cup white anchovies, drained of all oil (see Worth Knowing)

3 tablespoons champagne vinegar

3 cloves garlic, about 2 tablespoons

1 shallot, coarsely chopped, about 2 tablespoons

1 lemon

¼ teaspoon finely ground black pepper

¼ cup extra-virgin olive oil

4 cups mixed bitter greens (arugula, frisée, endive, mustard greens, kale)

Large-flake sea salt, such as Maldon, for garnish

1 (2-ounce) block pecorino cheese, for shaving

Bring the pork to room temperature and thinly slice 6 to 8 slices per serving, 24 to 32 slices total.

In a blender, combine the anchovies, vinegar, garlic, shallot, 1 teaspoon lemon juice, the pepper, and 1 tablespoon warm water and pulse to a coarse paste. With the blender running on medium speed, slowly drizzle in the oil.

Toss just enough dressing with the greens to lightly coat. Arrange the pork on plates, top with the salad, and garnish with coarse sea salt. Use a vegetable peeler to shave a few pecorino curls over each serving.

Slow-Smoked Pork Loin MAKES 2 TO 3 POUNDS

1 (2 to 3-pound) sirloin end
boneless pork loin

2 teaspoons kosher salt

1 teaspoon ground black pepper

Heat a smoker to 200°F.

Season all sides of the meat with the salt and pepper. Using apple wood, smoke the meat for 2 hours.

Allow to cool to room temperature in the smoker if using an electric smoker. If using a wood smoker, remove the pork from the smoker and cool to room temperature. Use immediately, or cover and refrigerate for a week or so.

Worth Knowing

White anchovies come packed in a vinegar and oil marinade. They have a much milder flavor than the more common salted anchovies in cans, and the two are not interchangeable. Look for white anchovies in gourmet markets.

For the pork, you want a loin that's 3 to 4 inches in diameter, from the sirloin end. A thinner piece will cook too quickly.

Think of the leftover pork like lunch meat. Slice it or chop it and use it in place of ham for sandwiches, on an English muffin, or scrambled with eggs. You can use it anywhere you would use ham or Canadian bacon.

INDIANAPOLIS-STYLE FRIED PORK LOIN SANDWICH

MAKES 4 SANDWICHES

Here's the pride and joy of Indianapolis, Indiana—a German pork schnitzel given the American hamburger-on-a-bun kind of love. In Indiana, they call this particular cut of pork a "tender loin," but it's actually a center-cut pork loin. It has zero fat, which makes it great for breading and frying. Pounding out the loin makes it thinner so the pork fries up faster and takes on more of the crunchy breading. I like to bread it with buttery cracker crumbs, which have just enough sugar and fat to brown quickly before the pork overcooks. I also like a big sesame seed bun, and some raw onion, mustard, and mayonnaise on the sandwich. You'll see folks add lettuce and tomato, but I don't think it improves the flavor. When all is said and done, it's a simple sandwich that proves you don't have to reinvent the wheel to put together something delicious. It's also my staff's favorite family meal at Gunshow.

8 ounces strip end pork loin, sliced into 4 even pieces

2½ tablespoons Dry Brine (page 22)

Canola oil for frying, about 1½ cups

⅓ cup Wondra flour

1 egg

1 cup buttermilk

1 sleeve Club crackers, finely ground

4 large white sandwich buns, preferably sesame seed

Yellow mustard

Mayonnaise

½ red onion, thinly sliced

Kosher dill pickles

Sprinkle both sides of the pork with the dry brine, then stack and wrap tightly in plastic wrap. Refrigerate for 4 hours or up to overnight.

Remove the plastic wrap and discard. Pat the pork dry with a paper towel and place each pork loin slice between sheets of plastic wrap. Gently and evenly pound until very thin but not falling apart.

Heat a large cast-iron skillet with ¼ inch of oil to 375°F. Line a baking sheet with a double layer of paper towels.

Spread the Wondra in a shallow bowl, lightly beat the egg and buttermilk in a second shallow bowl, and spread the cracker meal in a third shallow bowl. Using the 3-step breading method (see page 21), dust the pork with the flour, dip in the egg, and then coat with the crumbs. Fry the pork until golden brown, about 2 minutes on the first side, then flip and cook until golden brown on the second side, another minute or so. Transfer the pork to the prepared baking sheet to drain.

To build the sandwich, split the buns. Liberally slather mustard and mayonnaise on both sides of the buns and stack with the pork, onion, and pickles.

PORK SOUVLAKI WITH CUCUMBER SALAD

FEEDS 4

In 2011, Valerie and I honeymooned in Greece. The best meal we had was also the least expensive. We found this little hole-in-the-wall that had a wood-burning grill, a hand-cranked rotisserie, two hot-plate heating elements, and only four tables. It was run by one guy who began our pork souvlaki by walking next door to the butcher shop to procure a pork loin. He threaded the pork on skewers and grilled it over wood. That pork souvlaki was hands-down the best thing we ate in Greece. This recipe pays homage to that preparation by combining a traditional Greek pork souvlaki with the American penchant for gyros, which is grilled meat wrapped in puffy pita bread. It makes a satisfying sandwich. If you can find goat's milk yogurt, that will give the cucumber salad a little more tang and creaminess. But plain old cow's milk Greek yogurt works fine too.

1 tablespoon dried oregano

3 teaspoons kosher salt

1 tablespoon olive oil

2 teaspoons freshly squeezed lemon juice

3 cloves garlic, crushed

12 ounces boneless, tail end pork loin, cut into 1-inch cubes

1 Kirby/pickling cucumber, peeled and diced, about ¾ cup

¼ cup grape tomatoes, quartered

1 small red bell pepper, ribs and seeds removed, finely diced, about ¼ cup

1 jalapeño pepper, ribs and seeds removed, finely diced

4 pieces Greek-style flatbread or pocketless pita

1 tablespoon minced red onion

¼ cup Greek yogurt

Mix the oregano, 1 teaspoon of the salt, the olive oil, 1 teaspoon of the lemon juice, and the garlic in a zip-top bag and smush the bag together with your hands to combine. Add the pork and toss in the marinade, making sure all the pieces are covered. Squeeze out the air, zip the top shut, and marinate at room temperature for at least 2 hours.

Mix the cucumbers, tomatoes, bell pepper, jalapeño, and onion together with 1 teaspoon of the salt. Set aside while the meat marinates.

Heat a grill pan over high heat or an outdoor grill to medium-high. Skewer the pork onto 4 skewers and put on the grill. Grill until charred on one side, about 2 minutes, then flip, grilling until all sides are charred; the other sides will take a little longer, about 3 minutes per side. The meat should be somewhat firm and have an internal temperature of about 145°F when done. If you have room on the grill, grill the flatbread to soften it as you cook the pork; otherwise, when the pork is done, set aside to rest, tented with aluminum foil, and grill the flatbread just until you have nice charred grill marks on both sides.

Just before serving, stir the yogurt, the remaining 1 teaspoon lemon juice, and the remaining 1 teaspoon salt into the cucumber mixture and toss to combine.

Slide the meat from the skewers onto the flatbread and dress with the salad. Serve immediately.

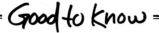

Good to Know

If you're using an indoor grill pan, crank it on high heat for the best sear marks. On an outdoor grill, medium-high heat works best.

"SLICING A WARM SLAB OF BACON IS A LOT LIKE GIVING A FERRET A SHAVE. NO MATTER HOW CAREFUL YOU ARE, SOMEBODY'S GOING TO GET HURT."

—ALTON BROWN

No. 5

BELLY AND RIBS

When I was on *Top Chef Las Vegas* in 2009, I only cooked pork belly one time. Yet, when I came home, I was known as the pork belly guy. Now, I get more requests for pork belly than for any other food. I'm not talking about just pork foods—I mean that people request pork belly from me more than any other food period.

After I came home from the show, we were buying whole, local hogs at Woodfire Grill. We wanted to use the whole pig, so we did put some pork belly dishes on the menu. I had developed the Braised Pork Belly (page 118) technique as a way to grill the belly without it catching fire from all the dripping fat. Using that as a base, we served pork belly every which way . . . with chiles and ginger alongside Asian dishes . . . basted in cider vinegar and served Southern style with slaw and braised greens . . . even dusted with Moroccan spices and served alongside couscous and curry. We dressed it up so many different ways that I eventually got sick of pork belly. So I took it off the menu.

Then all hell broke loose. People went stark raving mad. I heard comments, got nasty e-mails. One night, near the end of service, I was standing at the hostess stand checking reservations for the next night. It was a rare moment by myself, but I could feel someone staring into the back of my head. "Chef," I heard, as I turned around. Standing there was a middle-aged, conservatively dressed, bland-looking woman. "I just wanted to tell you how disappointed we were with our meal," she said. I thought she was joking, being sarcastic. "We have been trying to get in here for a month," she continued. "We watched you on the show, loved

you on the show, and came in with the expectation of having pork." We did have some pork loin on the menu at the time, so I replied, "What did you order?" She came back quickly, raising her voice, "I don't want a fucking pork chop. I want pork belly!" That shocked me. This woman looked so sweet and nurturing, I expected her to hand me a tray of warm cookies, but she had a mouth on her like a longshoreman just off the docks. Before I could explain why we'd taken it off the menu, she looked me up and down and started to really lay into me: "I think it's selfish of you. Who the fuck are you to take something off the menu that everybody is coming here to eat!" I was stunned at the words coming out of this woman's mouth. Here I was, getting chewed out by Betty Crocker.

Her husband shook my hand and told me how great the meal was, but after getting reamed by his wife, I knew something had to change. Pork belly went back on the menu the next day. And it stayed there until I left Woodfire Grill three years later.

When I opened Gunshow, I didn't take that particular preparation with me. After cooking something every day, seeing it all time, and eating it constantly, you start to lose interest. For years, that braised and grilled pork belly had been my go-to dish for off-property events and food festivals. In 2010, Grilled Pork Belly with Pickled Apples and Smoked Peanut Butter (page 120) was my go-to dish for the entire fall season. Over the years, I had served pork belly so many times, so many ways, that I started to forget what made it special.

In 2013, I got a reminder when one of the chefs at Gunshow wanted to create a little Chinese-style bun as a sandwich for the menu. We developed the filling with duck but quickly realized duck would be too expensive for a sandwich. Someone suggested pork belly, and everyone agreed it would work great. When we finished developing the dish and I tasted that first soft bun with the crispy exterior of the pork with its sweet red glaze and ginger flavor, and the molten interior of fat just melting on my tongue, and the ultra-tender meat, I remembered exactly why I and so many other people love pork belly. If it's done right, it's pretty fucking spectacular.

I'm happy to say that my estranged former love has now returned to my life. I'm pretty pumped about it. If you're new to pork belly, try your hand at the Buffalo Pork "Wings" (page 118). They're a crowd-pleaser and dead easy to make. From there, move on to White-Cooked Pork with Garlic Sauce (page 126), Sichuan-Style Twice-Cooked Pork Belly (page 116), and finally Grilled Pork Belly with Pickled Apples and Smoked Peanut Butter (page 120). You might just fall in love.

★ GOOD TO KNOW ABOUT ★
Pork Belly

IT'S WHERE BACON COMES FROM: When you're looking at a pig and you see the broad side, that's the belly. Pork belly actually sits just outside the portion of ribs known as spareribs. It's composed of fat, connective tissue, and meat all layered together like a lasagne. It's a mixed bag, and that's why people love it. In America, the belly is the most frequently consumed part of the pig because it's the cut that's cured to make bacon.

BUTCHERING IT: If you're taking a whack at butchering pork belly yourself, you'll find it on the underside of the pig, near the shoulder and leg. It's mostly fat with very little lean meat. First, trim away the cartilage and glands. Then, remembering that pork belly sits on the spareribs, picture the ribs behind the belly as a trimmed-up St. Louis rack. Mentally trace that outline on your pork belly and cut away the rack of ribs from the belly. If you cut close to the ribs and leave very little fat on the rack, what you're left with is the center-cut pork belly. You'll need to trim it up quite a bit to get to the usable part. The fattier ends are often made into salt pork (see below). But if you trim away everything but the "center-cut" section, you'll have yourself a nice, raw pork belly that can be used for Braised Pork Belly (page 118) and all the other pork belly dishes in this book.

BUYING IT: Let's say you're buying pork belly at the store. It probably won't be in the meat case, but it is available. You could call around, but it's easiest to just go to an Asian or Mexican market. Asians are ape shit for pork belly, so it's always there. Or try a farmers' market. Form a relationship with a local farmer if you can; the quality of the pork belly you'll get from a farmer will be better than anything you'll buy in a store.

COOKING IT: I like to cook pork belly with some moist heat first to render out some of its fat and dissolve its collagen into that magical substance known as gelatin. Gelatin is a big part of what tastes so good and rich in pork belly. I usually braise the belly, then allow it to cool overnight. The moist heat softens the meat and removes 15 to 20 percent of the fat, which is fine because there's more than enough fat to spare. Rendering the fat also softens the meat. At that point, the belly can be cooked any number of ways from frying to searing to roasting. Or you can keep braising it.

DECODING LABELS: Here's a quick label decoder for various foods related to pork belly:

Center-cut raw pork belly is the boneless broad side of a pig, often sold with skin attached and used to make bacon, such as House-Made Bacon, Three Ways (page 132).

Bacon is the food that drives vegetarians crazy and makes them reconsider eating meat again. Bacon is raw pork belly cured with either a wet cure or dry cure (commercial bacon is usually wet-cured because it's faster). Then it is smoked. However, bacon is not fully cured or cooked. It's not safe to eat raw, like salami. Bacon requires further cooking. It is usually sold with the skin removed.

Pancetta, like bacon, is dry-cured pork belly that is usually rolled before curing but sometimes cured flat. The big difference: Pancetta is not smoked. Pancetta also includes—usually but not always—subtle spices like cinnamon and black pepper. And it's fully cured, so pancetta is safe to eat without cooking. I find it benefits from cooking anyway. Use pancetta any way or anywhere you might use bacon (minus the smoke flavor).

Salt pork is the part of the belly that can't be used for bacon—the misshapen sides or ends that don't produce a beautiful slice of bacon. You cure these pieces by burying them in a barrel of salt. The salt pulls out all the moisture and creates a very dense, dry, salty piece of fat and meat. If a recipe calls for bacon or pancetta, salt pork is not an appropriate substitute because it has a completely different texture and flavor. Salt pork is disappearing from our culinary landscape, but it's a traditional American ingredient that's important to American food ways. It doesn't require refrigeration and keeps for months to years before going rancid.

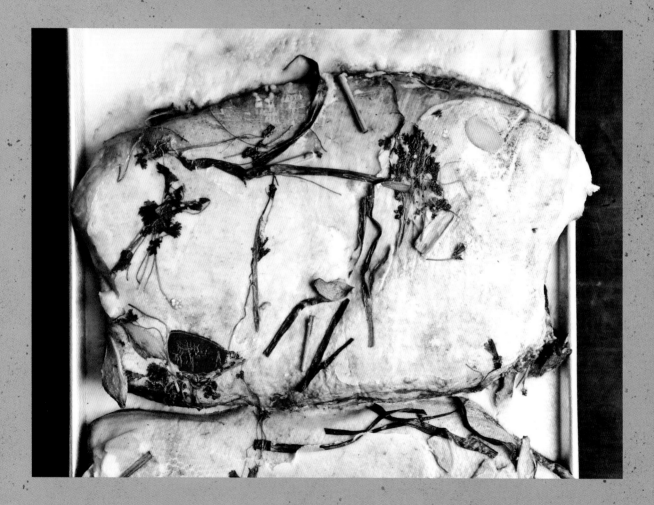

★ GOOD TO KNOW ABOUT ★
Ribs

WHERE THEY COME FROM: What is a rack of ribs? Picture a pig from an aerial view. The ribs spread out east to west from the backbone and then curve down and around the animal toward the belly. But when you buy a rack of ribs, you're not buying the entire rib cage. Butchers cut the rib cage in half crosswise to create different "racks" of ribs. Here's a label decoder:

Baby back ribs: No, they're not from baby pigs. What distinguishes baby back ribs is that they are connected to the backbone. From the aerial view, the baby back ribs spread east to west from the backbone and curve about halfway down the rib cage. This rack of ribs lies directly beneath the pork loin, so they're leaner than spareribs. They're also a bit smaller; hence the *baby* name. The meat tends to dry out easily, so I like to cook baby back ribs relatively quickly—less than 1 hour total cooking time.

Spareribs are my preferred cut of ribs. Picture the aerial view of the pig again and imagine the baby back ribs continuing down and around the animal. The lower half of the rib cage is what's cut into a rack of spareribs. They're larger and richer tasting than baby backs because they're closer to the belly than the loin. Spareribs are also a bit tougher, so they need some coaxing to get tender. Fortunately, the meat here is marbled with fat, so when you cook spareribs slowly at a steady temperature, the fat and

collagen melt, and you end up with very tender meat. At the lowest ends of the rib cage, the spareribs become hard cartilage and bone. These little triangular sections are called the rib tips, which are rarely sold on their own. More often rib tips are sold connected to a whole rack of spareribs. When the rib tips are removed from the rack, the rack looks perfectly rectangular and it's called a St. Louis cut. A lot of people prefer St. Louis–cut ribs, but I like spareribs with the triangular rib tips attached. You have to pick around thirty different pieces of cartilage there, but the meat is incredibly delicious.

Country-style ribs are not ribs at all because they're not cut from the rib cage. Country-style ribs are cut from one of two places: either the front end of the baby back rib section near the shoulder or the back end of the loin section that tapers down above the hind leg of the pig. Country-style ribs are more like pork chops than ribs because they have no bone (if cut from above the hind leg) or very little bone (if cut near the shoulder). They're easy to cook, but you can't swap these in for the other rib cuts called for in recipes. They just don't cook the same.

REMOVE THE MEMBRANE: Before you cook a rack of ribs, look for the sheer white membrane on the bone side of the rack. It's what gives the ribs a glossy look, like they're covered in white plastic wrap.

You want to remove the membrane. Don't ignore this step. It's extremely important for ensuring tenderness because the membrane never softens. Leaving it on can ruin a rack of nice tender ribs. Plus, I like to season both sides of a rack of ribs and the membrane prevents the seasoning from reaching the meat. Remove it by peeling up one corner, grabbing it with a dry kitchen towel, and pulling it off in one sheet.

USE A MINIMAL AMOUNT OF MOISTURE:
Everyone has their secret method for cooking ribs. I find the best results come from avoiding an excessive amount of liquid in the early stages of cooking. You want some moisture—usually in the form of steam—because it softens connective tissue and tenderizes the meat. But it also waters down the rich, meaty taste. Instead of steaming the hell out of them, I prefer to tenderize ribs by sustaining a consistent temperature throughout the cooking. That method gradually dissolves the collagen in the connective tissue and transforms it into gelatin, and the gelatin then continually and slowly bastes the meat, tenderizing it and improving its flavor. If you speed up that process with excess moisture and heat at the beginning, for example by wrapping the ribs in foil for a majority of the cooking time, the collagen dissolves too rapidly and just melts away. Ultimately, it's a matter of personal preference, but when people say, "These ribs fall off the bone," what I hear is, "These ribs are overcooked." If you like that wet, drippy taste in ribs, keep the ribs wrapped up when I say to unwrap them in the recipes in this book. Otherwise, unwrap them as directed so they have a chance to evaporate some excess moisture and concentrate their meaty flavor.

SAUCING AND SEASONING: What's the best way to season a rack of ribs—dry rub, sauce, or wet mop? The debate rages on in the barbecue world. Again, it's mostly personal preference. The only ingredients that will really penetrate the meat are salt and acid

(such as vinegar), both of which will break down the muscle fibers. Mustard, pepper, chili powder and other seasonings that we rub, brush, mop, or glaze onto the surface of ribs remain mostly on the surface. There just isn't much absorption. And you can't save overcooked ribs by basting or mopping them; the meat inside will still be overcooked. If you're using barbecue sauce, it goes on only at the end. That's a hard-and-fast rule. Nearly every barbecue sauce ever made has sugar in it, and when subjected to heat, that sugar will burn and make your ribs taste bitter. Save your saucing for the very end or for the table.

REST THE RIBS: Just like any other cut of meat, ribs have to rest when they come off the heat. If you slice them hot off the grill, you will waste all the work it took to get the ribs nice and juicy. Pitmasters will stack the racks on the cold side of the pit to let them rest so the meat can reabsorb the juices. Bottom line: Rested meat is juicier meat.

UNCLE CLINT'S BLUE RIBBON RIBS

MAKES 2 RACKS, ENOUGH TO FEED 4 TO 6

My Uncle Clint marked the beginning and end of summer by cooking ribs. We had them on Memorial Day and Labor Day. The meat would smoke all day long while we swam in the pool and played outside. By three o'clock in the afternoon, we'd sit down to eat. Clint has won barbecue competitions with these ribs, and I got so used to them that I now hold all ribs up to this standard. He doesn't wrap them in foil or bake them, steam them, or—God forbid—microwave them. That makes the meat too soft. He just puts them in a smoker and holds a steady temperature. That gives the ribs a concentrated flavor and just enough tenderness. Uncle Clint's barbecue sauce is a family secret, but this one emulates his. Don't get too hung up on the sauce, though. The key is a consistent temperature for the entire cooking time.

2 slabs St. Louis–cut pork ribs, about 2 pounds each

Kosher salt

Coarsely ground black pepper

Uncle Clint's Rib Sauce (recipe follows)

Heat a smoker to 290°F. Remove and discard the sheer white membrane from the underside of the ribs. The membrane will be slippery, so grab it with a kitchen towel to pull it off. Liberally season both sides of the ribs with salt and pepper, patting the seasoning into the meat. Slide the ribs onto a wire rack and put the rack in the smoker away from direct heat. Cook the ribs until they are tender and the meat begins to pull back from the ends of the bones, 3½ to 4 hours, rotating the slabs once or twice for even cooking.

At the end of cooking, brush the bone side of the ribs with the sauce, then flip and cook that side until nicely colored. Brush the meat side, then flip and cook that side until nicely colored. Repeat this process until the ribs have a nice glaze of sauce all over and the meat side is face up. Remove the ribs and let rest at room temperature for at least 30 minutes before serving.

You can cut the racks into 3 or 4-bone servings with sauce on the side or slice into single ribs, toss in sauce, and grill over high heat to char and crisp them even further.

Uncle Clint's Rib Sauce MAKES ABOUT 2 QUARTS

3 cups apple cider vinegar

2 cups dark beer, such as
    Guinness or other stout

2 cups ketchup

1 cup yellow mustard

½ cup molasses

½ cup packed dark brown sugar

½ cup honey, preferably sourwood

2 tablespoons tomato paste

1 tablespoon kosher salt

1 tablespoon ground black pepper

1 tablespoon garlic powder

1 tablespoon onion powder

1 teaspoon cayenne pepper

Combine all of the ingredients in a saucepan over medium-high heat. When the sauce begins to bubble, decrease the heat to low and simmer for 1 hour. Cool and store, covered and refrigerated, for up to 1 month.

Good to know

Sourwood honey has a floral aroma and tons of flavor. It comes from bees that pollinate the sourwood trees, aka Appalachian Lily trees, that grow in northern Georgia and North Carolina.

This all-purpose barbecue sauce tastes great on anything grilled. Slather it on grilled pork chops, Ham Burgers (page 162), or anything else that's seen some fire.

VIETNAMESE SPARERIBS WITH CHILE AND LEMONGRASS

FEEDS 12 AS AN APPETIZER

Like other Vietnamese restaurants, Nam Phuong in Atlanta serves pho, but their ribs are the best thing on the menu. The meat is tender with a crackly exterior. Nam Phuong uses flanken or crosscut ribs, which are like little rib nuggets, each with a bone inside. You can order different sauces, but my favorite is the chile and lemongrass. To bring you those flavors and textures, I steam-bake the ribs until tender and then broil and baste them with a puree of lemongrass, chiles, soy sauce, fish sauce, garlic, and sugar. A little rice on the side is perfect.

3½ pounds Asian-style (flanken) pork spareribs, about 36 pieces (see Worth Knowing)

2 teaspoons kosher salt

10 cloves garlic, peeled, about ¼ cup

1 stalk lemongrass, sliced, about ¼ cup

3 Thai bird chiles

¼ red onion, stem and root ends trimmed, cut into chunks

2 tablespoons sugar

2-inch piece fresh ginger, peeled and chopped, about 2 tablespoons

1 tablespoon fish sauce

1 tablespoon soy sauce

1 lime

¼ cup chopped fresh cilantro leaves

Heat the oven to 325°F.

Season the ribs lightly with 1 teaspoon of the salt and place on a broiler pan fitted with the broiling rack or a baking sheet fitted with a cooling rack. Add a ¼-inch depth of boiling water to the pan, wrap the ribs and pan tightly with foil, and cook until the ribs are pull-apart tender, 1½ to 2 hours. Basically, you're steaming the ribs.

In the bowl of a food processor fitted with the metal blade, combine the garlic, lemongrass, chiles, and onions and process for 30 seconds, until well chopped. Add the sugar, ginger, fish sauce, soy sauce, and the remaining 1 teaspoon salt and continue processing to a coarse paste, scraping down the sides of the food processor a couple times.

Adjust the rack in the oven to the highest setting and preheat the broiler.

Arrange the ribs, meat side up, on the rack and smear with some of the garlic paste. Broil the ribs until nicely caramelized, about 5 minutes. Watch carefully and when they start getting a little char on the tips, remove and flip them. Smear again with some of the paste and broil on the bone side for about 3 minutes. Flip, smear, and broil one final time so they are nice and crispy on the meat side, about 2 more minutes.

Using tongs, transfer the ribs to a cutting board and cut into single-bone pieces. Squeeze the lime into the pan drippings and stir to combine. Toss the ribs in the pan drippings and serve sprinkled with the cilantro.

Worth Knowing

Asian-style spareribs are cut across the bone, also known as flanken cut. You can find them at Asian markets or have your butcher cut them for you. Ask the butcher to cut the rack of ribs in thirds across the bones.

SLOW COOKER COUNTRY-STYLE RIBS

FEEDS 4

When I was a kid, the pastor in my local church, Doug Gilreath, told a story about how when he was young, his mom made ribs in a Crock-Pot. Apparently, they were one of his favorite foods. One day, he snuck a little out of the pot. He thought no one would notice. Then he grabbed a second little piece. As the story goes, he ended up eating most of the family's dinner that day. While I should have been hearing the moral of the pastor's story, all I could think was, "That's kinda weird. They made ribs in a Crock-Pot." The idea went against everything I believed about barbecue. But as time went on, I heard other people talk about "Crock-Pot barbecue," and I've come to understand the necessity. Maybe you live in an apartment and can't have a grill or smoker. To fill that need, this recipe provides the flavor of Uncle Clint's Blue Ribbon Ribs (page 110) in a greatly simplified form. For a full meal, serve the ribs with the Black-Eyed Peas with Jowl Bacon (page 217) and Basic Cabbage Slaw (page 29).

4 pounds country-style pork ribs

1 teaspoon kosher salt

½ teaspoon ground black pepper

2 tablespoons grapeseed oil or canola oil

¾ cup Uncle Clint's Rib Sauce (page 111)

3 tablespoons molasses

Pat the ribs dry and season both sides with the salt and pepper.

Heat a large skillet over high heat until smoking. Add the oil and swirl to coat. Brown the ribs on all sides, 3 to 4 minutes per side, until deep golden brown. Move the ribs to a plate and pour the oil out of the pan, then deglaze the pan with ½ cup water.

Mix the sauce, molasses, pan juices, and any juices from the rib plate in a large slow cooker. Add the ribs, cover, and cook on high for 2½ hours or low for 4 hours.

When the ribs are almost done cooking, preheat the broiler. Line a baking sheet with foil for easy cleanup. Place a rack in the pan and spray with nonstick spray. Transfer the ribs to the rack and brush with the sauce from the slow cooker. Broil until brown and crusty, about 3 minutes on each side. Brush again with sauce when the ribs come out of the broiler.

Reserve the remaining sauce from the slow cooker and serve with the ribs.

MEXICAN PORK RIBS IN SALSA VERDE

FEEDS 4 TO 6

People often grill or roast ribs, but I think they taste best cooked slowly. For this dish, also called *costillas de puerco*, you braise the ribs in seasoned water and then toss them in tomatillo sauce. It's a simple one-pot dish with a good balance of flavors. The acid in the salsa cuts the fattiness of the ribs, and the fat in the ribs carries the spices in the salsa. Using my not-so-vast knowledge of Mexican cuisine, I put together a quick pan-roasted tomatillo sauce here, but you could use another tomatillo salsa if you like. The ribs themselves braise unattended on the stovetop for about 2 hours. All in all, this is among the easiest and tastiest rib recipes in the book.

1 rack St. Louis–cut pork ribs

½ white onion, stem and root ends trimmed, cut into 2-inch wedges

1 tablespoon sugar

1 teaspoon kosher salt

2 cups Salsa Verde (recipe follows)

12 fresh white corn tortillas, heated

Remove and discard the sheer white membrane from the underside of the ribs. The membrane will be slippery, so grab it with a kitchen towel to pull it off. Cut the ribs into 3-inch-wide pieces; in the middle of the rack this will be 1 bone; toward the ends it will be 2 bones.

In a large Dutch oven, combine the ribs, onion, sugar, salt, and just enough water to cover the ribs. Bring to a boil over high heat, decrease the heat to low, cover, and simmer until tender, about 2 hours.

Using tongs, transfer the ribs to a baking sheet. Discard all but 1½ cups of cooking liquid. Stir the salsa into the cooking liquid in the pot and then return the ribs to the pot and toss to coat. Bring to a boil, and then decrease the heat to low and simmer for 5 minutes, tossing occasionally.

Served with the tortillas.

Salsa Verde MAKES 2 CUPS

6 tomatillos, papery skin removed

1 small onion, stem and root ends trimmed, cut into quarters

6 cloves garlic, peeled

1 jalapeño pepper, about 1 ounce

1 lime

¾ cup fresh cilantro leaves + more for garnish

1 tablespoon kosher salt

Heat a large cast-iron skillet over high heat and add the tomatillos, onion, garlic, and jalapeño. Dry-roast until the vegetables are charred on all sides, transferring piece by piece to a plate as they are done; the garlic will get done first, in about 8 minutes; the onion will take another 2 minutes; the jalapeño will take another 5 minutes; and the tomatillos will take about 5 more minutes; total cooking time will be about 20 minutes. Combine the vegetables in a blender. Add the juice of the lime, the cilantro, salt, and ¼ cup water. Blend until fairly smooth, about 30 seconds. Store, covered and refrigerated, for up to 1 month.

SICHUAN-STYLE TWICE-COOKED PORK BELLY

FEEDS 4

You know what I love most about Chinese cooks? They spend all day prepping but only five minutes cooking. Talk about efficiency! Until recently, I held off on learning how to make proper Chinese food. When I came around, this was one of the first dishes I tried my hand at making. It's not difficult, but you have to have all your vegetables and sauces prepped ahead because the cooking is lightning fast. The cornerstone of the dish is a raw pork belly that's braised first and then flash-fried until brown and crisp. It's a good option for a dinner party when you want to do most of the cooking before your guests arrive.

1 pound Braised Pork Belly
  (page 118)

1 tablespoon hot black bean
  paste (spicy fermented black
  beans)

1 teaspoon sweet bean sauce
  (Chinese brown bean paste)

1 tablespoon dry white wine

1 tablespoon sweet fermented
  soybean paste (doubanjiang)

1 teaspoon soy sauce

1 teaspoon red pepper flakes

1½ teaspoons sugar

½ teaspoon kosher salt

2 tablespoons grapeseed oil
  or canola oil

3-inch piece fresh ginger, peeled
  and finely julienned, about
  ¼ cup

1 leek, white part only, julienned,
  about 1 cup

1 bunch chives or garlic scapes,
  cut into 3-inch pieces, about
  1 cup

2 cups steamed white rice

Carefully peel the skin and top layer of fat from the braised pork belly and discard. Slice the belly into 16 equal pieces.

In a small bowl, mix the hot black bean paste and bean sauce to combine.

In a separate bowl, mix the wine, soybean paste, soy sauce, red pepper flakes, sugar, and salt to make a sweet wine sauce.

Heat a 12-inch skillet over high heat to smoking hot. Add the oil to the pan and return to smoking hot. Flash-fry the pork until starting to brown and crisp, about 1½ minutes; flip and cook for another 45 seconds. Transfer to a paper towel–lined plate. Add the ginger and the bean paste mixture and toss to coat. Toss in the leeks, chives, and sweet wine sauce and, shaking the pan, toss, toss, toss the vegetables, about 30 seconds. Add the pork back to the skillet and toss, toss, toss the mixture again, making sure the pork is well coated and mixed with the vegetables, about 1 more minute. Serve over the rice.

Good to Know

Bean pastes bring tremendous flavors to Chinese sauces and glazes. The names can be confusing, but you want three of the bean pastes here: hot black bean paste (aka spicy fermented black beans), sweet soybean paste (aka *doubanjiang* or sweet fermented bean paste), and sweet bean sauce (aka brown bean paste).

Garlic scapes are the curvy green stalks that grow from hard-neck garlic bulbs. They're available in farmers' markets and some grocery stores, mostly in the spring. If you can't find them, use scallions.

BACON POPCORN

MAKES ABOUT 12 CUPS

Save your bacon grease! My granny kept hers in an old Folgers coffee can and used it for all kinds of frying. It turns out bacon grease makes phenomenal popcorn. You might think the popcorn comes out overly bacony, but it just gets a light bacon flavor. For a little more bacon, I add pieces of cooked bacon to the popcorn here. Truth be told, I was never a huge fan of popcorn. It gets stuck in your teeth and there always seem to be too many unpopped kernels in the bottom of the bowl. On the other hand, my wife loves popcorn. So I developed this popping technique for her. Follow the directions here and most of the kernels should pop. Then I toss the popcorn with pieces of bacon and Parmesan cheese to boost the savory umami factor.

8 slices Belly Bacon (page 132)

⅓ cup yellow or white popcorn kernels

2 tablespoons freshly grated Parmesan cheese

1 teaspoon fine sea salt

½ teaspoon ground black pepper

Using scissors or a sharp knife, cut the bacon into ¼-inch pieces.

Heat a 5 to 6-quart Dutch oven (with a lid) over medium heat and add the bacon. Cook until browned and crispy, about 12 minutes. Using a slotted spoon, transfer the bacon to a paper towel–lined plate. Increase the temperature to medium-high and add a kernel of corn. When the corn pops, add the remaining corn and put the lid on, slightly ajar. Once the corn starts popping, shake the pan constantly. When the popping slows, remove from the heat and immediately pour into a large bowl. Toss in the bacon, cheese, salt, and pepper.

Good to know

If you're making bacon anyway, throw it in the popcorn as directed. It's an added bonus. But if you just have bacon grease, the popcorn will taste great without the pieces of bacon.

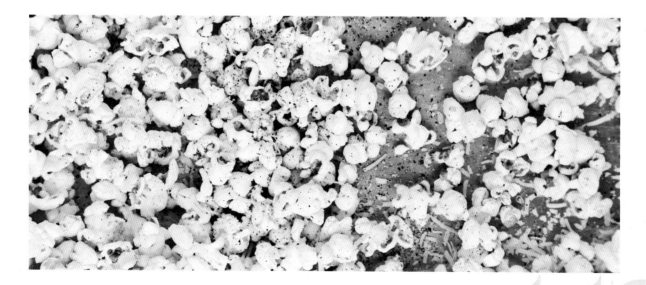

BUFFALO PORK "WINGS"

FEEDS 10 TO 12

In 2013, I was commissioned to serve a dish at the Georgia Dome during a Falcons game. While other chefs brought froufrou food to the football stadium, I brought something absurd: the pork wing. Chicken wings are my favorite junk food, and I figured they'd be even better with pork, especially during a football game. Here we have braised pork belly cut into chunks the size of hot wings, fried, and slathered in wing sauce. They're ludicrous and delicious at the same time. The fans seemed to like them. As I understand it, I hold the record for highest sales among guest chefs at the Georgia Dome. I'm also the only guest chef who worked his own station.

Canola oil for frying

2-pound slab Braised Pork Belly (recipe follows)

5 ounces Frank's RedHot sauce

2 tablespoons butter, cubed

Blue cheese or ranch dressing, for serving

Heat oil in a deep fryer to 375°F.

Trim the top layer of fat off the pork belly down to the first layer of meat. Cut lengthwise (the way you would slice bacon) into 1-inch-thick slices. Crosswise, cut the rest of the pork belly to make pieces about 4 inches long and 1 inch thick.

In a saucepan, heat the hot sauce over medium heat just until bubbling around the edges. Remove from the heat and whisk in the butter cubes one at a time until all are melted.

Fry the pork until crispy, about 5 minutes. Shake the fryer basket to remove excess oil. Drop the pork into the buttery hot sauce and toss to coat. Serve with blue cheese or ranch dressing.

Braised Pork Belly MAKES ABOUT 2 POUNDS

1 (2-pound) center-cut slab raw pork belly

2 tablespoons kosher salt

1 cup apple cider vinegar

Heat the oven to 300°F.

Rub both sides of the pork belly with the salt and lay flat, fat side up, in a baking dish that is just a little larger than the slab. Add the vinegar; it should come about halfway up the side of the meat. Wrap tightly with aluminum foil and braise in the oven for 3 hours.

Remove from the oven and let rest, wrapped in the foil, until the pork cools to room temperature. Remove from the pan, wrap in parchment and then foil, and refrigerate or freeze until ready to use (see Good to Know).

Good to know

The braised pork belly can be frozen for up 2 weeks. Thaw completely before using.

This braising technique makes a great starting point. I use it as the base for Sichuan-Style Twice-Cooked Pork Belly (page 116), White-Cooked Pork with Garlic Sauce (page 126), and Grilled Pork Belly with Pickled Apples and Smoked Peanut Butter (page 120).

GRILLED PORK BELLY WITH PICKLED APPLES AND SMOKED PEANUT BUTTER

FEEDS 4

This dish resulted from my improbable mission to grill pork belly. Normally, all the fat in pork belly would render into the fire of the grill, sending up an inferno. But I braise the belly first to melt away the fat—that's the secret. An initial braise allows the belly to grill up golden brown and crispy on the outside with an interior of molten fat and soft protein. It's so juicy it almost gushes. This was a signature preparation of mine at Woodfire Grill and remains so at Gunshow. You could serve the grilled belly with almost anything, but something acidic, like the pickled apples, helps cut through the fat. For the smoked peanut butter, I usually just put a bowl of peanut butter in a smoker, but I simplified the method here for home cooks. Apples love pork, peanut butter loves apples, pork loves smoke—it's a flavor love fest.

2 cups salted roasted peanuts

¼ teaspoon liquid smoke

¼ cup grapeseed oil or canola oil

1 cup All-Purpose Pickling Liquid (page 25)

1 Fuji apple

12 ounces Braised Pork Belly (page 118)

Kosher salt and ground black pepper

4 scallions, root and tough green ends trimmed, finely bias sliced, about ¼ cup

Using a Vitamix or high-speed blender, blend the peanuts on medium speed to a fine grind, about 30 seconds. With the blender running, drizzle in the liquid smoke and oil. Turn the blender off, scrape down the sides, and then return to medium-high speed and the mixture will come together into a smooth butter. You need to keep it on medium-high speed, as high speed will heat it and cause the oil to separate from the solids, causing it to "break." Store the peanut butter, tightly covered at room temperature, for up to 1 month.

Bring the pickling liquid to a boil over high heat. Peel, core, and dice the apple (¼-inch dice) into a small bowl and strain the hot pickling liquid over the top. Discard the solids. Spoon out 2 tablespoons of the pickling liquid to use later and refrigerate the apples until ready to serve.

Heat a grill pan over high heat.

Peel the skin and top layer of fat from the pork belly and discard. Cut into strips 3 inches long and ½ inch wide. Pat them dry and brush with the reserved pickling liquid. Season with salt and pepper and grill the pork belly until deep golden brown on one side, about 3 minutes. Flip, brush with more pickling liquid, and grill for another 2 minutes, or until golden brown.

Spoon about 2 tablespoons of the peanut butter across each plate, top with the pork belly, and garnish with the pickled apples, a little pickling liquid, and a sprinkle of scallions.

Worth Knowing

The better the peanuts, the better the butter. My favorite are the large oil-roasted Virginia peanuts.

If you don't have a high-speed blender, use high-quality natural (unsweetened) peanut butter without added oil and then process the peanut butter, liquid smoke, and oil in a food processor or blender until smooth.

You can use any remaining peanut butter for general use. Stir in 2 teaspoons honey and you're ready for a smoky PB & J!

You can make the pickled apples the day before and keep them refrigerated.

BLACK VINEGAR-GLAZED PORK BELLY BUNS

MAKES ABOUT 20 PORK BELLY BUNS (ENOUGH FOR 10 PEOPLE)

Here's one of the only restaurant recipes in this book. It comes straight from the Gunshow menu. The cooks created it as a group, but most of the credit goes to Brian Carson. He wanted to make a Chinese-style duck bun, but we all agreed it might be better with a different meat. At the time, we were sitting on a lot of pork belly, so we braised some belly in black vinegar. The sweet-and-sour glaze cut the richness of the pork belly, but it still needed spark and punch. We added some pickled carrots and braised red cabbage, and that did the trick. This pork bun is now one of Gunshow's most successful dishes.

PICKLED CARROTS

¼ cup Chinese black vinegar

1 tablespoon pickling spice

2 teaspoons granulated sugar

1 teaspoon kosher salt

1 cup carrots, julienned

RED WINE–BRAISED CABBAGE

½ small head red cabbage, finely shredded

2 cups red wine vinegar

1½ cups dry red wine

¼ cup granulated sugar

1 piece star anise

1 bay leaf

2 tablespoons kosher salt

PORK BELLY AND GLAZE

2½ cups Chinese black vinegar

¼ cup kosher salt

2½ pounds pork belly

½ cup granulated sugar

1 tablespoon light corn syrup

1 bunch scallions, trimmed

1 bunch cilantro

1 jalapeño pepper, split lengthwise

2-inch piece ginger, sliced into coins

4-inch stalk lemongrass, crushed and cut into 1-inch pieces

⅓ cup oyster sauce

Canola oil, for frying

10 Steamed Buns (recipe follows)

For the carrots, combine the vinegar, pickling spice, sugar, salt, and ⅓ cup water in a small saucepan. Bring to a boil and stir to dissolve the sugar. Place the carrots in a small bowl and strain the pickling liquid into the bowl. Discard the solids and let the carrots pickle, covered and refrigerated, for at least 2 days or up to 2 weeks.

For the cabbage, combine the cabbage, vinegar, wine, sugar, star anise, bay leaf, and salt in a nonreactive pan and simmer until tender and the cabbage looks deep purple in color, about 45 minutes. Keep warm until ready to use or cool, cover, and refrigerate for up to 2 weeks.

For the pork belly, preheat the oven to 275°F. Combine 1½ cups of the vinegar and the salt in a small saucepan and bring to a boil. Remove from the heat and stir until the salt is dissolved. Place the pork belly, skin side up, in a 9 by 13-inch baking dish and add the vinegar mixture. It should come about halfway up the belly. Cover tightly with foil and braise in the oven until fork tender, about 3 hours. Cool the belly to room temperature in the braising liquid, cover with parchment, and evenly weight the top to press the belly flat. (A same-size pan with some cans or jars on top works well.) Cover and refrigerate overnight or up to 1 week.

For the glaze, pour the sugar and corn syrup into a 2-quart saucepan. Stir in enough water so that the mixture looks like wet sand, about 2 tablespoons. Cook, without stirring, over medium heat until the mixture starts to caramelize on the outer edges, about 5 minutes. Check the mixture now and then and swirl the pan a little to even out the color. When the mixture turns dark amber, about 8 more minutes, remove from the heat and swirl until evenly dark. Stand back and carefully stir in the remaining 1 cup vinegar; it will sputter and the sugar will harden, which is okay. Keep stirring until the sugar dissolves into the vinegar.

Thinly slice the scallion greens and set aside to use later. Pick the cilantro leaves from the stems and set aside to use later. Add the white parts of the scallions and the cilantro stems to the vinegar mixture along with the jalapeño, ginger, and lemongrass. Simmer until the mixture reduces in volume by half, about 15 minutes. Stir in the oyster sauce and simmer until the mixture is slightly thickened, about 10 minutes more. Keep warm until ready to use, or cool, cover, and refrigerate for up to 1 week. Reheat the glaze just before using.

When ready to serve, finish the belly by starting at a corner and peeling the top, tough skin layer off the pork belly, just like peeling off a sticker, being careful to leave the fat cap beneath the skin intact. Cut the pork belly into ½-inch strips and then into 2-inch lengths. Each piece will be about 1½ ounces.

Line a baking sheet with a double layer of paper towels. Pour the oil into a wok or deep pan until the oil is 1½ inches deep. Heat the oil to 375°F. Working in batches, fry the pork belly strips until browned and crispy, about 3 minutes. Place on the prepared baking sheet to drain.

In a large, shallow bowl, toss the fried pork belly with three-fourths of the green onions and enough glaze to generously coat the belly. Split the steamed buns crosswise and layer each with a little cabbage, a slice of pork belly, and some pickled carrots. Garnish with the reserved scallion greens and cilantro leaves.

Steamed Buns MAKES ABOUT 20

1 tablespoon active dry yeast

¼ cup granulated sugar

3 cups all-purpose flour

2 tablespoons and 2 teaspoons dry milk powder

1 tablespoon kosher salt

½ teaspoon baking powder

½ teaspoon baking soda

¼ cup lard, melted

2 teaspoons grapeseed oil or canola oil + some for greasing the bowl

In a 2-cup measuring cup, dissolve the yeast in 1 cup warm (115°F) water. Stir in the sugar and let the mixture sit until it starts foaming and develops a head, just like a beer, about 5 minutes.

Continued

123

In the bowl of a stand mixer fitted with the dough hook, combine the flour, milk powder, salt, baking powder, and baking soda. Turn the mixer on low to combine the dry ingredients. With the mixer running, add the yeast mixture and mix until a wet dough forms, about 30 seconds. Add the melted lard in a slow steady stream and mix until the dough gets really tacky, about 2 minutes. Increase the speed to high and knead the dough in the mixer until the dough starts pulling away from the sides of the bowl, about 4 more minutes. Flour is pretty finicky; depending on the humidity, you may need to add just a tiny bit more flour, a teaspoon at a time, up to 1 tablespoon more, mixing about 30 seconds after each addition, until the dough come away from the sides of the bowl. The dough should be very soft and stretchy.

Dump the dough onto a floured work surface and knead a few turns, just to form a smooth ball.

Rub the dough ball with the oil and also wipe the insides of the mixer bowl with oil. Return the dough to the bowl, cover with oiled plastic wrap, and set in a warm place to proof until almost doubled in size, about 45 minutes.

Cut twenty 4-inch squares of parchment, spread them out on baking sheets and spray or brush the parchment with oil.

Dump the dough onto the work surface, punch down and knead a few turns to form a smooth ball. Using a bench knife, cut the dough in half and roll each half into a log about 2 inches wide. Cut each log into 10 portions. Roll each portion into a smooth ball and place on the parchment squares. When all the dough is rolled, cover with oiled plastic wrap and set in a warm place and let rise again until doubled in bulk, about 30 minutes.

Using the palm of your hand, flatten the buns to ¼-inch-thick disks, cover with the oiled plastic wrap and let rest until doubled in thickness, about 20 minutes.

Heat a wok or steamer filled with enough water to reach 3 inches from the bottom of the steamer basket and bring to a boil over high heat. Arrange 4 buns, still on the parchment squares, in a single layer in each steamer basket. Stack the baskets if you can, cover, and steam until the buns are set, about 8 minutes. The buns will be very shiny and smooth and will have almost doubled in bulk. If necessary, repeat steaming until all the buns are hot and set.

Good to Know

This recipe is great for a large gathering, but it has several components. It helps to have a game plan. Make the carrots and cabbage first—they will both keep for up to 2 weeks in the fridge. You can make the pork belly and glaze up to 1 week ahead. On the day you plan to serve this dish, do the buns first, since the dough has to rise several times and it takes a couple hours total. Then you can steam the buns, fry off the belly, toss it in the reheated glaze, and assemble the pork buns with the cabbage and carrots.

Chinese black vinegar is aged rice vinegar that turns solid black in color and develops deep, malty flavors. Look for it at your local Asian market or the international aisle of a well-stocked grocery store.

To trim a stalk of lemongrass, cut off the root end and the thin, dry green leaves until you're left with a 4-inch-long cylinder. Peel off any dry outer leaf layers and then crush the lemongrass with a heavy pan to release the essential oils. Cut the lemongrass crosswise into 1-inch pieces, and it's ready to use in this recipe.

WHITE-COOKED PORK WITH GARLIC SAUCE
FEEDS 4

Here's a good dish for warding off vampires. It's got a cup of garlic cloves pureed into a paste with rice vinegar, soy sauce, sesame oil, and chiles. This muddy paste gets seared in a pan for 30 seconds, then poured over pork belly, and it's topped with toasted peanuts and cilantro. The belly itself is sliced thin and "white-cooked," meaning it's just barely warmed through to get the fat moving. I know it sounds crazy, but it tastes amazing. Take a leap of faith with this one. It's a classic Chinese preparation, and if you're making another dish with Braised Pork Belly (page 118), you can use the ends and trim here. The belly doesn't need to be too pretty because most of it gets covered with sauce anyway.

8 ounces Braised Pork Belly (page 118), cut into 16 slices each ¼ inch thick

1 cup cloves garlic, peeled

¼ cup unseasoned rice vinegar

¼ cup soy sauce

1 tablespoon sugar

½ teaspoon kosher salt

¼ teaspoon sesame oil

1 Thai bird chile

¼ cup salted roasted peanuts

2 tablespoons grapeseed oil or canola oil

¼ cup fresh cilantro leaves

Using a rimmed dinner plate, spread the slices of pork belly around the plate all the way to the edge, cover, and set aside, letting the pork come to room temperature.

In a food processor fitted with the metal blade, process the garlic, vinegar, soy sauce, sugar, salt, sesame oil, and chile until it's the texture of a muddy paste, about 1 minute. With the processor running, drizzle in ¼ cup water.

Heat a skillet over high heat and quickly dry-roast the peanuts, about 30 seconds, just to warm through and really bring out the flavor of the nuts. Chop the nuts. Add the oil to the pan, heat until smoking hot, and add the garlic sauce. Stir gently until boiling, and cook for about 30 seconds. Spoon the garlic paste over the pork and sprinkle with the peanuts and cilantro.

CHINESE SPARERIBS, TAKE-OUT STYLE

MAKES 1 RACK, ENOUGH TO FEED 6 TO 8

I love the flavors and techniques of classic Chinese cuisine, but I'll be the first to admit that I have a soft spot for bastardized American-style Chinese food—especially the sticky, shiny red spareribs. They're my Uncle Richard's favorite too. He's a perpetual bachelor. As a kid, I would hang out at Uncle Richard's house and we'd eat piles of those ribs. He always ordered way too much—so much that the restaurant we ordered from, Hunan Village, sent him a Christmas card every year. Whenever I went in to pick up the ribs, they would always say, "Please tell Mr. Edwards he is our best customer." I figured it was time for me to pay homage to these ribs by cooking them myself.

1 rack St. Louis–cut pork ribs, about 2¾ pounds

½ cup hoisin sauce

½ cup soy sauce

¼ cup packed light brown sugar

2 tablespoons dry sherry

2 tablespoons seasoned rice vinegar

6 cloves garlic, minced, about 3 tablespoons

¼ teaspoon Chinese five-spice powder

2 teaspoons sesame oil

2 tablespoons sesame seeds

Remove and discard the sheer white membrane from the underside of the ribs. The membrane will be slippery, so grab it with a kitchen towel to pull it off. Cut the ribs into single-bone pieces.

In a medium bowl, combine the hoisin, soy sauce, sugar, sherry, vinegar, garlic, five-spice powder, and sesame oil, whisking until smooth.

Dip each of the ribs into the sauce to coat, shake off any excess sauce, and drop into a gallon-size zip-top bag. Squeeze the air out of the bag, zip close, and marinate the ribs in the refrigerator for a minimum of 3 hours or overnight. Pour the excess sauce in a jar, cover, and refrigerate until ready to cook the ribs.

Heat the oven to 325°F. Line a deep roasting pan with aluminum foil. Spray a rack generously with nonstick spray and place in the roasting rack. Lay the ribs in a single layer, meat side down, on the roasting rack and add a ¼-inch depth of very hot water to the bottom of the pan. This will create steam, which will keep the ribs moist. Cover tightly with foil and bake for 1 hour.

Remove the foil and generously brush the ribs with the reserved sauce. Bake, uncovered, for 30 minutes; remove from the oven, flip the ribs, and brush again. Return the pan to the oven until the ribs start getting really caramelized and crispy, another 30 minutes. Flip the ribs and baste one final time, sprinkle with the sesame seeds, and cook for an additional 10 minutes.

Good to know

The ribs can be made ahead and refrigerated in a covered container for up to 2 days. Sprinkle with sesame seeds and crisp them up in a hot (400°F) oven just before serving.

DEEP-FRIED BABY BACK RIBS

MAKES 1 RACK: ABOUT 12 RIBS

One day at Gunshow, I was joking about a nonexistent restaurant called Snack Attack and all the crazy-ass food we'd serve. The words deep-fried baby back ribs slipped out of my mouth. Baby backs aren't really my thing for barbecue, but everything tastes better fried, right? Once I uttered the concept, I had to try it. I rubbed a rack of baby backs with sugar and spices, baked it in foil, then cut the rack into individual ribs. Then I dunked the ribs in seasoned flour, buttermilk, and back in the flour before dropping them in the fryer. They came out looking like long skinny pieces of fried chicken, but inside was this amazingly tender, flavorful pork rib. I served them with ranch dressing and barbecue sauce. It was better than good. I realize how white trash this dish is, but the cooks at Gunshow have proclaimed it as their favorite recipe in the book.

¼ cup packed light brown sugar

1 tablespoon kosher salt

1 teaspoon ground black pepper

1 teaspoon smoked paprika

½ teaspoon granulated beef bouillon (or 1 cube grated on Microplane)

½ teaspoon garlic powder

⅛ teaspoon hickory smoke powder or liquid smoke

1 rack baby back ribs, about 2¼ pounds

Canola oil for frying

1 cup Seasoned Breading Mix (page 23)

1 cup whole or low-fat buttermilk

Sweet and Smoky Barbecue Sauce (page 28), pureed until smooth

Preheat the oven to 325°F.

In a small bowl, toss the brown sugar, salt, pepper, paprika, bouillon, garlic powder, and smoke powder to combine. If using liquid smoke, don't add it to this sugar mixture; you'll spread the liquid smoke on the ribs instead.

Pat the ribs dry and place on a sheet of heavy-duty aluminum foil that is twice the length of the racks. If using liquid smoke rather than the smoke powder, smear it across the meat using your finger. Be very careful, as liquid smoke is insanely strong; believe me, a little goes a long way, so spread it thin. Coat both sides of the ribs with all of the sugar mixture, wrap tightly in the foil, and place on a baking sheet. Cook for 1¼ hours. Remove from the oven and let cool in the foil.

Just before serving, heat a deep fryer or Dutch oven with a 3-inch depth of oil to 375°F.

Spread the breading mix in a shallow bowl. Unwrap the ribs and cut into single-bone pieces. One by one, toss the ribs in the breading mix, shake off any excess, dip in the buttermilk, shake off excess, and dip a final time in the breading mix. Fry the ribs, being careful not to overcrowd the fryer, until golden, about 3 minutes. Serve with the barbecue sauce.

PORK PHO

FEEDS 6 TO 8

I love traditional beef pho. When I'm under the weather, that's the soup I eat. It's hard to improve upon the original, but I wanted to try with this pork pho. The most recognizable pork cuts here are paper-thin strips of belly and shoulder floating in the broth. But the broth itself also develops rich texture from the gelatin in the pork feet and great flavor from the smoked ham hocks. It's a pork lover's paradise. You won't find all of these cuts in your corner Piggly Wiggly. But an Asian market could be a one-stop shop. Overall, the soup isn't hard to make; it just has a lot of ingredients. One of my favorite things about it is how you make it your own at the table. You can add basil, onions, sriracha, or whatever you like. Here, I set up the pho my favorite way, with chiles, Thai basil, a little black pepper, sliced raw onions, scallions, and cilantro.

4 pounds pork feet, sliced crosswise into 2-inch pieces

3 Vidalia onions

4-inch piece fresh ginger

6 whole cloves

4 star anise

2-inch piece cinnamon stick

½ teaspoon black peppercorns

2 smoked ham hocks

⅓ cup fish sauce

2 tablespoons light brown sugar

10 ounces pho (rice) noodles

2 jalapeño chiles

1 bunch Thai basil

1 bunch cilantro

1 bunch culantro (see Good to Know)

2 limes

1 tablespoon kosher salt

1 teaspoon hoisin sauce + more for garnish

1 teaspoon sriracha sauce + more for garnish

¼ teaspoon Accent seasoning

Finely ground black pepper

12 ounces very thinly sliced pork belly, cut into 2-inch strips

12 ounces very thinly sliced pork shoulder, cut into 2-inch strips

Place the sliced feet in a stockpot, cover with water, and bring to a boil. Boil for 2 minutes. Drain the feet in a colander and discard the cooking liquid.

Char 2 of the whole onions and the ginger over an open flame until blackened on all sides, 4 to 6 minutes. A gas burner works fine here. Using a towel, slide the charred skin off the onions; the inside will retain some of the smoky flavor. Peel the charred ginger, discarding the skin and leaving the ginger in one piece.

Wrap the cloves, anise, cinnamon stick, and peppercorns in a piece of cheesecloth and tie it shut.

Rinse the feet, and the stockpot, and return the bones to the pot. Add the charred onion and ginger, ham hocks, fish sauce, brown sugar, and spice bundle. Cover with 6 quarts water and bring to a boil. Skim with a ladle to remove the scum and residue that rises to the top, then decrease the heat to low and simmer gently for 3 hours. Continue to skim every 30 minutes.

Continued

Soften the noodles in warm water for 30 minutes. Drain and discard the soaking liquid.

Peel and slice the remaining onion in half, stem to root end, cut the halves in half crosswise, and thinly slice each quarter lengthwise. Thinly slice the jalapeño into rings. Pinch the basil, cilantro, and culantro into small sprigs.

Strain and reserve the pork foot broth, discarding the solids. Stir 2 tablespoons lime juice, the salt, hoisin, sriracha, and Accent seasoning into the broth. Return the broth to the pot and bring to a boil.

Transfer 2 cups of the broth to a separate pot and bring to a rolling boil. Add the soaked noodles and cook until tender, 2 to 3 minutes.

Transfer a serving of cooked noodles directly to each large serving bowl. Top with some jalapeño slices, onion slices, a pinch of black pepper, 2 ounces of each meat, and some of the basil, cilantro, and culantro. Ladle the boiling broth to cover each serving and finish with a drizzle of hoisin and sriracha. Garnish with additional herbs and a large wedge of lime.

Good to know

Culantro is the Mexican name for sawleaf, an herb in the parsley family with aromas of cilantro, basil, and mint. You could substitute it with Vietnamese mint, aka Vietnamese coriander, *laksa* leaf, or *rau ram*.

If you tell a butcher you need some pig's feet, he or she will probably say, "Here, just take them." There isn't a big demand for them, but trotters make incredible broth.

HOUSE-MADE BACON, THREE WAYS

MAKES 2 TO 3 POUNDS

If you have a smoker, it's pretty easy to make bacon at home. Take a raw pork belly, cure it in salt, sugar, and spices for 2 weeks, then smoke it with hickory wood and low heat for 8 hours. You can do the same thing with pork jowls to make Jowl Bacon and with boneless pork shoulder to make Cottage Bacon (Kansas City–style bacon). See the photos on page 14. I use Belly Bacon in everything from House-Made Bacon BLT (page 135) and Sweet Potato Pancakes with Maple-Braised Bacon (page 136) to Banoffee Trifle with Candied Bacon (page 140) and Bacon-Molasses Chipwiches (page 143). The KC–style bacon turns up in Cottage Bacon Croque Monsieur (page 57) and the Jowl Bacon in Black-Eyed Peas with Jowl Bacon (page 217). You can substitute the Belly Bacon with store-bought bacon in a pinch. Just be sure to buy dry-cured, wood-smoked bacon, preferably unsliced. Benton's bacon makes a good choice.

¾ cup kosher salt

½ cup packed light brown sugar

1 tablespoon ground black pepper

1 tablespoon Espelette pepper or hot paprika

¼ teaspoon ground cinnamon

1 teaspoon curing/pink salt

1 (3-pound) pork belly with skin or 1 (2-pound) boneless pork butt or 2 pounds boneless pork jowl

Combine the salt, brown sugar, black and red peppers, cinnamon, and curing salt in a gallon-size zip-top bag. This can't be made ahead as it will clump and cake; you need to mix it fresh each time.

For Belly Bacon, add the pork belly to the curing mix and completely coat the meat with the cure, rubbing it into all sides, nooks, and crannies. Squeeze and/or suck as much air out of the bag as possible, and then zip it shut and compact the meat into one end of the bag. Wrap the bag tightly with freezer or masking tape around the top and sides of the bag. Put the meat package into another zip-top bag, seal, and place in the refrigerator. It's always a good idea to label the parcel with what it is and the date. Keep refrigerated for 14 days, turning the bag over every day to make sure the cure and juices are evenly distributed.

Remove the meat from the bag, discard the bag, and rinse the meat to remove all excess cure and juices. Using paper towels, pat the meat completely dry. Place the meat on a plate and refrigerate, uncovered, for another 2 days. The low humidity in the refrigerator will help to dry the meat. Since the meat has already cured, there is no spoilage concern at this point.

Preheat a smoker to 180°F. Place the meat directly on the rack in the smoker, turn the heat off completely, and smoke for 8 hours. You will not be using heat, only smoke. Remove the bacon from the smoker and cool completely before slicing. To store, keep refrigerated in an airtight bag or container for up to 1 month or frozen for up to 6 months.

For Cottage Bacon, follow the same directions as above, using the boneless pork butt in place of the pork belly. If you have a larger pork butt, scale the curing mixture in equivalent proportions. For instance, for

a 4-pound pork butt, double the amount of curing mix. The curing salt removes moisture, concentrates flavors, prevents bacterial growth, and keeps the meat "pink." The exact proportions are important for flavor and texture and to avoid spoilage. Keep in mind that cottage bacon is a little more like ham because it has much less fat than traditional belly bacon.

For Jowl Bacon, follow the same directions above, using the boneless pork jowl in place of the pork belly. Since pork jowl is lower in fat (about 50 percent fat vs. 75 percent fat for pork belly), it doesn't cook up like traditional belly bacon. For the best results when cutting jowl bacon into strips, slice the bacon very thinly. Weigh down the strips in the pan until they are crisp, and then turn and weigh them down again until cooked through.

Good to Know

If you have a vacuum sealer like FoodSaver, vacuum-pack the pork instead of putting it in a zip-top bag. You'll get a slightly deeper cure.

To smoke the bacon on a kettle grill, use hickory wood shavings and indirect heat: Just split the grill in half and place the pork opposite the shavings so they're not directly over the heat.

HOUSE-MADE BACON BLT

MAKES 4 SANDWICHES

This sandwich is all about the awesome flavor of House-Made Bacon (page 132). I use 4 thick-cut slices per sandwich. The bacon likes to burn because of the sugar in the curing mix, so start it in a cold pan over medium heat. For the bread, I prefer a buttery loaf like challah. Brioche works too. I butter the bread and toast it, slather it with Duke's mayonnaise, and then add two pieces of bacon per slice of bread. For the lettuce and tomato component, I like a nice salad of baby arugula, little tomatoes cut in wedges, and simple lemon vinaigrette with some pecorino cheese. Putting the salad in the middle of the sandwich keeps the bread from getting soggy.

16 thick slices Belly Bacon (page 132)

2 tablespoons butter

8 (½-inch-thick) slices crusty white bread

2 tomatoes

¼ cup finely grated pecorino cheese

½ teaspoon extra-virgin olive oil

¼ teaspoon freshly squeezed lemon juice

Kosher salt and ground black pepper

1 cup arugula

¼ cup mayonnaise

Starting with a room temperature pan, arrange the bacon in a single layer and place over medium heat. Cook for 4 minutes, flip, cook for another 4 minutes, flip again, and cook for another 2 minutes. The bacon should be crispy on the edges. The homemade bacon will not be like store-bought and will tend to burn as the fat renders. Watch carefully and turn it as needed to get the bacon crispy on the edges. You don't want to render all of the fat out. Transfer to a paper towel–lined plate and repeat the process until all of the bacon is cooked. Remove the pan from the heat, add the butter, and swirl until melted into the drippings.

Adjust the rack in the oven to the highest setting and preheat the broiler to high. Brush a baking sheet with the buttery bacon drippings and brush one side of each slice of bread with the drippings. Place the bread, brushed side up, on the baking sheet. Toast the bread until the edges start to brown, about 2 minutes. Flip the bread and brush with the buttery bacon drippings. Return to the oven and toast until the edges start to brown, another 2 minutes or so.

Cut the tomatoes into thin wedges. In a bowl, gently toss the tomatoes, cheese, olive oil, lemon juice, and salt and pepper. Add the arugula and toss once again to coat.

For each sandwich, spread 2 slices of toast with mayonnaise, layer 1 slice with 2 strips of bacon, one quarter of the tomato salad, another 2 strips of bacon, and top with the remaining toast. Using a serrated knife, slice on the diagonal and serve.

SWEET POTATO PANCAKES WITH MAPLE-BRAISED BACON

FEEDS 6 FOR BREAKFAST (OR 24 AS AN APPETIZER)

This dish goes beyond your traditional pancakes with a side of bacon. The sweet potato pancakes become a backdrop for the real star, thick-cut maple-braised bacon. You start with a thick slab of bacon, preferably Belly Bacon (page 132), get the bacon real crisp in a heavy griddle, and then add maple syrup and Coca-Cola. As the bacon braises, the acid in the Coke tenderizes it. And, oh yeah, you save the rendered bacon fat for cooking the pancakes. This is not diet food. I like to serve the maple-braised bacon right on the sweet potato pancakes and top the whole thing with a couple fried eggs. It's an over-the-top, indulgent Sunday morning brunch to enjoy before you head off to the couch.

1 jumbo sweet potato

8 ounces Belly Bacon (page 132) or slab bacon

¾ cup maple syrup

¾ cup Coca-Cola

2 tablespoons sherry vinegar

1½ cups all-purpose flour

1 tablespoon baking powder

1 teaspoon freshly grated nutmeg

½ teaspoon kosher salt

2 eggs

1¼ cups whole milk

Preheat the oven to 375°F. Bake the sweet potato until fork-tender, about 40 minutes.

Slice the Belly Bacon across the grain into ½-inch strips. Cut each strip into 3 pieces; each piece will be about 3 inches long.

Heat a cast-iron skillet over medium heat, add the bacon, and cook for 7 minutes, until the bacon just starts to get golden brown. Flip the bacon and place a bacon press or the bottom of a clean smaller skillet on the bacon and press to ensure even cooking and prevent curling. Cook for another 7 minutes, until crispy and browned. Mostly, you're just rendering off some of the fat in this step and adding a little color, which will translate into more flavor in the final dish. Pour the bacon drippings from the pan and reserve. Return the bacon to the pan, add the maple syrup, Coca-Cola, and vinegar, and bring to a boil over high heat. Decrease the heat to low, cover, and simmer for 20 minutes. Uncover, increase the temperature to high, and reduce the liquid to a syrupy consistency, about 8 more minutes.

Sift the flour, baking powder, nutmeg, and salt into a large bowl. Peel the sweet potato and mash it in a medium bowl until smooth. Break the eggs into a 2-cup measuring cup and gently whisk to break up the yolks. Add the milk and stir to combine. Add the milk mixture to the sweet potato mash and stir until blended. Whisk in ¼ cup of the reserved melted bacon drippings. Gradually stir the egg mixture into the dry ingredients just until incorporated, being careful not to overmix, which would develop too much gluten in the flour and make the pancakes tough. The batter will be a little bit thicker than traditional pancake batter, resulting in a creamier pancake. Let the batter rest for 10 minutes at room temperature.

Preheat an electric griddle to 300°F. Brush the griddle with butter. Spoon ¼ cup of pancake batter onto the griddle for each pancake. Cook until bubbles start forming and the top of the pancakes starts to dry out, about 2 minutes. Flip the pancakes and cook for another 2 minutes. This will take a bit longer than traditional pancakes due to the sweet potato. You want the pancakes to be a light golden brown and fully cooked through. Adjust your temperature on the griddle if the pancakes are browning too fast and are still gummy in the center.

Place 2 pancakes on each plate, top with a slice of bacon, and spoon some syrup across the top.

Good to know

To serve this as an appetizer, make 2-inch pancakes and cut the bacon into 1½-inch slices.

CANDIED BACON

MAKES 1 POUND: ABOUT 16 SLICES

I was out of town having breakfast at a diner one day, and along with the scrambled eggs and hash browns on the menu, I saw candied bacon. Bring it on! I'd been playing with different ways of candying bacon—like coating the bacon in liquid sugar—but it never came out crisp enough. When the candied bacon came to the table, it was thick cut with a gorgeous sheen and tasted nice and crispy. "How do you make this?" I asked the waitress. She said they just sprinkle brown sugar on it and bake it. Duh—sometimes chefs overthink things. This is one of the simplest preparations in the world to make. Definitely give it a try. I also use this as a dessert component in Banoffee Trifle with Candied Bacon (page 140) and Bacon-Molasses Chipwiches (page 143).

1½ cups packed light brown sugar

1 teaspoon kosher salt

1 pound Belly Bacon (page 132), sliced and chilled

Preheat the oven to 350°F. Line 2 baking sheets with parchment.

Combine the brown sugar and salt and place in a pile on another baking sheet. Separate the bacon into single slices and, one by one, lay the bacon in the sugar mixture and press to crust it on both sides, patting so the sugar adheres. You should have a fairly thick layer of brown sugar on both sides of the bacon. Spread in a single layer on the parchment-lined baking sheets. Sprinkle any remaining sugar over the bacon. Bake until the sugar melts, bubbles, and turns a deep brick red color, 18 to 20 minutes; the bacon will start to curl. If using thick-sliced bacon, after 18 minutes increase the oven temperature to 400°F and bake until crispy and deep brick red in color, another 10 minutes or so. Remove from the oven and immediately transfer to a baking sheet lined with nonstick foil or a silicone mat. Serve immediately or let cool and refrigerate in an airtight container for up to 1 week.

Good to know

If you replace the Belly Bacon with store-bought bacon, buy a thick-cut dry-cured bacon smoked with real hickory wood.

During recipe testing, Gena Berry went one step further with this candied bacon and turned it into Crack Bacon, a wicked addictive snack. To make it, just add 1½ teaspoons cayenne pepper, 2 teaspoons Espelette pepper, and 1 teaspoon ground black pepper along with the sugar and salt in the recipe. It tastes best baked and served immediately. But you can get a jump on prep by mixing up the spice mixture ahead of time and spreading it on the prepared baking sheets. Then just coat the bacon in the seasoning, bake, and serve.

BANOFFEE TRIFLE WITH CANDIED BACON

FEEDS 6 TO 8

My restaurant Gunshow has no investors. To raise money I did a series of fundraising dinners all over the country. I customized the menu for each group—except for dessert. I'm not much of a pastry chef, so I stuck with my slam-dunk combo of bananas, toffee, and candied bacon. I made it several different ways. At first, I plated it as a deconstructed modernist dessert. Then in Seattle I served a much bigger group of folks and the modernist plating turned out to be too time-consuming. Out of sheer necessity, I made it into a trifle, and that's what made the dish even more successful. It's a layered dessert of vanilla custard, Candied Bacon (page 139), crushed shortbread cookies, fried bananas, toffee caramel, and chocolate ganache. You can totally make this at home. The layering makes it look awesome in a glass dish. Serve it with coffee and your friends will think you're badass.

4 tablespoons butter

1 cup packed light brown sugar

1 cup heavy cream, divided

1 teaspoon fine sea salt or table salt

¼ teaspoon vanilla extract

Canola oil for frying

3 bananas

5 ounces 65% chocolate, chopped

12 ounces shortbread cookies

2 cups vanilla custard or pudding (see Good to Know)

16 strips Candied Bacon (page 139), chopped, 2 pieces reserved for garnish

To make the caramel, melt the butter in a saucepan over medium-high heat. Add the brown sugar and stir to combine. Bring to a boil and stir in ¾ cup of the cream. Return to a boil and decrease the heat to a low simmer. Simmer, swirling occasionally, until the mixture reaches 235°F, about 10 minutes. Remove from the heat and stir in the salt and vanilla.

Heat the oil in a deep fryer to 350°F.

Peel the bananas and fry until deep golden brown, 8 to 10 minutes. Transfer to a paper towel–lined plate to cool.

Heat the remaining ¼ cup cream in a small saucepan just to a boil, then remove from the heat and stir in the chocolate until melted.

Place the cookies in a large zip-top bag, squeeze out any excess air, and roll with a rolling pin a few times to make very coarse crumbs; you should have about 3 cups.

You can make one large trifle bowl or individual servings in 8-ounce canning jars. To assemble, layer one-third of the cookie crumbs, half the custard, half the bacon, half the fried bananas, half the caramel, and the chocolate; continue layering on the remaining custard, bacon, bananas, and one-third of the crumbs; top with the remaining caramel and crumbs. Serve immediately or cover and refrigerate for up to 1 day. Cut the reserved bacon into long strips and garnish each serving with a strip.

Good to know

You can replace the chocolate with ¾ cup semisweet chocolate chips.

Use your favorite vanilla custard or pudding here; store-bought will work but homemade is better.

BACON-MOLASSES CHIPWICHES

MAKES 12 SANDWICHES

A few years ago, Paula Deen invited me on her television show to cook an all-pork menu. The dessert I created looks simple but is kind of a pain in the ass to make. It has three parts: ginger-molasses cookies, candied bacon, and ice cream made with the bacon. The cookies are my granny's classic gingersnaps, but a little undercooked so they're still soft. For the ice cream, you fold in candied bacon and then freeze it on a rimmed baking sheet so you can punch out circles matching the cookies. Paula took one bite of this chipwich and fell in love. She took another chipwich to her husband at work and a third to her daughter-in-law. The staff told me she never ate the food on her show, so I guess that's a pretty solid endorsement of this recipe.

3 egg yolks

½ cup sugar

½ teaspoon vanilla extract

1¼ cups heavy cream

½ cup chopped Candied Bacon (page 139), about 8 slices

24 Ginger-Molasses Cookies (recipe follows)

Line a baking sheet with parchment paper.

In a stand mixer fitted with the whisk attachment, whisk the yolks, sugar, and vanilla until very thick and light lemon colored, about 3 minutes. Transfer this mixture to another bowl. Add the cream to the mixer bowl and whisk on medium-high speed until the beater leaves soft peaks when lifted, about 2 minutes. Fold ½ cup of the whipped cream into the yolk mixture, then fold the yolk mixture into the remaining whipped cream. Fold in the candied bacon. Spread on the prepared baking sheet, cover with plastic wrap, and freeze until firm. It won't freeze as solid as hard ice cream but will be a little softer, known as *semifreddo*.

Using a round cookie cutter the size of your cookies, punch out 12 rounds of the *semifreddo* and sandwich each round between 2 cookies. Eat immediately or wrap in parchment and freeze for up to 1 day. Thaw for about 5 minutes before eating.

Continued

Ginger-Molasses Cookies MAKES 24 COOKIES

2¼ cups all-purpose flour

1 teaspoon baking soda

2 teaspoons ground cinnamon

1½ teaspoons ground ginger

¼ teaspoon ground cloves

½ teaspoon fine sea salt

¾ cup (1½ sticks) butter, softened

⅓ cup packed light brown sugar

⅓ cup granulated sugar

1 egg

⅓ cup molasses

Raw, demerara, or turbinado (coarse) sugar, for rolling

Whisk together the flour, baking soda, cinnamon, ginger, cloves, and salt in a medium bowl.

In the bowl of a stand mixer fitted with a paddle attachment, beat the butter on medium speed until light and fluffy, about 2 minutes. Slowly add both sugars and beat until light and fluffy, another 2 to 3 minutes. Decrease the speed to medium-low, add the egg, and mix until well incorporated, about 30 seconds. Add the molasses and mix until well incorporated, about 30 more seconds. Remove the bowl from the mixer and, using a rubber spatula, fold in the flour mixture just until incorporated. Chill the dough for at least 30 minutes.

Preheat the oven to 375°F. Line baking sheets with parchment paper.

Place the raw sugar in a small bowl. Using a ½-ounce scoop, scoop the dough into balls and roll lightly to form a smooth ball. Dip each dough ball into the sugar and toss to cover completely. Place 2 inches apart on the prepared baking sheets and bake until the cookies have flattened slightly and have just started to crack and puff, 8 minutes. You want these cookies to be just a tad underbaked, so they have a moist center. Remove from the oven, lift the baking sheet about a foot over the counter, and drop the sheet squarely on the counter, giving the cookies a nice smack. This will help them spread and flatten just a tad more, making them the perfect consistency for the sandwiches. Cool completely on the baking sheets.

Good to Know

You can make and freeze the candied bacon *semifreddo* up to 2 weeks in advance. Just keep it tightly covered in the freezer.

MAPLE-BACON ICE CREAM

MAKES ABOUT 1 QUART

While it's not my No. 1 flavor, people go crazy for bacon ice cream. They ask me about it all the time. They make a more complicated version at Morelli's, the ice cream place I help out at in Atlanta. But I simplified the process here, so all you need to do is steep some chopped-up bacon in your base cream mixture and then pull out the bacon with a slotted spoon, leaving behind all that smoky, bacony goodness. This preparation actually works better with store-bought wet-cured bacon because a homemade bacon or Benton's bacon would be way too smoky and overpower the ice cream.

1¾ cups heavy cream

¾ cup half-and-half

⅔ cup Grade B maple syrup

3 thick slices uncooked bacon, cut into 4-inch pieces

1 teaspoon kosher salt

4 egg yolks

In a medium pan, heat the cream, half-and-half, maple syrup, bacon, and salt almost to a boil. Turn the heat off but leave the pan on the burner and let the bacon steep for 30 minutes. Use a slotted spoon to remove and discard the bacon.

In a medium bowl, whisk the egg yolks until thick. Whisk ½ cup of the warm cream mixture into the yolks, and then whisk the yolk mixture into the cream. Turn the heat to medium-high and cook, stirring frequently, until the mixture thickens slightly and coats the back of a spoon, about 5 minutes.

Strain the custard through a fine-mesh sieve into a metal bowl and chill thoroughly. Freeze in an ice cream maker according to the manufacturer's instructions, but only to soft-serve consistency. Be careful not to overchurn, as the ice cream will go from smooth to grainy.

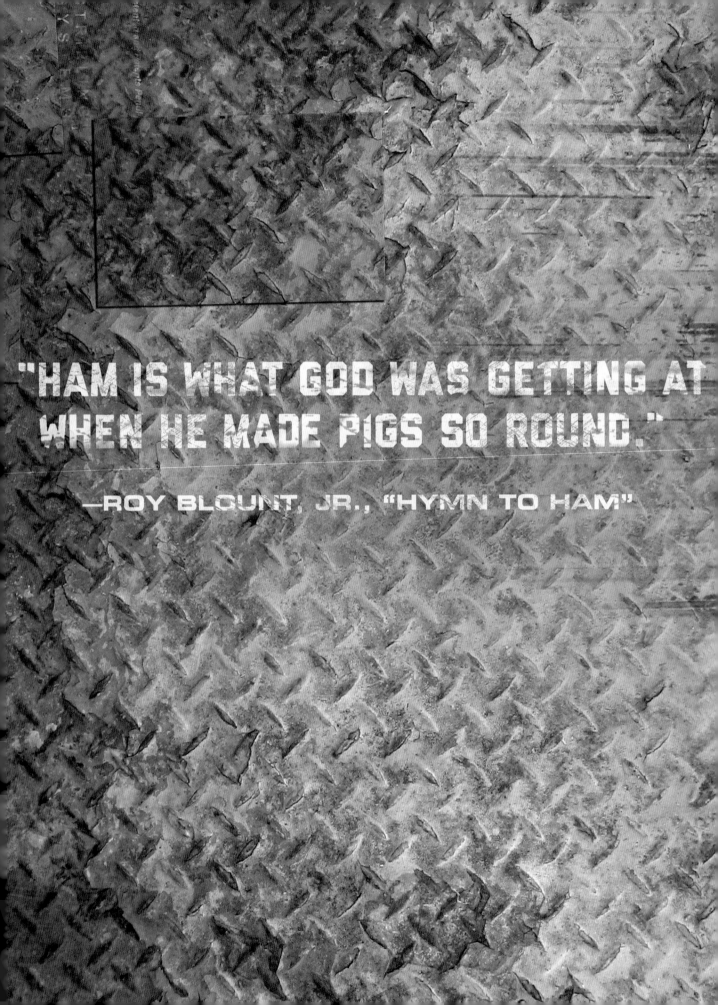

"HAM IS WHAT GOD WAS GETTING AT WHEN HE MADE PIGS SO ROUND."

—ROY BLOUNT, JR., "HYMN TO HAM"

№ 6

HAMS

I feel like a confession is in order. As a kid, I didn't really like ham. Given the choice between turkey and ham at Thanksgiving, I'd choose turkey; between roast beef and ham at Christmas, I'd choose roast beef; and between a ham sandwich and a bologna sandwich, I'd always choose bologna.

We had lots of ham around the house. But it was usually a baked ham baked waaaaaaay too long until it was bone dry. Or we had the cheapest deli ham you could possibly buy. My opinion of ham was not very high. I loved pork in general but never had much of a soft spot for this particular cut.

Later in life, I thought, maybe I should look into ham a little more closely. As a teenager, I was eating at my favorite barbecue place, Fresh Air Barbecue in Jackson, Georgia. I was chatting with a woman there about how juicy their barbecue is and asked, "Do you guys just cook pork shoulder or do you smoke other cuts?" She looked me right in the face and said, "We only cook hams." I was shocked. "Hams?" Not cured ham, obviously, but just the back leg. "Why?" I asked. "Our opinion is that the ham is more flavorful than the shoulder," she said. "We think cooking shoulders alone produces barbecue that's too fatty. Cooking a whole bone-in ham produces the best end result." I was impressed. Their barbecue was not the least bit dry. Clearly a juicy, succulent ham could be accomplished.

Fast forward a few years, I'm cooking professionally at the Ritz-Carlton in Atlanta, and I'm exposed for the first time to prosciutto di Parma.

In the Gillespie household, we had no prosciutto di Parma, so I had zero experience with it. In came this gorgeous prosciutto aged 24 months. I was terrified. Getting this hotel chef job was like moving from AAA baseball to the big leagues. I didn't want to mess anything up—and this was an expensive piece of meat. The chef, Matt Swyckerath, told me to slice the prosciutto. I pulled out my knife and started slicing. "What are you doing?" asked Chef. I thought for a split second, then put the prosciutto on the meat slicer. After three slices, he looked at me and said, "What are you, retarded? Take off the rind first!" Then he yelled at me for slicing it too thick. After a decent amount of waste, I managed to get a proper, paper-thin slice of prosciutto. To my amazement, rather than continue to scold me, Chef said, "Now eat it." I didn't realize that it was safe to eat. It didn't look cooked. "Eat it like it is," he said.

I remember, like yesterday, just how salty it was. I wasn't expecting that. I thought it would taste more akin to wet-brined Virginia ham. Instead, it had an intense saltiness like country ham. The taste was incredibly concentrated with flavorful nuances of sweet, nutty—acorny, really. And that funkiness common to all cured meats. Most impressively, the fat just melted on my tongue. That texture blew me away. I'd never had a piece of meat sliced so thin that I didn't have to chew. I just put the prosciutto in my mouth, the fat dissolved at body temperature, and the tiniest movements of my tongue made the prosciutto fall apart.

It was such an emotional experience for a cook. I got exposed to something I'd never seen or tasted before. Then I understood why it was so expensive. Even though I was a total rube at the time, I could tell how unique and special this ham was.

Two minutes before that experience, if you'd asked me whether I liked ham, I would have said, "It's okay." But ever since then I've been saying, "I love it."

Even if you're not a fan of ham, give these recipes a try. They use everything from prosciutto and serrano ham to country ham and baked ham. If you're feeling adventurous, take a raw pig leg, cure it, smoke it, and bake it into Old-School Baked Ham (page 160). Or, to go the quick route, just buy a baked ham to use in the recipes here like A Really Good Ham Sandwich (page 161) and Overstuffed Ham and Cheese Omelet (page 169). I use some raw cuts from the leg here, too, for dishes like Chicken-Fried Pork Steak (page 158). This chapter celebrates all the delicious ways you can enjoy the rear leg of a pig.

★ GOOD TO KNOW ABOUT ★
Ham

WHAT IT IS: A ham is the hind leg of a pig. It's called a ham when it's raw and a ham when it's cured or cooked. In the recipes, I make it clear when I'm talking about raw ham, cured ham, or cooked ham. Raw ham is the starting point, but unless you're curing it, you rarely work with a whole raw ham. For one thing, it's massive. A full-grown hog raised for market generally has a ham on it weighing 30 to 60 pounds. To make Old-School Baked Ham (page 160) from scratch, I call for a 10-pound raw ham, which is a little easier to work with.

HAM IS LEAN: Like pork shoulder, the ham consists of a collection of different muscles. But unlike shoulder, the ham muscles are lean and tender, not tough and fatty. That's because the leg muscles are so large that no one muscle has to bear the weight of the entire animal. It's a common misconception that ham is a fatty cut of meat. That's just not true. Almost all of the fat on ham is surface fat that can be easily trimmed away—and more often than not, it is trimmed away. The leg meat itself is very lean. For cooks, this means that ham is not quite as forgiving as shoulder. Ham meat is so lean that it can dry out. The key to juicy, tender ham is gentle, consistent, moist heat.

TRY A PORK LEG STEAK: Pork leg is one of my absolute favorite parts of the animal. If you're good with a knife, I encourage you to separate out the leg muscles, pull off the connective tissue, and cook with one of the muscles. The singular muscles are so lean that they cook up more like pork loin. But unlike pork loin, they're full of flavor. Carving out one of these leg muscles is the secret to my Chicken-Fried Pork Steak (page 158).

BEHIND THE LABELS: Why is pork labeling so confusing? I have no idea. But here's a guide to the different types of ham you're likely to encounter:

Fresh ham is the raw hind leg of a pig, otherwise known as a raw ham. You probably won't see it in the store. Maybe around the holidays you'll see whole fresh hams. To procure this cut, ask a farmer or butcher to cut a raw ham for you.

Ready-to-cook ham is the cured and smoked hind leg of a pig. Curing is what gives ham its rosy pink color, and smoking evaporates some excess moisture and adds flavor. But the meat is not yet safe to eat raw. It must be cooked. You can buy ready-to-cook ham, aka wet-brined ham, at the store. This type of ham is ready for further cooking, such as baking to make baked ham (see below), or further smoking. If you follow the recipe for Old-School Baked Ham (page 160), the first two steps (curing and smoking) take you to this point of having ready-to-cook ham. But if you want to skip those steps, you could get a store-bought ready-to-cook ham and proceed with the recipe to make your baked ham.

Baked ham comes in lots of different varieties in grocery stores with labels like honey-baked ham, honey-roasted ham, Black Forest ham, and tavern ham. They're all wet-cured hams that are smoked and/or fully cooked. This type of ham is safe to eat. Make a sandwich, make an omelet, or heat it up and carve it for Easter. Serve it with a giant wedge of pineapple if you like. Baked ham is ready to heat and eat.

Dry-cured ham represents a different curing method than wet-cured ham. Prosciutto, serrano,

Westphalian, and country ham are all dry-cured hams. While wet-cured baked hams use heat to kill bacteria, dry-cured hams rely on salt to remove moisture from the meat, which removes the moist environment that bacteria like to grow in. All dry-cured hams can be eaten safely without further cooking because they have been dehydrated with salt for months. I use dry-cured country ham to make Ham Burgers (page 162) and Country Ham Breakfast Strata (page 171); serrano ham to make Serrano Ham Croquettes (page 165); and prosciutto to make Ham-Wrapped Snapper (page 152) and Arugula, Fig, and Prosciutto Bundles (page 167). Keep in mind: Dry-cured ham and baked ham are not the same. They can't be swapped for one another. Dry-cured ham has a much more concentrated ham flavor.

HAM-WRAPPED SNAPPER

FEEDS 4

Pork doesn't always have to be the star of the show. It's perfectly happy as a supporting actor or even as part of the crew. That's one of the things I love about it. A few years ago, I'd been looking for a way to grill halibut over a superhot fire without drying out the fish. Prosciutto was just the thing. It's a handy wrapper and the fat melts and bastes the fish, keeping it moist. Plus, it's got that intense salty porkiness that punches up the flavor of the fish. I call for snapper here, but you could use halibut, grouper, black bass, black cod, or any sturdy white fish less than 1 inch thick. Ham wrapping is a good grilling technique to have in your back pocket. Try it on vegetables too.

4 center-cut snapper fillets, about 6 ounces each

Kosher salt and ground black pepper

4 paper-thin slices prosciutto

4 scallions

2 cloves garlic, peeled

Leaves from 4 sprigs fresh thyme or basil (cut basil leaves into chiffonade)

2 tablespoons extra-virgin olive oil + more for garnish

1 lemon

Aged balsamic vinegar or balsamic glaze, for garnish (see Good to Know)

Pat the fish dry. Lightly sprinkle the top of the fillets with salt and pepper. Lay each fillet atop a single slice of prosciutto. Trim and discard the root ends and dark green parts from the scallions. Slice the white part of the scallion into 4-inch lengths, cut lengthwise down the center, and continue cutting into very thin sticks. Slice the garlic into paper-thin slices. Spread the scallions, garlic, and herbs among the fillets and wrap the prosciutto tightly around the fish, arranging so the prosciutto seam is under the fillet and will stay closed. Secure with a toothpick on both sides.

Heat a grill to medium. Brush the bottom/seam side of the fillets with some of the oil and place, seam side down, on the grill. Close the grill lid and cook for 5 minutes, until the prosciutto starts to get crispy. Brush the tops with a little more oil and, using a fish spatula, carefully flip the fillets. Close the grill and cook for another 3 minutes, then turn 45 degrees to a hot part of the grill to create nice grill marks; close the grill and cook for another 2 minutes, or until the fillets are fully cooked through.

If using a stovetop grill pan, heat over high heat, decreasing the heat to medium after you place all the fillets on the pan. Cover with a domed pot lid to trap the heat and cook the fish through to the center, about 4 minutes. Brush with oil, carefully flip, cover, and grill for another 3 minutes, then turn 45 degrees and place on a hot part of the pan to create nice grill marks, and cook for another 2 minutes.

Serve with a big squeeze of lemon and a nice drizzle of olive oil and balsamic glaze.

Good to know

Aged balsamic vinegar is mellower and more complex tasting than the cheap stuff. You can also use balsamic glaze, a type of boiled-down balsamic that's thicker and sweeter.

CHICAGO-STYLE MEAT LOVER'S PIZZA

MAKES TWO 10-INCH PIZZAS: PLENTY FOR 8 PEOPLE

New York–style pizza has a thin crust, a thin layer of sauce, and a thin layer of cheese. Chicago style is completely different. This pie has a thick crust, a thick layer of sauce, and a thick layer of cheese. The dough goes into a big pie pan (cast iron makes it extra-crispy), the cheese goes over the crust first, then you put the toppings over the cheese, and a thick layer of sauce on top. By the time you're done filling it up, it really is more like a pizza "pie." And it's damn good. With smoked ham, bacon, hot Italian sausage, pepperoni, and coppa (capocollo), this version has all three of my favorite food groups: pork, pork, and more pork.

1 tablespoon active dry yeast

1 tablespoon sugar

10 tablespoons butter

3¼ cups all-purpose flour

½ cup finely ground white cornmeal

4 teaspoons kosher salt

2 tablespoons olive oil

8 ounces Belly Bacon (page 132) or store-bought bacon, finely diced

1 large Vidalia onion, cut into ¼-inch dice, about 3 cups

2 teaspoons light brown sugar

1½ teaspoons red pepper flakes

1 teaspoon dried oregano

¾ teaspoon dried thyme

1 tablespoon dried minced garlic

42 ounces chunky crushed tomatoes, 5¼ cups

1 pound mozzarella cheese

8 ounces provolone cheese

2 links hot Italian sausage, about 7 ounces total

8 ounces thinly sliced smoked ham

4 ounces thinly sliced pepperoni

3 ounces thinly sliced coppa (capocollo)

½ cup freshly grated Parmesan cheese

Dissolve the yeast and sugar in 1⅓ cups warm water (about 115°F).

Melt 3 tablespoons of the butter.

In the bowl of a stand mixer fitted with a dough hook, combine the flour, cornmeal, and 2 teaspoons of the salt. With the mixer on low speed, add the yeast mixture and mix for 1 minute. Continue mixing and drizzle the melted butter into the dough. Increase the speed to medium and knead the dough until completely combined and in one mass, about 2 minutes. The dough will take a little bit to come together, then it will "whop, whop, whop" in the bowl. That's when it is done. Rub the dough ball with some of the olive oil, cover with plastic wrap, and set in a warm place until the dough has doubled in size, about 1 hour.

Heat a 2-quart, heavy-bottomed saucepan over medium heat. Add 3 tablespoons of the butter and swirl until melted. Add the diced bacon and cook for 2 minutes, stirring to even the cooking. When the bacon starts to brown, drain over a bowl, reserving the drippings and transferring the bacon to a paper towel–lined plate. Measure ¼ cup of the drippings back into the pan and add the onions, the remaining 2 teaspoons salt, the brown sugar, red pepper flakes, oregano, and thyme. Cook until the onion is soft and translucent, about 5 minutes. Add the dried garlic and tomatoes and simmer, covered, over low heat until thick, about 45 minutes. Stir a couple times to prevent sticking.

Smear a little olive oil onto your rolling pin, punch down the dough, and roll into a rectangle about 13 by 18 inches. Soften the remaining 4 tablespoons butter so it is easily spreadable. Using an offset spatula, smear the softened butter evenly across the crust, not quite to the edge. Roll the dough, jelly roll style, and pinch the ends and side seams closed. Using the rolling pin, roll out the log to flatten it, and then cut in half. Fold each piece into thirds and then shape into a round. This process will result in an ultra-crispy, flaky, buttery crust. Rub the balls with olive oil, cover, and refrigerate until doubled in size, about 1 hour.

Preheat the oven to 425°F. Grate the mozzarella and provolone and toss to combine.

Remove the casing from the sausage and cut lengthwise into quarters, then into 1-inch pieces. Heat a skillet over medium-high heat, add the sausage, and cook through, about 4 minutes.

Roll each dough ball into a 13-inch round. Generously brush the bottom and sides of two 10-inch cast-iron skillets with oil and drop a dough round into each skillet, pressing it into the pan and all the way up the sides. Divide the toppings between the skillets and layer in this exact order: mozzarella and provolone cheeses, sausage, ham, bacon, pepperoni, and coppa. Using your hands, press the toppings into the crust to compact. Divide the sauce between the skillets and spread evenly over the top. Sprinkle the Parmesan over the top. Bake until the crust is nicely browned and the filling is bubbly, about 35 minutes. Let stand for 15 minutes before slicing and eating.

Good to Know

It's easiest to make this dish in stages. You can make the tomato sauce well in advance and refrigerate for a few days or freeze it for a few months. The dough can be left to rise in the refrigerator for several hours or overnight instead of at room temperature. Get those two steps done and then layering and cooking the pie will be easy.

Dried garlic is preferred over fresh here. Instead of the hot bite of fresh garlic, you get a milder garlic flavor with some sweetness.

LEMON-RICOTTA TORTELLINI IN HAM BROTH

FEEDS 8

Here's my cheater method for making fresh pasta: wonton wrappers. I know, I know. They're not as good as fresh pasta dough. But if you live in, say, Sheboygan, Wisconsin, and can't get amazing fresh pasta at the corner market and don't have time to make the dough and roll it out yourself, wonton wrappers work. They're essentially 3-inch squares of egg noodle dough ready-made for ravioli and individual lasagna. I'm playing on classic Italian tortellini with the broth here but using pork. In the pasta filling and the *brodo*, the pork is smoked ham hocks, one of the unsung heroes of the pork world. Ham hocks bring savory, smoky, salty, and meaty to the party all at once. Ricotta and lemon bring the sweet and sour.

1 bunch chives

²/₃ cup shredded ham from Ham Broth (page 27)

1 cup whole-milk ricotta cheese

1 tablespoon finely grated Parmesan cheese + more for garnish

Kosher salt

1 lemon

1 small clove garlic, peeled and mashed, about ½ teaspoon

1 egg

40 wonton wrappers or fresh pasta sheets, cut into 3½-inch squares

2 cups Ham Broth (page 27)

Finely slice 1 tablespoon of the chives, reserving the rest of the chive spears for garnish. In a small bowl, stir together the tablespoon of chopped chives, ½ cup of the shredded ham, the ricotta, Parmesan, 1 teaspoon salt, ½ loosely packed teaspoon finely grated lemon zest, ½ teaspoon lemon juice, and the garlic.

In a small bowl, beat the egg with 1 tablespoon water to make an egg wash.

Working in batches, lay out the wonton wrappers in a single layer and brush egg wash around the edges of each. Drop a teaspoon of the ham filling into the center of each square and fold corner to corner into a triangle, pressing together the edges. Bring the 2 points from the long end of the triangle together around your finger and press to seal. (See photo.)

Heat the ham broth to a low simmer in a saucepan.

Bring a large pot of water to a rolling boil and add enough salt to make it seawater salty, about 2 tablespoons. Drop the tortellini into the water, stir briefly to prevent sticking, and cook until they float, about 4 minutes. Ladle about ¼ cup broth into the bottom of each pasta plate or shallow bowl. Add 5 tortellini right from the cooking water (use a slotted spoon or spider to drain) and garnish with Parmesan cheese, the remaining shredded ham, and a few chive spears.

Good to Know

The tortellini freeze really well. Just seal them in freezer bags and freeze them for up to 2 months. Then you can heat them in the broth as mentioned above (without changing the cooking time), or serve them with tomato sauce or Alfredo sauce.

CHICKEN-FRIED PORK STEAK

FEEDS 4

This is a crazy idea turned into a recipe. Chicken-fried steak is normally made with beef eye of round, a lean, dense, inexpensive cut from the back ass of the animal. I always wanted to make it with pork because it just sounded awesome. I use the same cut from the pig—the ham—and cut it into fillets like beef tenderloin. You could serve these pork steaks with anything and they'd be delicious. Some people have chicken-fried steak for dinner. Some for breakfast. My personal favorite is with a bowl of spicy turnip greens. Or enjoy it with Fatback Fried Corn (page 221) and Basic Cabbage Slaw (page 29).

4 pork leg fillets, about 4 ounces each, run through the cuber (see Worth Knowing)

3 eggs

1½ cups Seasoned Breading Mix (page 23)

Kosher salt and ground black pepper

Grapeseed oil or canola oil for panfrying

1½ cups milk

½ teaspoon freshly squeezed lemon juice

⅛ teaspoon Accent seasoning

Pat the pork dry.

Beat the eggs and pour them into a shallow bowl or plate large enough to hold one fillet. Spread 1¼ cups of the seasoned breading mix on a large plate. Season the fillets aggressively on both sides with salt and pepper.

Heat ¼ inch oil in a large, deep skillet over high heat until almost smoking.

Using the 3-step breading method (see page 21), bread the fillets, shaking off any excess: Dredge in the breading, dip in the egg, then dredge again in the breading. Add the breaded fillets to the skillet, and cook for 2 minutes. Flip and cook for 3 minutes. Place on a rack over a baking sheet and tent with aluminum foil to keep warm.

Carefully pour the excess oil from the skillet and reserve, leaving the browned bits in the pan. Measure 2 tablespoons of reserved oil back into the skillet. Return to medium heat and stir in the remaining ¼ cup seasoned breading mix. Stir, scraping all the browned bits into the flour and oil, and cook for 1 minute, or until the mixture is bubbling. Slowly stir in the milk just until combined and thick. Stir in the lemon juice and Accent seasoning. Decrease the heat to low and cook for another 2 minutes, stirring occasionally.

Serve the fillets slathered with gravy.

Worth Knowing

The muscles in a pig's leg are pretty large, and you can separate them by pulling off the connective tissue. For this recipe, use any single pork leg muscle and cut it crosswise into fillets like a beef tenderloin fillet. Ask your butcher to run the pork leg fillets through the cuber, a meat-tenderizing machine that looks like a steamroller with spines. You'll get a more tender chicken-fried steak that way.

OLD-SCHOOL BAKED HAM

MAKES ONE 10-POUND BAKED HAM

Most people think of baked ham as something you buy at the store. Well, I'm gonna show you how to make it. It's not hard, and it blows away any ham you'll ever buy in a supermarket. You get a raw pork leg from a farmer or butcher, soak it in salt water for a week, smoke it at a low temperature for 3 hours, and then bake it for another 3 hours. This is how my mother and grandmother always made baked ham. I use this basic baked ham as the basis for all sorts of dishes like A Really Good Ham Sandwich (page 161) and Overstuffed Ham and Cheese Omelet (page 169). But if you want to skip the brining and smoking steps, you could start with a genuine Smithfield ham and simply bake it at home, as directed here.

2½ cups packed light brown sugar

2 cups kosher salt

2 pounds sweet onions, about 3 medium, cut into quarters

1 cup garlic cloves, peeled

2 tablespoons whole cloves

1 cinnamon stick

6 allspice berries, about 2 teaspoons

1 tablespoon + 2 teaspoons curing/pink salt

Ice cubes

1 (10-pound) fresh ham (bone-in rear leg of pig)

Non-scented heavy-duty plastic garbage bag

5-gallon heavy-duty bucket or cooler just large enough to hold the ham

Combine 2 cups of the brown sugar, the kosher salt, onions, garlic, cloves, cinnamon, and allspice berries with 1 gallon water in a large pot. Bring to a boil and stir to dissolve the sugar. Remove from the heat and stir in the curing salt. Add 1 gallon ice cubes to cool the brine. Place the ham in the plastic bag and cover with the brine, press all the air out of the bag, and secure tightly with a twist tie. Place the bag in the bucket and cover with ice. You may need to weigh the ham down to keep it fully submerged in the brine. Let the ham brine for 7 days, making sure to check and replenish the ice to keep it below 40°F during the entire brining time.

Remove the ham from the brine, rinse, and pat dry. The exposed meat should be bright pink because of the curing salt. Discard the brining liquid. Refrigerate the ham, uncovered, overnight.

Set your smoker on the lowest setting—you don't want more than 100°F— and cold-smoke the ham, with the baffles closed, on full smoke for 2 hours.

Preheat the oven to 325°F. Cut 2 sheets of heavy-duty aluminum foil twice the length of your ham and fold together to make a square sheet. Lay the cured and smoked ham in the center of the foil and rub all over with the remaining ½ cup brown sugar. Wrap tightly in the foil and place on a baking sheet or in a roasting pan lined with foil. Bake to an internal temperature of 155°F, about 15 minutes per pound (about 2½ hours for a 10-pound ham). Slice or chop to use like you would store-bought baked ham.

Good to Know

Want a fully cooked, ready-to-eat smoked ham? To make a hot smoked ham instead of a baked ham, follow the directions above through the process of cold smoking. Then set the smoker to 200°F and proceed to hot-smoke the ham to an internal temperature of 155°F, about 4 hours more.

A REALLY GOOD HAM SANDWICH

FEEDS 4

My Pennsylvania friends were always telling me about Primanti Bros. sandwiches in Pittsburgh. So I went there to try one. All the sandwiches come with fries and slaw packed between two thick slabs of Italian bread. You pick your protein, which includes everything from hot sausage and salami to pastrami, corned beef, steak, and sardines. I got ham. It was a killer sandwich, but I thought it would be even better with better-tasting ham. I make my version with scraps from Old-School Baked Ham (page 160). You could also use slices of any decent wet-cured, smoked, bone-in ham. I also like a spread of 3 parts mayo, 1 part yellow mustard, and ½ part horseradish for spunk. With the ham, cheese, fries, coleslaw, and thick-cut bread, this is definitely a two-hander sandwich.

3 tablespoons Duke's mayonnaise

1 tablespoon yellow mustard

1 teaspoon prepared horseradish

1 slicing tomato

Kosher salt and ground black pepper

1¼ pounds Old-School Baked Ham (page 160), sandwich sliced, but not too thin

6 ounces sliced cheese (I like American; provolone and Swiss are good, too)

1 loaf fresh, soft Italian bread, cut into ¾-inch slices

Basic Cabbage Slaw (page 29)

Pork Fat Pommes Frites (page 223)

In a small bowl, combine the mayonnaise, mustard, and horseradish. Set aside.

Slice the tomato ¼ inch thick, place on a paper towel–lined plate, and sprinkle with salt and pepper.

Heat a skillet or griddle over medium-high heat. Place the ham in the skillet and heat for 30 seconds. Flip, add the cheese to the warm ham, and grill just until the cheese melts.

To build your sandwiches, slather the mayonnaise mixture on both the top and bottom slices of bread, pile on the ham and cheese, and top with a hefty spoonful of slaw, a tomato slice, and a few piping-hot fries. Press the top slice of bread right on the fries and smash down just a little.

Worth Knowing

Italian bread comes in so many forms. What you're looking for here is a soft, chewy loaf with a tight crumb and a chewable crust. You don't want a loaf with a super-chewy crust and a ton of big holes throughout the crumb. That kind of Italian bread has its place, but not in a sandwich.

HAM BURGERS

FEEDS 4

It may come as a surprise, but I'm not a huge fan of burgers. I did, however, have an amazing cheeseburger as a teenager at an old-fashioned soda shop in a pharmacy. We were on vacation in North Carolina, at the Grandfather Mountain Highland Games. Down in the town of Boone, three things made that burger great: 1) It was cooked on a flattop, which I prefer over grilled burgers. 2) It was not just beef. It had a sausagelike texture. 3) It had quickly grilled onions. This burger recipe has all those elements and more. It's a mix of ground beef and pork (leg or shoulder works fine), and each sandwich has two big patties with melted Gouda cheese, tarragon aioli, and a sliver of dry-cured ham. Don't forget the side of Pork Fat Pommes Frites (page 223).

1¼ pounds 80% lean ground pork

12 ounces 85% lean ground beef

Kosher salt and ground black pepper

½ teaspoon garlic powder

½ teaspoon onion powder

1 cup apple cider vinegar

⅔ cup sugar

¼ cup pickling spice (see Good to Know)

1 red onion, peeled and sliced into ¼-inch rings

¼ cup Duke's mayonnaise

2 tablespoons chopped fresh tarragon

1 teaspoon finely minced garlic

4 King's Hawaiian sandwich buns

3 tablespoons butter, softened

4 thin slices country or serrano ham

8 slices smoked Gouda cheese

In a large bowl, combine the pork, beef, 1 tablespoon salt, 1 teaspoon pepper, and the garlic and onion powders. Mix well (using clean hands is the best way). Divide the mixture into 8 balls, each about 4 ounces, and refrigerate until chilled through and firm, about 30 minutes.

In a small saucepan, combine the vinegar, sugar, pickling spice, and 2 teaspoons salt, and bring to a boil. Separate the onion rings into a small bowl and strain the hot pickling liquid over the top. Discard the solids.

In a small bowl, stir together the mayonnaise, tarragon, garlic, 2 teaspoons pickling liquid, and a pinch of salt until well combined. Set aside.

Heat a griddle over high heat. Spread the cut sides of the buns with butter and place, butter side down, on the griddle. Cook the buns until browned and toasty, being careful not to let them burn, 1 to 2 minutes. Transfer the buns to a plate and spread each with the tarragon mayonnaise.

Spread the ham on the long edge of the griddle and heat through, about 1 minute. Flip the ham and, using tongs, transfer half the onions to the top of the ham. The liquid from the onions will hit the griddle and steam. Flip the ham so the onions are directly on the griddle and the ham is on top. The steam will soften the onions and release some of the liquid into the ham. Leave the ham stacks on the griddle.

Evenly space 4 of the burger balls on the hot griddle about 3 inches apart. Using a wide, heavy, flat grill press or spatula, smash the patties flat . . . I mean really smash them flat; you might want to use a towel and place your hand on top of the spatula to really spread them out. Cook for 2 minutes. Scootch the 4 ham stacks to the center of the griddle and flip one of your flattened burgers on top of each stack. Smash again, pressing the meat into the ham-onion mixture. Top with a slice of cheese and cook for another 2 minutes. Transfer these patties to the bottom buns, cheese side up, and tent with foil to keep warm. Repeat the cooking and pressing process with the remaining 4 burger balls, topping each of these with a slice of cheese once you flip them. Stack the cheeseburgers on the hamburger stacks, put the tops on, and give them a nice smash down to compact.

Good to know

Most grocery stores carry pickling spice. Look for it in the spice aisle.

My favorite burger buns are King's Hawaiian. They have the perfect soft but not-too-soft texture and just enough sweetness to enhance the meat. Not every market carries them, but I have seen them in Walmart, of all places.

GRANNY'S HAM AND NAVY BEAN SOUP

MAKES 3 QUARTS

Every week, we had this brothy pot of beans and some fresh corn bread in our house. It's a humble soup, but a few key steps make it really tasty. First, use dried beans, not canned. Second, save the ham bone from a country ham or Old-School Baked Ham (page 160). I like to freeze leftover ham bones and then stick the bones in the beans. They add incredible flavor to the broth. Third is a signature ingredient in the Appalachian cooking of the South: salted fatback. Most people would look at this soup and think there's dairy in it. That's the kind of creaminess you get from fatback. The buttery texture and salty, porky taste can't be replicated by anything else. Corn bread is also a must here for dipping in the broth. I wish I could share my corn bread recipe, but Granny would disown me. She's fine with me sharing some family recipes, but others are sacred. If you held me at gunpoint, I'd give you the combination to the safe at my house before I'd give out the recipe for my family's corn bread.

2 cups dried navy beans, picked over

1 large onion

2 stalks celery

1 carrot

8 ounces fatback

1 ham bone

4 cups Ham Broth (page 27)

2 dried bay leaves

Kosher salt and ground black pepper

Soak the beans in water for at least 8 hours or overnight.

Peel the onion and cut into 8 wedges. Remove and discard the strings from the celery and cut into 2-inch pieces. Peel the carrot, slice in half, and cut into 2-inch pieces. Cut the fatback into 2-inch pieces.

Drain and rinse the beans and add them to a large Dutch oven along with the onions, celery, carrots, fatback, ham bone, ham broth, bay leaves, and 4 cups water. Place over high heat, cover, and bring to a boil. Decrease the heat to a simmer and cook until the beans are tender, about 1½ hours. The mixture will look creamy. That is the fatback working its magic. It's the key ingredient, so do not substitute.

Using tongs, fish out the fatback and bay leaves and discard. Pull the ham bone out and shred the meat into the soup, saving a little for garnish. Season to taste with salt and pepper.

Good to Know

All the vegetables are cut into big chunks here and then left in the soup. They're extra-good if you get a chunk in your bowl.

SERRANO HAM CROQUETTES

MAKES 24 CROQUETTES

I've had these tapas multiple times in Spain and the United States, and they remain one of my favorites. I can't get enough of the crispy exterior, but here I emphasize the creaminess inside. Mashed potatoes, Manchego cheese, and bits of dry-cured serrano ham form the dough. You roll it into balls, bread it in panko crumbs, and fry them. The croquettes taste amazing as is, but they're even better with a smoky tomato mayonnaise for dipping. I set up the recipe so you can make everything in advance and fry the croquettes right before serving them. Perfect for a party.

1½ pounds Yukon gold potatoes

1 large head roasted garlic, about 12 cloves (see Good to Know)

3 eggs

¾ cup heavy cream

4 ounces thin-sliced serrano ham, chopped into 1-inch pieces

1 teaspoon kosher salt

¼ teaspoon freshly grated nutmeg

5 ounces Manchego cheese, grated on large holes of box grater

½ cup all-purpose flour

2 cups panko bread crumbs

Canola oil for frying

½ cup Smoky Tomato Aioli (recipe follows)

Preheat the oven to 400°F. Bake the potatoes directly on the oven rack until fork-tender, 45 to 55 minutes. When cool enough to handle, peel and run through a ricer or food mill. You want 3 cups mashed potatoes.

Mash 6 of the garlic cloves; you should get about 2 tablespoons. Reserve the remaining roasted garlic for the aioli. Beat 1 egg in a small bowl.

In a medium saucepan, combine the cream, ham, mashed garlic, salt, and nutmeg and heat just until bubbles form around the edge. Remove from the heat and stir in the potatoes. Stir in the cheese and aggressively beat until well combined. Mix in the beaten egg. Spread on a baking sheet and refrigerate until chilled and firm, about 1 hour, or cover and refrigerate overnight.

Break the other 2 eggs into a bowl and beat; these will be used for breading. Using a 2-ounce (¼-cup) scoop, scoop the potatoes and gently and lightly roll into balls. Measure the flour into a small bowl and the panko into another small bowl. Using the 3-step breading method (page 21), dip the potato balls in the flour, egg, and then panko. You can set the breaded croquettes on a cooling rack for 15 minutes or cover and refrigerate them for 1 hour before frying.

Heat oil in a deep fryer to 375°F. Line a baking sheet with paper towels and top with a cooling rack. Carefully drop the potatoes into the fryer, without crowding, and fry until deep golden, about 3 minutes. Transfer to the cooling rack, cool for 2 minutes, and then serve immediately with the tomato aioli.

Continued

Smoky Tomato Aioli MAKES ABOUT 2¼ CUPS

¾ cup canned crushed tomatoes

¼ cup freshly squeezed lemon juice

3 egg yolks

6 cloves roasted garlic, mashed, about 2 tablespoons (see Good to Know)

2½ teaspoons kosher salt

1 teaspoon ground black pepper

1 teaspoon smoked paprika

1 cup grapeseed oil or canola oil

½ cup extra-virgin olive oil

In a small bowl, combine the tomatoes and lemon juice.

Blend the yolks in a blender on medium speed for 20 seconds. Add half the tomato mixture, the garlic, salt, pepper, and paprika and blend until smooth, about 30 seconds. With the blender running on medium-high speed, drizzle in the grapeseed oil, drop by drop at first, then in a very slow stream; then slowly drizzle in the olive oil. The mixture will be very thick. With the blender running, add the remaining tomato mixture. Taste and add a little more salt as needed. This is best after it sits and tightens up overnight and the flavors have time to bloom. Taste before serving and add a little more salt or lemon juice if you think it needs it. Refrigerate for up to 1 week.

Good to know

It's easiest to make the croquettes and aioli the day before you plan to serve, and then fry the croquettes and serve them right away with the aioli. Both the croquettes and aioli improve in flavor after sitting overnight.

These are small-plate portions good for a first course or light supper. For smaller appetizer-size portions, use a smaller scoop, such as a 1-ounce (2-tablespoon) scoop.

To fill out the plate, serve these with Pork Fat Pommes Frites (page 223), My Version of Bacon Explosion (page 189), and/or Deep-Fried Baby Back Ribs (page 128).

To roast a head of garlic, cut off about ¼ inch from the top to expose some of the cloves and place on a square of foil. Drizzle a little olive oil over the cloves, then wrap in the foil. Roast at 350°F until soft and browned, about 45 minutes. Let cool in the foil, then unwrap and squeeze the roasted garlic from the skins.

ARUGULA, FIG, AND PROSCIUTTO BUNDLES
FEEDS 4

Figs make it California cuisine. That was always our joke in the kitchen. Put anything on a plate, slice some figs alongside it, and it's California cuisine. Whatever you call it, anything with figs and prosciutto is going to be good. This preparation is not in any way complicated or time-consuming. It's just a rolled-up salad. Arugula is one of my all-time favorite greens, and I love it wrapped up with figs in sheets of dry-cured ham with a drizzle of balsamic vinegar. You get a bite of peppery, salty, sour, sweet, and savory all at once. If figs aren't in season, you can use apples instead.

6 cups arugula

⅓ cup celery leaves

Kosher salt and ground black pepper

1 lemon

1 tablespoon extra-virgin olive oil + more for drizzling

8 fresh Brown Turkey figs

8 paper-thin slices prosciutto

3 tablespoons balsamic glaze (see Good to Know)

Block of Parmesan cheese, for shaving

In a medium bowl, toss the arugula and celery leaves with a pinch of salt and pepper, ¼ teaspoon lemon juice, and the olive oil.

Trim the stems and slice the figs lengthwise into about 4 slices each.

Cut 4 pieces of parchment paper about 2 inches longer than and double the width of your prosciutto slices. For each serving, on each parchment sheet, arrange 2 slices prosciutto with the short ends toward you, overlapping a bit on the long ends. Divide the figs between the prosciutto slices, piling them on the short ends that are closest to you. Divide the arugula and pile on the figs. Start rolling the prosciutto into a bundle, jelly roll style, using the ends of the parchment to pull the meat up and over the arugula into a pretty tight bundle; the prosciutto should wrap around the arugula with extra so it will stay bundled. Cut each bundle on the diagonal and serve drizzled with balsamic glaze and olive oil. Use a vegetable peeler to shave curls of Parmesan cheese over the top.

Continued

Good to Know

Balsamic glaze is boiled-down balsamic vinegar with a syrupy consistency and sweet taste. To make it at home, just boil balsamic vinegar in a saucepan until reduced and syrupy. It will reduce by about half, so start with twice as much vinegar (start with 6 tablespoons vinegar to get 3 tablespoons glaze). If you like it sweeter, add a little sugar to the vinegar (about 1 tablespoon sugar per 4 tablespoons vinegar).

If figs aren't in season, replace them with two Fuji apples. Peel the apples and cut them in half around the core, then thinly slice them from end to end.

Most people throw out celery leaves, but they're delicious! Think of them as a spunkier parsley. Use them like an herb when you want the taste of celery without the crunch.

OVERSTUFFED HAM AND CHEESE OMELET

FEEDS 1 OR 2

In culinary school, one of our instructors, Chef Hammond, was the former executive chef at Brennan's in Houston. He was adamant about properly cooked eggs, and I wanted to share everything I learned so you can enjoy a properly cooked omelet. First: Finely chop your fillings—ham and scallions here. Second: Match your eggs to your pan. I like a generous 3-egg omelet in a 10-inch pan, but if you have an 8-inch pan, make a 2-egg omelet instead. Third: The omelet should taste creamy and not too firm. I whip a little mascarpone into the eggs to make sure they stay creamy and to give the omelet a light texture. Finally, a proper omelet should not be brown. Adjust the heat so it stays a light canary color. Some people roll their eggs over the filling, but you have to get the egg layer very thin for it to roll, and the eggs are more likely to overcook. I'm a folder.

3 eggs

1 tablespoon mascarpone or whipped cream cheese

⅛ teaspoon kosher salt

2 teaspoons butter

4 ounces Old-School Baked Ham (page 160) or other baked ham, finely diced

4 scallions, roots and tough greens trimmed, thinly sliced

2 ounces sharp cheddar cheese, finely grated

2 thin sandwich slices American cheese

Break the eggs into a 2-cup measuring cup, add the mascarpone and salt, and blend with an immersion blender until fluffy, about 1 minute, making sure the cheese is completely incorporated into the eggs.

Heat a 10-inch nonstick skillet over medium heat. Add 1 teaspoon of the butter and swirl to melt. Add the ham and cook, tossing occasionally, until the ham just starts to brown, a little more than a minute. Add half the scallions and toss, cooking for another 30 seconds. Transfer the ham and scallions to a plate and reserve. Return the skillet to the heat, add the remaining 1 teaspoon butter, and swirl to melt and cover the bottom of the skillet. Add the eggs and, using a heatproof rubber spatula and starting at the outer edge of pan, scrape the eggs toward the center of the pan, letting the runny eggs fill out to the edges. When you finish going around the pan, there should still be a little creamy egg on top. Add both cheeses and the ham-onion mixture and let the eggs cook for another 30 seconds.

This is a one-fold omelet. Gently slide half the omelet onto the serving plate and, in a single motion, tilt and pull the pan up and over the plate, folding the other half onto the first half. Garnish the top with the remaining scallions.

COUNTRY HAM BREAKFAST STRATA
FEEDS 8 TO 10

Here's what to make for your next Sunday brunch. It's mostly bread, milk, and eggs baked into savory Italian bread pudding. A rustic sourdough loaf works best. It soaks overnight in the milk and eggs, so the bread needs to be sturdy. As with an omelet, you can fill a strata with whatever you like, but if you're not a born-and-bred Southerner, here's the perfect place to get more comfortable with dry-cured country ham. Onions, peppers, and Parmesan complement the ham. I like some chopped collards in there too. The strata comes out almost like a cake that you can cut into slices. A little salad on the side makes the perfect go-with.

1-pound loaf sourdough bread, cut into 1-inch cubes, about 3 quarts

8 eggs

2⅓ cups half-and-half

6 ounces country ham, finely diced

2 tablespoons bacon grease (see Good to Know)

2 cups julienned collard greens (optional)

1 small onion, cut into ¼-inch dice, about ½ cup

1 small red bell pepper, stem and seeds removed, cut into ½-inch dice, about ½ cup

5 scallions, root ends trimmed, thinly sliced, about 1 cup

3 ounces Parmesan cheese, freshly grated

Preheat the oven to 325°F. Spread the bread on a baking sheet and toast until crispy but not browned, about 8 minutes.

In a large bowl, whisk the eggs with the half-and-half until well combined. Gently fold in the bread cubes, cover, and refrigerate overnight.

Preheat the oven to 350°F (325°F if using convection). Butter a 9 by 13-inch baking dish.

Place a large skillet on the stove, add the ham, and turn the temperature to high. Add the bacon grease and toss with the ham until melted. Cook, tossing frequently just until the ham starts to crisp, about 3 minutes. Add the collards and cook until wilted, about 2 minutes. Stir in the onions and peppers and toss and cook until the onions are translucent, about 2 minutes.

Remove the bread that has been soaking overnight and fold in the scallions, cheese, and cooked vegetables. Spread the egg mixture in the prepared dish and cover with aluminum foil. Bake for 30 minutes, then remove the foil and bake until set, puffed, and golden brown, another 15 minutes or so. You can test it with a toothpick; when it comes out clean, it's done. The eggs will deflate quickly, which is fine.

Good to Know

If you don't already, save your bacon grease! When it's warm, pour it into an airtight container, cover, and refrigerate it for up to 1 week. It makes a great cooking fat. You can substitute butter or oil if you like.

"A HIGHBROW IS THE KIND OF PERSON WHO LOOKS AT A SAUSAGE AND THINKS OF PICASSO."

—A. P. HERBERT

SAUSAGES AND SUCH

People think bacon is my favorite type of pork. But anyone who knows me will tell you that given the choice between bacon and sausage, I'll always choose sausage. One of my first loves was the patty sausage at the Waffle House. It's aggressively seasoned with red pepper flakes and black pepper. With a waffle drowned in maple syrup and those spicy sausages on top, I was one happy camper.

Everyone has food memories, but I seem to have an exceedingly large amount of sausage memories. I remember the first time I put yellow mustard on sausage with a biscuit. That's when I realized just how well the acidic-fatty combo works. I remember my dad grilling bratwurst whenever his buddies came over to play darts or cards. He knew how to grill the sausages without bursting the skins, and having one of those grilled brats made me feel like part of the group.

Most of all, I remember all the awesome sausages my granny cooked. I often had breakfast at her house before school. Fatback, ham, and sausage were always on offer. I'd break up the sausage and drop the little pieces right into my grits. If Granny would let me, I'd spoon the sausage pan drippings over the top. That's my all-time favorite breakfast.

Granny also kept cooked sausage patties in lard in sealed jars. It's an old-fashioned way of making them last longer. You just pull the sausages out of the fat and warm them in a pan.

The best sausages came around Christmastime. Every year, an old-school sack sausage would show up in the mail. It was packed in what looked like a muslin sock twisted at the top and tied with twine.

Granny would unwrap the sausage, cut the little chub into thick medallions, and fry them up in her cast-iron pan for breakfast. It was just enough sausage for the whole family for one meal, and everyone would say things like, "Oh, wow, that's really good. Where did it come from?" No one could remember. I thought it was from one of Pa's sisters (Pa being my grandfather).

Whoever sent it knew what they were doing. The sausage was coarse but it didn't crumble up like most coarse sausage. The meat was denser and held together when sliced. You could taste the sage, black pepper, ground chiles, and Christmas spices like nutmeg and clove. The color was firebrick red—even when you browned the sausage, it stayed red. It was fresh sausage, but the sack must've hung in the smokehouse because the muslin looked all hazy brown on the outside and the meat tasted like hickory. This sack sausage was so different and so special that I waited for it all year long. Right after Thanksgiving break from school, I would be primed. I knew it would be coming soon.

Then, sometime in my teens, the sack sausage just stopped showing up. Granny said, "Oh, 'so-and-so' passed away."

That year was definitely not my favorite Christmas. Ever since, I've dreamed about this sausage and tried to re-create it. The Hot and Spicy Sausage (page 186) is my latest attempt. It's the best one yet. Not perfect, but close. It still lacks that sharp, tangy taste I remember. Maybe the sack sausage was fermented for a few days before being smoked.

I'll try fermenting it next time, but for now, there are plenty of other sausages to enjoy. I like exploring them all. If I go to a German place, I order sausage. If I go to an Irish place, I try the sausage. At a BBQ place—even if it's known for brisket—I'm ordering the sausage. I'm so passionate about this food that I want to share my favorite sausage recipes. Making sausage isn't hard. It's just ground meat and spices. All the recipes here can be made with a basic grinder and stuffer. You don't need to measure the pH or worry about curing the sausages or regulating the humidity. These are simple recipes you can make at home. Grind up some pork shoulder and spices, and you've got the sausage for Spicy Sausage and Kale Soup (page 195). Add some pork fat and beer, and you're halfway to making Sheboygan-Style Beer Brats (page 180). Change the spices and switch the beer to Scotch ale, and you've got Scottish-Style Bangers (page 178). There's no end to what you can do with ground pork—from stuffing it into casings to laying it in a baking dish with a topping of creamy mashed potatoes for Pork and Lamb Shepherd's Pie (page 196).

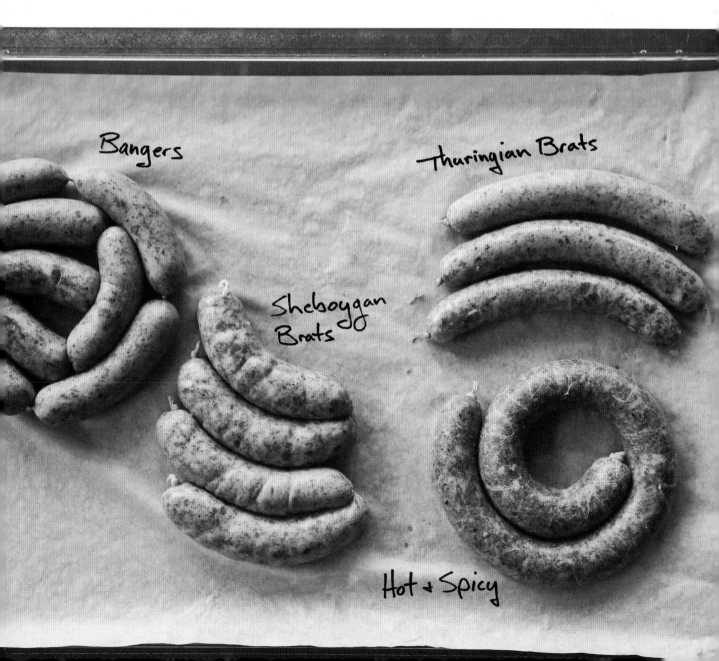

Bangers

Thuringian Brats

Sheboygan Brats

Hot & Spicy

GOOD TO KNOW ABOUT
Sausage

TEMPERATURE: This is the No. 1 culprit for failed sausage. Keep everything as cold as possible. The meat, fat, grinder, bowls, and even your hands have to be kept cold. That's because sausage, at its most basic, is a mechanical emulsification of meat, fat, and water. You force the three together, and that emulsion happens easily when everything is ice cold.

SANITATION: Cold temperatures are safer. Sanitation is paramount in sausage making, and bacteria doesn't grow well in cold environments. To keep everything sanitary, run your bowls and meat grinder parts through the dishwasher before you chill them. It's better to take steps to ensure that everything is pristinely clean. Wipe down every surface and wear gloves when you're handling the meat and grinding equipment. Accomplish all the steps of sausage making as expeditiously as possible. The more things sit on the counter, the more they warm up. If the phone rings, put the meat and fat back in the fridge before you proceed. Keep things cold and work quickly.

MEAT-TO-FAT RATIO: The standard ratio of meat to fat in sausage is 70 to 75 percent meat to 25 to 30 percent fat by weight. Stay in that range and your sausage will stay nice and juicy instead of getting dry.

MIXING: After grinding, mixing the meat and fat helps them emulsify (blend and stay together). You can mix in a food processor or stand mixer. I prefer the stand mixer because it creates less friction, which keeps everything cold. You can also put a bowl of ice water below the mixer bowl to keep things chilled. Most sausages also include ice water to lower the temperature of the mixture and help emulsify the ingredients. Plus, water and fat emulsify more easily than protein and fat. Ice water is like the deal maker, playing a vital role in bringing everything together.

TROUBLESHOOTING: If your meat mixture starts to look grainy and the liquid separates out from the meat, you've mixed too fast or the mixture has warmed up. There's no quick fix, so keep everything cold. Coarse sausages don't often have this problem, but finely ground sausages like Thuringer-Style Rostbratwurst (page 182) separate more easily. What you're looking for is a complete and total blending of all the ingredients. The mixture should look pasty and sticky, almost like bread dough.

TASTING FOR SEASONING: Always take a little bit of the raw ground sausage and cook it to taste whether there's enough seasoning. Once you move on, there's no adjusting the seasonings later. You can cook the sausage in a frying pan, but poaching

is best. If you fry the sausage, you concentrate the flavors. Poaching is closest to the final cooking method for most sausage, whether it's bratwurst or pâté. Just drop a piece of the raw meat mixture in barely simmering water and poach it until it is no longer pink. Then taste it for seasoning. Keep in mind that items served cold (like pâtés and terrines) need to be seasoned more aggressively than those served warm (like grilled bratwurst). That's because hot temperatures bring out the flavors of seasoning while cold temperatures mute the flavors.

CASINGS: More often than not, I use natural hog casings for link and coiled sausage. Sometimes I use sheep casings. Synthetic casings are also an option, but I prefer natural casings because they tend to hold in the meat juices better. A natural casing is the intestinal lining of an animal. Don't worry—it's flavorless when you buy it. Casings keep in a tub of water in the refrigerator for months. But they do eventually go bad. You can buy natural sausage casings and other sausage-making supplies like curing salt, grinders, and so forth from online sausage supply houses. I get mine from Butcher Packer.

AIR BUBBLES: Every now and then when stuffing sausage, you'll get a blowout. Air gets caught in the casing and, as the meat goes in, pressure busts a hole in the casing, and sausage comes flying out. Don't stress about it. Try to keep air bubbles out of

the sausage as you work, but if you do get a blowout, squeeze the sausage out of the broken area, tie off the end away from the blowout like tying a balloon, and keep stuffing. You can also pop any little air bubbles you see as you work to prevent them from getting bigger.

STORAGE: Fresh sausage mixtures should be used, cooked, or frozen within a day or two of being made. If you're freezing sausage, 2 months is about the maximum. After that, you lose flavor and quality. The issue is that when you grind meat, you expose more surface area to oxygen and to potentially harmful bacteria. Just think about each cube of meat as having 6 sides. When you grind it, the meat will then have thousands of sides. That's why it's best to grind meat fresh and use the sausage or cook it as soon as possible. That also explains why the only restaurants that will serve you a hamburger cooked below medium doneness are those that grind their meat the day they cook it.

RESTING: As with any meat, resting is a critical component of cooking up juicy sausages. The moment you cut open the casing, the meat juices will spill out everywhere. If the sausage is still piping hot, you'll negate all the work you did creating a moist meat emulsion. Let sausages rest until they are warm—not hot. If necessary, you can always reheat them a little.

SCOTTISH-STYLE BANGERS

MAKES 10 LINKS

In the United Kingdom, you might find this all-purpose sausage alongside eggs for breakfast, potatoes for lunch, or vegetables for dinner. At the Stone Mountain Highland Games northeast of Atlanta, the sausages are served on firm bread with English Colman's mustard. Bangers are not hard to make. It's basically ground pork and pork fat with some bread crumbs and seasonings like sage, black pepper, and cloves. In this Scottish version, I add Scotch ale for a dark malty note. The bangers blister up beautifully on a charcoal grill and the skin crisps up to the point of bursting. Or just brown them in a hot pan.

Hog sausage casings

Ice cubes

2 tablespoons kosher salt + more for icing the work bowl

1½ pounds pork butt, cut into 1½-inch cubes

8 ounces solid pork fat, cut into 1½-inch cubes

1 onion, chopped (1 cup), about 5 ounces

1 tablespoon rubbed sage

2 teaspoons finely ground black pepper

¼ teaspoon cayenne pepper

½ teaspoon ground ginger

⅛ teaspoon ground cloves

¾ cup Scotch ale, chilled

1 cup coarse bread crumbs or panko

1 tablespoon butter

Coarse mustard, for serving

Chill all parts of a meat grinder fitted with the coarse die, your work bowls, a baking sheet, meat, and all ingredients before starting. I can't stress enough how important it is to work with really, really cold ingredients and to keep them cold during the entire sausage-making process. Cold temperatures help the meat mixture emulsify properly. If you've got to take a break between steps, pop your equipment and ingredients back in the refrigerator.

Rehydrate your casings in a bowl of cold water for about 30 minutes, then run fresh cold water through to rinse out any impurities and to make them easier to work with. Always keep the casings submerged in cold water.

Prepare your work bowls: Half fill a very large bowl with ice, sprinkle with kosher salt, and add 2 cups ice water; this bowl will create an ice bath for the mixer bowl as it catches the sausage as it's coming from the grinder. Nestle the work bowl and paddle attachment into the ice bath.

Toss the pork butt with the pork fat, onion, 2 tablespoons salt, sage, black pepper, cayenne, ginger, and cloves and grind into the mixer bowl. Fit the mixer bowl with the pork and the wet paddle onto the mixer, add the ale and the bread crumbs, and mix on medium speed just until the mixture is well combined. Place the ground mixture back in the refrigerator.

Line the chilled baking sheet with parchment paper; this will be the pan you lay your sausages on as you're filling them. Fit your sausage stuffer with a ¾-inch stuffer tube, spray or grease the tube, and slide the casings over the tube. Tie the end of the casing and feed the sausage through the stuffer into the casings. Twist off the sausages every 4 inches, alternating twisting directions. Prick any visible air bubbles with a toothpick and gently squeeze out any air. If there aren't any air bubbles, prick each length randomly 3 times to allow the moisture to escape. Separate the sausages so they are not touching and refrigerate, uncovered, overnight. You want the sausages to dry out and set up before cooking.

Heat a sauté pan over medium heat, add the butter, and swirl to melt. Add the bangers and cook until browned on all sides and cooked through, 10 to 12 minutes. Serve with coarse mustard, or more traditionally over mashed potatoes (bangers and mash).

Good to know

These sausages will keep refrigerated for up to 3 days or packaged airtight and frozen for up to 6 months.

SHEBOYGAN-STYLE BEER BRATS

MAKES 6 TO 8 LINKS

To a German person, a bratwurst from Sheboygan, Wisconsin, is not bratwurst. However, German immigrants did develop Sheboygan-style brats, adapting their traditional sausage recipes for more rugged American tastes. The sausage is a 75:25 ratio of pork to fat and one of the easiest in the book to make. Just grind some pork shoulder with onions, garlic, salt, pepper, and nutmeg, and then whip the mixture with ice-cold beer. After stuffing and resting the sausages overnight, you poach them in a pan of beer and onions on the grill, sear them over the fire, and serve them in buns with mustard. It's the perfect food for tailgates, backyard barbecues, Sunday afternoons, or just about anytime.

Hog sausage casings

Ice cubes

2 tablespoons kosher salt + more for icing the work bowl

1½ pounds pork butt (shoulder), cut into 1½-inch cubes

8 ounces solid pork fat, cut into 1½-inch cubes

½ onion, cut into ¼-inch dice, about ½ cup

8 cloves garlic, peeled

1 tablespoon finely ground black pepper

1 teaspoon packed freshly grated nutmeg

½ cup cold lager-style beer, such as Bud or PBR + some for drinking

Chill all parts of a meat grinder fitted with the fine die, your work bowls, a baking sheet, meat, and all ingredients before starting. I can't stress enough how important it is to work with really, really cold ingredients and to keep them cold during the entire sausage-making process. Cold temperatures help the meat mixture emulsify properly. If you've got to take a break between steps, pop your equipment and ingredients back in the refrigerator.

Rehydrate your casings in a bowl of cold water for about 30 minutes, then run fresh cold water through to rinse out any impurities and to make them easier to work with. Always keep the casings submerged in cold water.

Prepare your work bowls: Half fill a very large bowl with ice, sprinkle with kosher salt, and add 2 cups ice water; this bowl will create an ice bath for the work bowl as it catches the sausage as it's coming from the grinder. Nestle the work bowl into the ice bath.

Toss the pork butt with the pork fat, onion, garlic, 2 tablespoons salt, pepper, and nutmeg and grind into the iced work bowl. Using a sturdy spoon, aggressively stir the beer into the ground pork just until the mixture starts getting sticky, about 1 minute. Place the ground mixture back in the refrigerator.

Line the chilled baking sheet with parchment paper; this will be the pan you lay your sausages on as you're filling them. Fit your sausage stuffer with a ¾-inch stuffer tube, spray or grease the tube, and slide the casings over the tube. Tie the end of the casing and feed the sausage through the stuffer into the casings. Twist off the sausages every 5 inches, alternating twisting directions. Prick any air bubbles with a toothpick and gently squeeze out any air. Separate the sausages so they are not touching and refrigerate, uncovered, overnight. You want the sausages to dry out and set up before cooking them. You can grill them, panfry them, or poach them.

Good to Know

The brats will keep refrigerated for up to 3 days or packaged airtight and frozen for up to 6 months.

To serve these as Sheboygan-Style Bratwurst Sandwiches: Heat a grill to medium-high. Pour 3 bottles (12 ounces each) lager-style beer into a deep roasting pan and add 10 cloves garlic and 2 large onions sliced into ½-inch rings. Bring to a low boil right on the grill, and cook until the onions soften, about 15 minutes. Add the sausages and enough water to cover, then bring the liquid to a simmer and poach until the sausages are cooked through, about 15 minutes. Transfer the sausages and onions to the grill grate and cook just until grill-marked, about 4 minutes. Serve the sausages on soft buns with the grilled onions, poached garlic, and yellow mustard.

THURINGER-STYLE
ROSTBRATWURST

MAKES 10 TO 12 LINKS

Germans excel at a few specific things: beer, car engines, and sausages. They'll make six or seven variations on a single sausage recipe, and each one will be distinct. What makes this recipe unique is very finely ground meat that's mixed with water until it emulsifies into a smooth, creamy paste. In the German state of Thuringia, they flavor the sausage with wild oregano that grows in the area. I use marjoram and sage to replicate the aroma. Another characteristic is that the meat is stuffed into narrow casings, so the finished sausage looks long and skinny instead of short and fat like Scottish-Style Bangers (page 178).

Narrow hog sausage casings, about 29-millimeter diameter

Ice cubes

2 tablespoons kosher salt + more for chilling the work bowl

1½ pounds pork butt, cut into 1½-inch cubes

8 ounces solid pork fat, cut into 1½-inch cubes

1 onion, chopped, about ¾ cup

1 ounce garlic cloves, about 8

2 tablespoons fresh marjoram leaves

2 teaspoons packed lemon zest

1 teaspoon rubbed sage

1 teaspoon finely ground black pepper

¼ teaspoon ground mace

Chill all parts of a meat grinder fitted with the fine die, your work bowls, a baking sheet, meat, and all ingredients before starting. I can't stress enough how important it is to work with really, really cold ingredients and to keep them cold during the entire sausage-making process. Cold temperatures help the meat mixture emulsify properly. If you've got to take a break between steps, pop your equipment and ingredients back in the refrigerator.

Rehydrate your casings in a bowl of cold water for about 30 minutes, then run fresh cold water through them to rinse out any impurities and to make them easier to work with. Always keep the casings submerged in cold water.

Prepare your work bowls: Half-fill a very large bowl with ice, sprinkle with kosher salt, and add 2 cups ice water; this bowl will create an ice bath for the mixer bowl as it catches the sausage as it's coming from the grinder. Nestle the clean mixer bowl and the paddle attachment for your mixer into the ice bath.

Toss the pork butt with the pork fat, onion, garlic, 2 tablespoons salt, marjoram, lemon zest, sage, pepper, and mace and grind into the mixer bowl. Fit the mixer bowl and the wet paddle onto the mixer, add 1 tablespoon ice water, and mix on high speed until the mixture is sticky like dough and just starting to come together, but stop before it shapes into a ball. Place the ground mixture back in the refrigerator.

Line the chilled baking sheet with parchment paper; this will be the pan you lay your sausages on as you're filling them. Fit your sausage stuffer with a ½-inch stuffer tube, spray or grease the tube, and slide the casings over the tube. Tie the end of the casing and feed the sausage through the stuffer into the casings. Twist off the sausages every 6 inches, alternating twisting directions. These sausages should resemble standard hot dogs in width and length. Prick any air bubbles with a toothpick and gently squeeze out any air. Separate the sausages so they are not touching and refrigerate, uncovered, overnight. You want the sausages to dry out and set up before cooking.

Preheat a grill or grill pan on medium heat and grill the sausages until nicely marked on all sides, about 10 minutes. Move to a cooler part of the grill, cover, and grill until cooked through to an internal temperature of 155°F, another 5 minutes or so.

Keep in Mind

These sausages can be covered and refrigerated for up to 3 days or packaged airtight and frozen for up to 6 months.

It's the mark of a good griller to grill sausages without bursting the casings.

Two serving choices here: on a bun or, my preference, on a plate with German-style mustard. The spicy mustard helps showcase the flavors in the sausage itself.

PORK AND RAISIN CRÉPINETTES

MAKES 12 CRÉPINETTES

A crépinette is a French charcuterie of seasoned sausage encased in caul fat (lacy beef fat) and pan-seared. It's almost like a fat-wrapped pork burger. I first tried them in Paris during a culinary school trip and loved the slightly sweet flavor. Later, at Fife restaurant in Portland, Oregon, I made some lamb crépinettes but only for a short time. Then, two years ago, I made pork and apple crépinettes for a fundraising event at the Moores Cancer Center in San Diego. The TSA decided that my 500 crépinettes looked like a bomb, inspected my cooler, destroyed it in the process, and repacked the sausages in a plain cardboard box. All 500 servings were destroyed! I am now more determined than ever to turn people on to this delicious sausage. Here's my pork and raisin version. I love these crépinettes over a puree of potatoes or turnips.

Ice cubes

2 tablespoons + 2 teaspoons kosher salt

1½ pounds pork butt, cut into 1½-inch cubes

1 large onion, chopped, about 1½ cups

2 ounces garlic cloves, about 16

6 ounces golden raisins, about 1 cup

2 teaspoons red pepper flakes

1 teaspoon finely ground black pepper

½ teaspoon ground cardamom

Caul fat

Chill all parts of a meat grinder fitted with the coarse die, your work bowls, a baking sheet, meat, and all ingredients before starting. I can't stress enough how important it is to work with really, really cold ingredients and to keep them cold during the entire sausage-making process. Cold temperatures help the meat mixture emulsify properly. If you've got to take a break between steps, pop your equipment and ingredients back in the refrigerator.

Prepare your work bowls: Half fill a very large bowl with ice, sprinkle with 2 tablespoons kosher salt, and add 2 cups ice water; this bowl will create an ice bath for the work bowl as it catches the pork as it's coming from the grinder. Nestle the work bowl into the ice bath.

Toss the pork butt with the remaining 2 teaspoons salt, the onion, garlic, raisins, red pepper flakes, black pepper, and cardamom and grind into the mixer bowl. Portion the ground mixture into 3-ounce balls and refrigerate on the chilled baking sheet.

Stretch the caul fat into a single layer on a work surface and, one by one, slightly flatten each ball into a 3-inch disk and wrap each completely with fat, just like you're wrapping a present, overlapping a little to make sure it's sealed. Cut the caul fat as needed. Turn each disk over and twist a few times to seal the overlapping pieces.

Heat a sauté pan over medium-high heat, add the crépinettes, working in batches if needed, not crowding the pan too much, and cook until they're nicely browned on each side, about 3 minutes per side. Decrease the heat to medium, cover the pan, and cook to an internal temperature of 150°F, another 5 to 7 minutes. Remove from the heat, leave the lid on, and let rest for 5 minutes.

Good to know

The crépinettes will keep refrigerated for up to 3 days or frozen in individual airtight packages for up to 6 months.

HOT AND SPICY SAUSAGE

MAKES ABOUT 2 POUNDS

When I took over at Woodfire Grill, I inherited sausage grinders, stuffers, and other equipment from the former chef, Michael Tuohy. This was one of the first sausages I made, a cross between Cajun andouille and generic Italian sausage. It's a loose sausage in the recipe below, but I also like to stuff it into casings and smoke it (see Worth Knowing). Use the loose version anywhere you want a generic loose sausage with a little kick. The smoked version can be used like andouille sausage—in gumbo, étouffée, or other rice dishes. Or just grill the cased and smoked version and serve it in rolls with onions and peppers for sausage sandwiches.

Ice cubes

3 tablespoons kosher salt

2 pounds pork shoulder, cut into 1½-inch cubes

6 fresh sage leaves, finely chopped, about 2 tablespoons

2 teaspoons red pepper flakes

2 cloves garlic, finely minced, about 1 teaspoon

1 tablespoon rubbed sage

1 teaspoon ground black pepper

1-inch piece fresh ginger, peeled and finely grated, about 1½ teaspoons

¼ teaspoon cayenne pepper

½ teaspoon curing/pink salt

Chill all parts of a meat grinder fitted with the fine die, your work bowls, meat, and all ingredients before starting. I can't stress enough how important it is to work with really, really cold ingredients and to keep them cold during the entire sausage-making process. Cold temperatures help the meat mixture emulsify properly. If you've got to take a break between steps, pop your equipment and ingredients back in the refrigerator.

Prepare your work bowls: Half fill a very large bowl with ice, sprinkle with 2 tablespoons kosher salt, and add 2 cups ice water; this bowl will create an ice bath for the work bowl as it catches the sausage as it's coming from the grinder. Nestle the work bowl into the ice bath.

Toss the pork shoulder with the fresh sage, red pepper flakes, garlic, rubbed sage, black pepper, ginger, and cayenne and refrigerate until thoroughly chilled.

Remove the chilled pork and sprinkle with the remaining 1 tablespoon kosher salt, the curing salt, and ½ cup ice water and toss to combine. Grind into the work bowl. Using gloved hands, thoroughly mix the ingredients together.

Heat a small skillet over medium-high heat. Pinch a small piece of sausage from the bowl, thoroughly cook, and taste. Adjust the seasoning as necessary.

Worth Knowing

This sausage works best made at least a day ahead. You can cover it tightly in plastic wrap for about a day. For longer storage, vacuum-seal and refrigerate it for up to 4 days or freeze it for up to 1 month.

To make Spicy Smoked Sausage, make and chill the Hot and Spicy Sausage. Using a ¾-inch stuffer tube, stuff the meat into rehydrated hog casings in one long piece. Prick randomly with a toothpick and remove any visible air bubbles, and place in the refrigerator overnight to dry. You want a nice sticky coating on the casing so the smoke will stick and penetrate the meat. Smoke with full smoke at 190°F to an internal temperature of 150°F, about 30 minutes.

MY VERSION OF BACON EXPLOSION

MAKES TWENTY ½-INCH THICK SLICES

Let me just say: I have seen the Bacon Explosion at its origin point. A few years ago, I helped build some Web-based cooking shows with Jason Day and Aaron Chronister, the guys who eventually produced *The Bacon Show*. These guys are competitive BBQ veterans from Kansas City, and they created the Bacon Explosion. It's a dish of highly seasoned loose Italian sausage layered with cooked bacon and barbecue sauce that's wrapped in a lattice of bacon strips and smoked. It's absurd—and absurdly delicious. My version includes cheddar cheese and charred jalapeños. I hope this rendition pays tribute to the original but also inspires you to create your own. You could stuff this with cotton candy and it would taste good. Go nuts!

---

24 thick slices Belly Bacon (page 132) or other bacon (see Good to Know)

2 pounds Hot and Spicy Sausage (page 186), chilled

8 ounces cheddar or Monterey Jack cheese, grated

⅓ cup Sweet and Smoky Barbecue Sauce (page 28) + more for serving

6 jalapeño chile peppers, charred, peeled, sliced lengthwise, stems and seeds removed (see Good to Know)

Lay a 12 by 18-inch piece of aluminum foil on your work surface, with the 12-inch side toward you. Using 16 strips uncooked bacon, make an 8-inch square lattice weave in the center of the foil (think apple pie lattice).

Using scissors, cut the remaining 8 slices bacon into ¼-inch pieces and cook, stirring occasionally, in a cast-iron skillet over medium heat until crispy, 12 to 15 minutes. Transfer to a paper towel–lined plate and allow to drain.

In a bowl, combine the sausage with one-quarter of the grated cheese and 3 tablespoons of the barbecue sauce. Pat the sausage mixture onto the center of the lattice, leaving a 1-inch border around all sides. Fold the jalapeños out flat and spread across the center of the sausage, then sprinkle the diced bacon and the remaining grated cheese over the jalapeños.

Lift the edge of the foil closest to you up and over, folding the lattice-backed sausage up and over the jalapeños, bacon, and cheese, almost to the edge. Using your hands and working quickly, tuck the edges up and under the bottom and around the ends, nice and tidy, so that the loaf is fully encased in bacon. Wrap tightly in the foil and chill for at least 1 hour and up to 24 hours, until firm.

Heat a smoker to 225°F. Unwrap the chilled loaf and hot-smoke at 225°F to an internal temperature of 160°F, about 1½ hours.

Continued

Adjust the oven rack to the second highest setting and preheat the broiler to high.

Place the loaf on a sheet pan lined with aluminum foil and brush with the remaining barbecue sauce and broil until the bacon starts to brown and curl, about 4 minutes. Slice and serve as you would a meat loaf, with additional sauce on the side.

Good to Know

You can replace the Belly Bacon (page 132) with store-bought thick-cut bacon, such as Wright block pack.

To char the jalapeños, place them in a smoking-hot cast-iron pan or on a grill until blackened all over. Let cool, then peel and cut the pepper flesh from the core.

I like to slice this and serve it like meat loaf. Or slice it thin and serve in a biscuit or as a decadent topping for a hamburger.

AMERICAN CRUNCHY TACOS WITH SPICY GROUND PORK

MAKES 12 TACOS

I grew up eating gringo beef tacos with onions, lettuce, shredded cheese, and taco sauce. My favorite was at Los Avina, a Mexican place just down the road from Locust Grove, where I grew up. This recipe is modeled after those tacos. The crispy taco shells are one of the things people love about American-style tacos. I make the shells myself, but you could use the store-bought prebent ones. I also like to grind the pork fresh because the meat stays juicier that way. The spice blend is like homemade taco spice with ancho powder, onion, garlic, salt, and hot paprika. I usually add MSG, too. I have to admit, I'm a fan of MSG. It has its uses, and this is one of them. Nothing else adds quite the same savory flavor, and it elevates the taste of everything else. But I've left it out here for the squeamish.

- 1 pound boneless pork shoulder, cut into 2-inch cubes
- 2 tablespoons ancho chili powder
- 1 tablespoon Espelette pepper or hot paprika
- 1 tablespoon kosher salt
- 1 teaspoon ground black pepper
- 1 teaspoon garlic powder
- 1 teaspoon onion powder
- 2 tablespoons grapeseed oil or canola oil
- Juice of 1 lime
- ¼ cup sour cream
- 12 corn taco shells (see Good to Know)
- ½ cup diced tomato
- ½ cup finely shredded lettuce
- ½ cup grated cheddar cheese
- ¼ cup finely diced onion

Fit a meat grinder with the medium die and refrigerate. Pat the pork dry and toss with the chili powder, Espelette pepper, salt, black pepper, garlic powder, and onion powder. Refrigerate until well chilled, at least 1 hour, or partially freeze for 20 minutes. You want the grinder and the meat well chilled before grinding. Pass the meat and any excess spices through the grinder.

Heat a heavy-bottomed skillet over high heat, add the oil, and heat until it shimmers. Add the ground pork and spread over the bottom of the pan. Cook the pork, stirring gently and leaving some clumps, until it is cooked through, 3 to 4 minutes. Remove from the heat.

Stir the juice from the lime into the sour cream in a small bowl.

Spoon 2 tablespoons pork into each taco shell. Garnish with the tomato, lettuce, cheese, onion, and some lime crema.

Good to Know

Look for crisp taco shells at your local Hispanic market. Or make your own: Let your corn tortillas dry at room temperature overnight so they absorb less frying oil. And if you're smart, buy a metal mold to fry the corn tortillas in. They cost 20 bucks and fry 4 shells at a time. Or do it the manual way. Heat oil in a deep fryer to 350°F. With a pair of tongs, grasp the tortilla in the middle, dip one half into the fryer, then flip and dip in the other half. Finally, pinch the top of the tortilla together and place the bottom of the tortilla into the fryer to create a U-shaped taco shell.

It's best to grind your own pork for this recipe. Preground meat will deflate and compact when you mix the spices in, and you never know what cuts of meat go into the preground product. For this recipe, you really want the fat and moisture you'll get from pork butt (shoulder).

PORK AND APPLE PASTIES

MAKES 8 PASTIES

Meat pies, hand pies, pasties . . . call them what you like. Either way, they're delicious. One year, I made it a point to try every version I could from Scottish meat pies to Cornish pasties to hand pies from Montana. Cornish pasties were my favorite. The filling is super-savory and the dough flaky and crisp. We're talking about a little half-moon-shaped pie—slightly larger than an empanada—that you can eat for lunch, dinner, or anytime on the go. The classic fillings are beef chuck, beef suet, and roots like turnips, potatoes, and carrots seasoned with warming spices such as mace and coriander. They're great for stretching the meat in the house, and the perfect place to use up scraps. Of course, I prefer pork for the meat—any lean cut will do—along with some salt pork to intensify the flavors. In the crust, a little lard creates flakiness and amplifies the sweet-savory pork and apple combination.

1 teaspoon sugar

1 teaspoon salt

2½ cups all-purpose flour +
more for rolling the dough

½ cup (1 stick) butter, cubed and
well chilled

6 tablespoons lard, chilled

6 ounces lean pork, such as loin
or tenderloin

1 small rutabaga

1 carrot

1 small Granny Smith or Fuji
apple, peeled and cored

1 small Vidalia onion, peeled,
root and stem ends trimmed

2 ounces salt pork, cut into
¼-inch dice

2 tablespoons demi-glace or
twice-reduced Chicken Stock
(page 26; see Good to Know)

2 teaspoons kosher salt

½ teaspoon ground black
pepper

⅛ teaspoon ground mace or
freshly grated nutmeg

1 egg

Dissolve the sugar and salt in ⅓ cup ice water. Measure the flour into the bowl of a food processor fitted with the metal blade. Scatter the butter over the flour and drop the lard by teaspoons into the flour. Pulse just until the fat is incorporated into the flour and small pea-size pieces remain. Turn the processor on and add the ice water, processing just until a ball forms, about 30 seconds. Dump the crust into a gallon-size zip-top bag and form into a ball. Flatten and refrigerate until well chilled and firm, at least 1 hour.

Trim the fat and connective tissue from the pork. Place in the freezer to get the meat really cold.

Peel and cut the rutabaga and carrot into ¼-inch sticks and then slice into ⅛-inch pieces, so you end up with thin slices, not cubes. You want about ½ cup rutabaga and ¼ cup carrot. Dice the apple and onion into ¼-inch cubes; you want about ½ cup each.

Slice the pork really, really thin, then dice it into tiny cubes and toss with the salt pork, demi-glace, rutabaga, carrot, apple, onion, salt, pepper, and mace.

Preheat the oven to 400°F.

Beat the egg with 1 tablespoon water to make an egg wash.

Divide the dough into 8 equal portions and roll each into a ball. Flour your work surface and roll the dough into thin circles, a little less than ⅛ inch thick. Place a nonstick cooking mat onto a baking sheet. Lay the dough circles out and brush the edges with egg wash. Mound ⅓ cup of the filling into the center of each dough circle, fold into half-moons, and crimp with your fingers to seal the edges. Using a fork, crimp the edges again to seal—you don't want a blowout! Brush the tops with the egg wash and, using a very sharp knife, make three 2-inch slashes in the top of each pie, to allow steam to escape while cooking.

Bake for 20 minutes. Decrease the heat to 350°F, rotate the baking sheet, and bake for another 20 minutes, until the filling is bubbling and the pastry is nicely browned.

Good to know

You can buy demi-glace in Whole Foods and some grocery stores. Or make twice-reduced Chicken Stock (page 26) by boiling the stock until it reduces in volume by half and then by half again. So start with ½ cup stock, and boil it down to ¼ cup, then to 2 tablespoons total volume.

I like to serve these with HP Sauce, a classic condiment from the British Isles. It's like dark American ketchup with spunk.

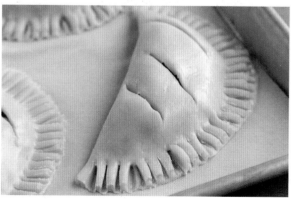

SPICY SAUSAGE AND KALE SOUP
MAKES 3 QUARTS

This is my mom's all-time favorite thing that I make. If she's sick, I get a call to make this soup. If she has a few days off at home, I get a call to make the soup. For family functions, I get the call. She first had something like it at the Olive Garden when I was a teenager. She came home and said, "Kevin, you need to figure out how to make this!" She drove me to the Olive Garden—40 minutes away—specifically so I could taste this soup. It's basically potato soup with sausage and greens in it. I've been making some version of it now since I was 15 years old. I like the soup kind of brothy. The potato just thickens it up a little bit. I also like black lacinato kale, but you could use other greens if you like.

1 pound boneless pork shoulder, cut into 2-inch cubes

2½ cups ¼-inch-diced Vidalia onion

8 cloves garlic, thickly sliced, about ¼ cup

1 tablespoon Espelette pepper or hot paprika

1 tablespoon + 1 teaspoon toasted fennel seeds

2 teaspoons kosher salt

1 teaspoon red pepper flakes

2 tablespoons extra-virgin olive oil + more for garnish

3 Yukon gold potatoes, halved and then sliced into ¼-inch slices, about 3 cups

2 quarts Chicken Stock (page 26)

1 cup freshly grated Parmesan cheese + more for garnish

4 cups packed sliced kale leaves, preferrably black lacinato kale, tough ribs removed

1 tablespoon sherry vinegar or apple cider vinegar

Refrigerate the pork until well chilled; the fat should be solid and firm. Chill your meat grinder and the large die. Toss 1¼ cups of the onion, 2 tablespoons of the garlic, the Espelette pepper, fennel seeds, salt, and red pepper flakes with the pork and mix well. Chill until ready to grind. Assemble the meat grinder and grind the pork into a large bowl.

Heat a large Dutch oven over medium-high heat. Add the olive oil and swirl to cover the bottom of the pan. Add the ground pork, stirring gently until it just starts to brown, about 5 minutes. Add the remaining 1¼ cups onion and 2 tablespoons garlic and cook, stirring occasionally, until the onions start to caramelize, about 5 minutes. Your sausage should be crumbly. Add the potatoes and toss to coat with oil. Add the chicken stock, bring to a boil, cover, and decrease the heat to low. Cook until the potatoes are cooked through and are just starting to break apart, about 20 minutes. Remove the lid, add the cheese and kale, and cook until the kale is completely wilted, about 10 minutes.

Just before serving, stir in the vinegar. Garnish each bowl with additional Parmesan cheese and a heavy drizzle of olive oil. The oil and other garnishes take the soup from ho-hum to over the top.

Good to Know

When I really want to up the flavor here, I add a little Aromat, a seasoning blend made from dried nutritional yeast, mushrooms, MSG, and salt. It's canned umami and delivers 100 percent pure savory flavor.

PORK AND LAMB SHEPHERD'S PIE

FEEDS 10 TO 12

I have a soft spot for British food. Few people will admit that. But some of the dishes Brits make are really great. Roast beef, Yorkshire pudding, and shepherd's pie come to mind right away. I used to frequent a little Irish pub when I lived in Portland, Oregon, and they had a really solid shepherd's pie. It had the right ratio of filling to topping (about 60:40); they used lamb in the filling; the topping was creamy; and they baked it in individual pans until golden brown. It was very successful, but I always thought, "You know what would make this even better? Pork." Too much lamb in shepherd's pie can be overwhelming—too barnyardy—but pork mellows out the filling and makes it a little sweeter.

2¾ pounds Yukon gold potatoes, peeled and cut into large, uniform chunks

Kosher salt

½ cup (1 stick) butter, cubed

½ cup half-and-half

4 ounces sharp cheddar cheese, grated

2 egg yolks, lightly beaten

3 tablespoons grapeseed oil or canola oil

2 pounds ground pork

1 pound ground lamb

8 ounces button mushrooms, trimmed and sliced

1 small onion, cut into ¼-inch dice, about 1 cup

3 stalks celery, cut into ¼-inch dice, about ½ cup

2 carrots, peeled, cut into ¼-inch dice, about ½ cup

1 tablespoon Worcestershire sauce

2 teaspoons fresh thyme, minced

1 (6-ounce) can tomato paste

¼ cup all-purpose flour

3½ cups Chicken Stock (page 26)

2 teaspoons ground black pepper

¼ teaspoon ground cinnamon

¼ teaspoon ground mace or freshly grated nutmeg

⅛ teaspoon ground cloves

2 cups petite peas

Preheat the oven to 350°F.

Boil the potatoes in salted water until fork-tender, about 30 minutes. Turn the heat off and dump the potatoes into a colander. Add the butter and half-and-half to the hot pan. Put the potatoes through a ricer or food mill; you should have about 4 cups. Using a whisk, whip the potatoes into the half-and-half mixture until the butter is melted; you'll have loose mashed potatoes. Whisk in the cheese until melted and then whisk in the egg yolks until completely incorporated. Taste and add salt if needed.

Heat a 5-quart Dutch oven or large deep cast-iron pan over high heat, add the oil, and heat until shimmering. Crumble the pork and lamb into the pan and brown, stirring occasionally with a wooden spoon or paddle, about 3 minutes. Add the mushrooms and cook, stirring occasionally, until browned, about 4 minutes. Stir in the onion, celery, and carrots and cook for another 2 minutes. Lower the heat to medium, add the Worcestershire, thyme, and tomato paste, and stir until the meat is coated. Stirring constantly, cook until the mixture starts to caramelize, another 2 minutes.

Sprinkle in the flour and stir until incorporated. Add the stock, scraping all the browned bits into the sauce, and stir until it starts to thicken. Add 1 tablespoon salt, the pepper, cinnamon, mace, and cloves and bring to a low simmer. Continue stirring and cooking; the mixture tends to stick, so keep scraping the bottom until the sauce thickens and resembles spaghetti sauce, about 5 minutes. Remove from the heat and fold in the peas.

Gently pour the potato mixture over the top, carefully smoothing out to the edges of the pan, making sure to completely seal the top. Bake until the potatoes are set and nicely browned and the edges are bubbly, about 25 minutes. It will be like molten lava at that point. Let it rest so the sauce can cool off and tighten up for about 20 minutes before serving.

Good to know

Even super-chef Marco Pierre White admits that frozen peas are better than fresh. English peas convert their sugars to starch the second you pick them. Unless you're working with fresh peas straight off the vines, frozen is the better choice.

Got leftovers? No problem. You can refrigerate this dish for nearly a week: Cut out squares and reheat them individually or reheat the whole dish.

CHONCHOS IN PONCHOS
MAKES 8 HEARTY OR 16 BITE-SIZE SNACKS

These are my gringo Mexican pigs in a blanket (*choncho* means "chunky" or "chubby"). I brought them to a Cinco de Mayo party one Sunday, and they disappeared in seconds. It's a very highbrow recipe that starts with Pillsbury crescent roll dough. You know it's classy when you start with that! Just slit some smoked sausages, stuff them with Jack cheese and jalapeños, and then wrap them in the dough. Brush with garlic butter and bake the little piggies. A final sprinkling of cheese and smoked paprika is the gourmet touch. Viva Mexico!

3 tablespoons butter

1 teaspoon chopped garlic, about 1 small clove

8 ounces spicy smoked Cajun sausage or kielbasa, casing removed

4 ounces Monterey Jack cheese, cut into ¼ by 1½-inch slices

1 long jalapeño pepper, sliced into thin rings

1 (8-ounce) tube refrigerated crescent roll dough

⅓ cup crumbled cotija cheese or other mild cheese

¼ teaspoon smoked paprika

Preheat the oven to 350°F. Line a baking sheet with parchment paper.

In a small pan over medium heat, melt the butter and stir in the garlic.

Cut the sausage into 2-inch lengths. Split each piece of sausage lengthwise down the middle, stopping just before you cut all the way through. Hold the sausage open and stuff with 1 slice of Monterey Jack and 2 slices of jalapeño.

Remove the crescent rolls from the tube and separate into triangles. Place 1 piece of sausage lengthwise on the wide end of each piece of dough. Fold the ends toward the center, burrito style, and roll to completely cover the sausage. Pinch the edges of the dough closed. Place on the baking sheet, brush each roll with the garlic butter, and sprinkle with the cotija. You'll need to press the cheese into the dough using your fingers.

Bake for 12 to 15 minutes, until golden brown. Remove from the oven, sprinkle with the smoked paprika, and serve warm.

Good to know

Use Conecuh sausage if you can. It's a high-quality pork sausage sold all over the United States. Or use any good-quality, coarsely ground smoked pork sausage the size of a fat hot dog.

These snacks are perfect for eating during a football game or at a cookout. You can prep them ahead, refrigerate them, and cook them just before serving. If you have leftovers, heat them on a baking sheet in a 400°F oven. But don't wrap or cover them while heating or they will get soggy.

For bite-size portions, cut the crescent roll triangles in half. Split the 2-inch lengths of sausage completely in half lengthwise, and then split the halves just down to the skin so they'll open up. Stuff with a smaller piece of Monterey Jack, some jalapeños, wrap, and bake as directed.

CURRIED PORK SAMOSAS

MAKES ABOUT 14 LARGE OR 42 MINI SAMOSAS

I went to elementary school with a kid named Bhavesh. He was first-generation Indian American, and in first grade, for Mother's Day, we made a cookbook as a class project for all the kids' moms. My mom still has the book—she keeps all that family stuff. I was flipping through it a few years ago and came across Bhavesh's mom's samosas. Of course, I had to try the recipe. It was so good, I riffed on it here by adding ground pork. Yes, I know that Hindus don't eat pork. But samosas made with ground pork, potatoes, and peas spiced with garlic, ginger, and chiles are absolutely delicious. For the wrapper, I use egg roll wrappers, which are pretty close to samosa dough and a lot easier to use.

Canola oil for frying

3 medium Yukon gold potatoes, about 12 ounces total

2-inch piece fresh ginger, peeled and minced, ¼ cup

8 cloves garlic, minced, ¼ cup

2 tablespoons Madras curry powder

1 small jalapeño pepper, stem and seeds removed, cut into chunks

¼ cup grapeseed oil or canola oil

8 ounces ground pork shoulder (70% lean)

2 teaspoons kosher salt

2 teaspoons freshly squeezed lemon juice

½ cup frozen petite peas

1 egg

1 package 5-inch square egg roll wrappers (for large) or 3½-inch square wonton wrappers (for bite-size)

Coriander Chutney Dipping Sauce (recipe follows)

Heat oil in a deep fryer to 350°F. Alternatively, pour about 4 inches of oil in a Dutch oven and heat to 350°F.

Pierce the potato skins with a fork and then bake the potatoes in a preheated 400°F oven until fork-tender, 50 to 60 minutes. Alternatively, microwave them on full power for about 10 minutes. Let cool slightly, then grate on the largest hole of a box grater, discarding the skins.

In a food processor fitted with a metal blade, process the ginger, garlic, curry powder, and jalapeño for about 20 seconds, just to combine. With the motor running, drizzle in the ¼ cup oil to form a chunky paste. Scrape the curry paste into a heavy-bottomed skillet and place over high heat. Reserve the processor bowl. As the mixture starts to heat and fry, shake the skillet back and forth. Cook for about 1 minute, or until the mixture stays together in a blob. With a spoon, stir the pork, salt, and lemon juice into the curry mixture until well blended, and then remove the skillet from the heat. The hot curry paste and residual heat from the pan will cook the pork. Stir the potatoes into the pork until well combined, and gently fold in the peas.

Beat the egg with 1 tablespoon water to form an egg wash. Lay the wrappers in a single layer on your work surface and brush the edges of each with egg wash. Place about 3 tablespoons of the pork mixture onto the upper corner of each wrapper (or 2 teaspoons if using the smaller wonton wrappers). Fold the corner over the filling, fold in the sides, and roll up the samosa "egg roll" style. Brush the edge closed with a little more egg wash. Repeat with the remaining wrappers and filling.

Deep-fry, making sure not to crowd the fryer, until browned and crispy, about 3 minutes. Serve with the dipping sauce.

Coriander Chutney Dipping Sauce

MAKES ABOUT 1½ CUPS

1 onion, peeled and cut into quarters

2 jalapeño peppers, stems removed, sliced

¼ cup grated fresh coconut, grated on medium holes of a box grater (see Good to Know)

2 tablespoons grapeseed oil or canola oil

1 tablespoon yellow mustard seeds

1 cup fresh cilantro leaves (see Good to Know)

1½ teaspoons kosher salt

¼ teaspoon tamarind paste

In a food processor fitted with a metal blade, combine the onion, peppers, coconut, and oil and process until a paste forms. Scrape the paste into a heavy-bottomed skillet and place over high heat; reserve the processor bowl. Cook just like the samosa filling; as the mixture starts to heat and fry, shake the skillet back and forth. Cook until the mixture stays together in a blob, a little more than 2 minutes. Add the mustard seeds, cooking and tossing for another 30 seconds. Remove from the heat and return the mixture to the food processor. Add the cilantro, salt, and tamarind and, with the processor running, drizzle in just enough ice water to form a spoonable sauce, about ½ cup. Store covered and refrigerated for up to 1 week.

Good to Know

Traditional samosas are folded into a pyramid shape, but it's tough to get the shape right, so I just roll them into cylinders like egg rolls to make it easier.

Look for Madras curry powder in the glass bottles in the spice aisle. Or use any good-quality curry powder.

You can use unsweetened grated coconut for the sauce. Just place it in a small bowl, add 2 tablespoons water, cover, and microwave for 1 minute.

Don't be thrown off by the names here. Cilantro and coriander are the same plant. Cilantro is the fresh herb. Coriander is the dried spice. Some folks also call the herb fresh coriander.

CRISPY PORK MEATBALLS WITH SWEET AND SMOKY SAUCE

MAKES 24 MEATBALLS; FEEDS 6 AS AN APPETIZER

You may have seen me make some version of these meatballs before. On *Top Chef Las Vegas*, we had a challenge to make a TV dinner, and I drew *The Sopranos*. So I made Italian meatballs. Lo and behold, it won the challenge! It's a simple recipe (lots of bread is the secret to tenderness), but I switch things up here by frying the meatballs and serving them with a sweet and sour barbecue sauce. Deep-fried sausage—how can you go wrong? Think of them as Swedish meatballs made American.

1 pound boneless pork shoulder, cut into 2-inch cubes, well chilled

1 small onion, cut into ¼-inch dice, about ½ cup

6 cloves garlic, thickly sliced, about 2 tablespoons

2 tablespoons Espelette pepper or hot paprika

1 tablespoon + 2 teaspoons kosher salt

1 tablespoon Worcestershire sauce

1 teaspoon ground black pepper

1 teaspoon dried oregano

6 fresh sage leaves, chopped, or 1 teaspoon rubbed sage

3 sweet King's Hawaiian sandwich buns

1 egg

1½ cups canola oil for frying

2 cups Sweet and Smoky Barbecue Sauce (page 28)

In a large bowl, combine the pork, onion, garlic, Espelette pepper, salt, Worcestershire, black pepper, oregano, and sage. Refrigerate until well chilled; the fat should be solid and firm. Chill your meat grinder and the large die. Assemble the meat grinder and grind the pork.

Tear the buns into shreds into a food processor fitted with a metal blade. Process the buns to coarse crumbs. In a separate bowl, whisk the egg and stir in the crumbs until all the egg is absorbed. Add the ground pork and mix to combine. Pinch off 1-ounce pieces and shape into meatballs, about 1½ inches around.

Line a baking sheet with a double layer of paper towels.

Heat a large skillet over medium-high heat. Add ¼ inch oil and heat to 300°F. Working in batches, add the meatballs in a single layer and cook until brown and crispy, about 2 minutes. Flip, cook for another 2 minutes, and continue cooking and turning until browned and crispy on all sides, a total of about 6 minutes. Transfer to the baking sheet to drain. The meatballs will be a little browner than you think they should be . . . this is right; you really want a nice crust. They won't be quite cooked through when you remove them, but they will finish cooking as they cool and when you drop them in the sauce.

Heat the sauce to a low simmer in a large saucepan, drop the meatballs into the sauce, and heat through, about 5 minutes.

=== *Good to know* ===

To make classic Italian meatballs, use one-third each ground pork, veal, and beef and simmer the meatballs in tomato sauce.

RUSTIC PORK TERRINE WITH SPICY MUSTARD AND VEGETABLE PICKLES

MAKES ABOUT THIRTY ³/₈-INCH-THICK SLICES

French cooks like to use up pork scraps by making pâtés and terrines. In old French cookbooks, you see recipes for elaborate multilayer terrines topped with aspic and served on a silver platter. This one is more rustic and known as *pâté grand-mère* (your grandmother's pâté). It's easier to make at home with some coarsely ground meat, seasonings, and a loaf pan. The recipe still has several steps, but once it's done, the terrine keeps in the fridge for about a week. You can pull it out at a moment's notice and serve slices with the mustard and pickled vegetables. Or make a patty melt into a pâté melt by serving it inside a toasted cheese sandwich.

2½ pounds boneless pork shoulder

1 carrot, peeled and julienned

1 turnip, peeled and julienned

1 cup All-Purpose Pickling Liquid (page 25)

2 eggs

¼ cup half-and-half

2 tablespoons bread flour

2 tablespoons + 1 teaspoon kosher salt

1 teaspoon finely ground black pepper

¾ teaspoon ground allspice

¾ teaspoon ground cloves

¾ teaspoon freshly grated nutmeg

1 shallot, finely chopped, about 2 tablespoons

2 tablespoons whole-grain mustard

2 tablespoons Dijon mustard

2 tablespoons mayonnaise

1 tablespoon capers, minced

1 teaspoon freshly squeezed lemon juice

Pinch of ground white pepper

Pinch of sugar

1 small celery root, peeled and julienned, about 1½ cups

¼ cup celery leaves

Refrigerate the pork until well chilled; the fat should be solid and firm. Chill your meat grinder and the fine die.

In a saucepan, combine the carrot, turnip, and pickling liquid. Bring to a boil for 2 minutes, then remove from the heat and let the vegetables cool in the pickling liquid. Cover and refrigerate overnight.

Whisk the eggs in a small bowl and stir in the half-and-half. Measure the flour into a separate bowl and slowly add the egg mixture, whisking until the flour is dissolved and there are no lumps. Slow is the key here!

Cut the pork into 1-inch cubes. In a large bowl, toss the pork with the salt, pepper, allspice, cloves, and nutmeg. Pass the mixture through the chilled meat grinder fitted with the fine die. Using gloved hands, mix the shallot and the egg mixture in with the ground pork.

Heat a small skillet over medium-high heat. Pinch a small piece of the pork from the bowl and thoroughly cook. Taste and adjust the seasoning as necessary.

Preheat the oven to 300°F.

Cut a piece of cardboard to fit just inside the top of your terrine mold, wrap it in foil, and save for later use. Your terrine mold should be long and slender; the one we use is a 1½-quart (11½ by 2½ by 3 inches high) terrine mold. Another long, slender 1½-quart mold or Pullman loaf pan will work. Fill the mold or pan with very hot water and let sit for 5 minutes.

Bring 2 quarts water to a boil.

Place the pork in the work bowl of a stand mixer fitted with the paddle attachment. Mix on high speed until the meat takes on a sticky, stretchy texture like bread dough, about 1 minute. This step creates a great texture and takes it from a pork meat loaf to a terrine.

Empty the water from the terrine mold, dry, spray with nonstick spray, and line with plastic wrap, leaving a 5-inch overhang on each side. This heating of the mold makes your pork easier to compact and wrap. Spoon the pork into the mold and press down to smooth the top. Using gloved hands, poke two fingers down in five intervals through the pork; this will help eliminate air bubbles. You want the pork to be very compact in the mold. Fold the plastic wrap over the top of the pork, one side at a time, like you're wrapping a present; again, you want to eliminate all air bubbles and make a tight packet. Place the lid on the mold. Alternatively,

wrap with aluminum foil and place in a towel-lined roasting pan (you want the sides of the pan to come up almost to the top of the terrine mold). Place the roasting pan in the oven and add enough boiling water to come halfway up the side of the terrine mold. Cook to an internal temperature of 155°F, about 1½ hours. Carefully remove the terrine from the water bath and place on a cooling rack, leaving the water bath in the oven to cool so you can safely remove it from the oven.

Place the reserved cardboard on the terrine when it comes out of the oven. Using cans, weigh the top of the terrine, cool to room temperature, and then refrigerate, weighted, overnight.

Remove the weights and the cardboard and, using the plastic wrap on the long edges, carefully lift the terrine from the mold.

In a small bowl, whisk together the coarse and Dijon mustards.

In a medium bowl, stir the mayonnaise, capers, lemon juice, white pepper, and sugar to combine, and toss in the celery root and celery leaves.

Slice the terrine and serve cold or at room temperature with the pickled vegetables, celery root rémoulade, and blended mustard.

Worth Knowing

If you have some pork scraps in the kitchen, you can use the trim here instead of pork shoulder. Aim for a meat-to-fat ratio of 70 percent meat to 30 percent fat by weight.

The cooked terrine can be covered and refrigerated for up to 1 week before serving.

MOSAIC PORK TERRINE
MAKES ONE 12-OUNCE LOAF; ABOUT 18 THIN SLICES

If you've made the Rustic Pork Terrine with Spicy Mustard and Vegetable Pickles (page 204), try this next. It's a little more sophisticated—not particularly hard, but more avant-garde. Instead of grinding the seasoned meat, you cut the meat into chunks and "glue" the chunks together in a loaf shape. You need transglutaminase (meat glue) to hold the meat together and a sous-vide machine to cook the terrine. That's the avant-garde part. This terrine comes out with a beautiful cobblestone pattern that looks really cool when you slice it. The meat is seasoned with garam masala, which plays well off the pickled peaches on the side.

2 small pork tenderloins, about 2¼ pounds

3 teaspoons kosher salt

2 teaspoons garam masala

¾ teaspoon ground black pepper

About ¼ cup transglutaminase (see Good to Know)

2 peaches

1 cup All-Purpose Pickling Liquid (page 25)

Completely trim all the fat and connective tissue from the pork and discard; you should have 2 pounds cleaned, trimmed tenderloin for the terrine. Cut the pork into 1-inch cubes and spread on a baking sheet. Sprinkle with 2 teaspoons of the salt, 1 teaspoon of the garam masala, and the pepper. Toss to combine and then spread in a single layer and let sit until liquid starts beading out of the meat, about 30 minutes.

Mix the remaining 1 teaspoon salt and remaining 1 teaspoon garam masala in a small bowl.

Arrange the meat in a single layer so all sides are touching each other, and, using a sieve, dust with enough transglutaminase so you have a complete, even dusting, like a light snow. This isn't a measured amount; you just need to completely dust the top of the meat. Let rest for 10 minutes.

Using gloved hands, toss the meat to distribute the transglutaminase; it will be sticky and tacky. You must use gloves, as the transglutaminase will stick to your hands like Super Glue and create a big mess otherwise. Pack and shape the meat into a loaf; really compact it together, making sure it's all meat on meat with no air bubbles in the middle. Tear a long sheet of plastic wrap and place your loaf along the long edge. Sprinkle the masala mixture on all sides. Wrap with plastic wrap to form a tight loaf, smacking it on the counter a few times to knock out any remaining air bubbles. Wrap into a log about 3½ inches in diameter,

making sure there are no visible air bubbles, and wrap with a second piece of plastic wrap, tightly twisting the ends to close. Prick a few holes around the loaf so all air can escape and hang the loaf overnight (at least 24 hours) in the refrigerator over a bowl.

Remove the plastic wrap and vacuum-seal the meat in a plastic pouch. Cook on a rack in a 140°F water bath with an immersion circulator for 3 hours. Remove the pouch and let cool to room temperature, and then refrigerate overnight.

Peel and dice the peaches into ¼-inch pieces and place in a bowl. Bring the pickling liquid to a boil and strain it over the peaches. Cover and refrigerate overnight.

Thinly slice the terrine and serve with the pickled peaches.

Good to know

Transglutaminase is also called meat glue, and that's exactly what it does: It glues meat together in the absence of starch or other binders. It's a harmless enzyme. Look for it online at shops such as modernistpantry.com.

"PORK FAT RULES!"

—EMERIL LAGASSE

№ 8

ODDS AND ENDS

"Nothing goes to waste." I always thought that was a beautiful idea. But it's a double-edged sword. I grew up a good ol' boy in the South, and we had to eat everything to survive. In my family, bits and pieces of animals like intestines and tripe were not celebrated as some sort of high gastronomy. They were a symbol of poverty. We ate the guts because we didn't have anything else.

Sometimes those bits and pieces still carry a stigma. But I'm a firm believer in "nothing goes to waste." When I started cooking at Woodfire Grill, we got in whole hogs and I made it a point to use everything—not just to respect the animal's life but also to challenge ourselves to create something delicious out of scraps. I looked through Fergus Henderson's book, *The Whole Beast*, to get inspired, and we created all kinds of delicious dishes using pork cheeks, trotters, and crispy pig ears and tails.

I love every last morsel on a pig. But I don't want to go too far afield here with oddball cuts like pig hearts and kidneys. I do use trotters in my Pork Pho (page 129). You just can't get a rich mouthfeel in that soup from anything but gelatin, and pig's feet have that in spades. Mostly, however, these recipes stick with more familiar pork trimmings like fatback, lard, pork rinds, and ham hocks.

People say that Southerners eat lots of pork. The truth is, we use small bits of pork for flavor. Most Southern dishes are not based on a giant pork roast or a large quantity of meat, but rather include a small quantity of some flavorful piece of pork like bacon, ham hocks, or fatback. Without those little bits, a dish might be completely ordinary. Just look at my Granny's Ham and Navy Bean Soup (page 164). It's nothing special at first, but she adds fatback, which slowly melts and gives the soup a creamy texture and deep, porky taste you can't get with any other ingredient.

If you're only familiar with supermarket cuts of meat, it's okay to be trepidatious about trying the odds and ends from any animal. But, in all honesty, there's no good reason to throw away good food. Taste my Pork Osso Buco (page 213) and you'll see that pork shanks are absolutely worth eating. Or if you're tired of boring French fries, try the Pork Fat Pommes Frites (page 223). Frying in lard gives the potato another reason to live. These recipes show you that enjoying pork isn't just about grilling chops and baking ham. Every part of a pig can create truly delicious food.

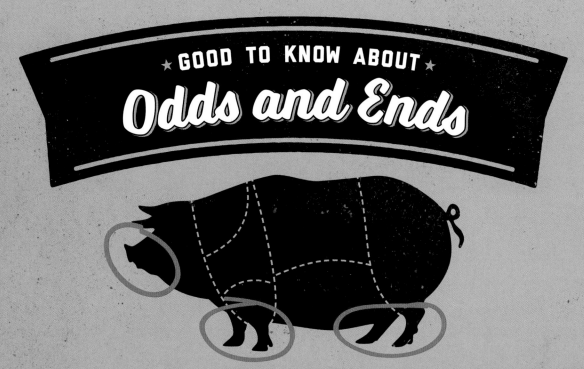

★ GOOD TO KNOW ABOUT ★
Odds and Ends

FATBACK VS. SALT PORK: These two items are made in a similar fashion: They are immersed in salt to wick away moisture, prevent bacterial growth, and make them last. The major difference is where they come from on the animal. Fatback, as the name implies, is the fat from the back of a hog, specifically the part that faces northward above the ribs. Salt pork, on the other hand, is from a fatty part of the belly—a part that's sometimes called "streak of lean" because it has one streak of lean running through all the fat. Before using it, salt pork is soaked in water to remove some of the salt, but fatback is just sliced and cooked. Traditionally, fatback is cured with the rind still intact, so that's removed first because it gets as hard as a rock during curing. The marquee difference between these two items is flavor: Salt pork has a more pronounced meaty flavor. Fatback tastes creamier with a slightly funky flavor and produces a buttery texture in whatever you're cooking. It's what differentiates the cooking of the Appalachian Mountains from the coastal South and the plantations. Fatback is what carries you through the winter when the pig has already been slaughtered, the chops have been eaten, and there isn't much meat left.

LARD: Before we had vegetable oil, pork fat was the cooking liquid of choice. Lard is still a great frying oil and one of the best baking fats. Every true-blue old-fashioned Southern lady will tell you that lard makes a more tender piecrust than butter. Just keep in mind that lard sold on shelves in grocery stores is a heavily refined product loaded with preservatives. It's so refined that, to my tongue, it doesn't taste like much of anything. I don't recommend it for the Pork Fat Pommes Frites (page 223) or any recipe in this book calling for lard. I suggest you render lard yourself at home. It's not hard. Just dice up the pork fat, put it in a heavy pot with some water, and cook it until the water boils off, leaving behind the rendered pork fat. The liquid fat should be crystal clear, and when it cools and sets up, it will be a beautiful porcelain white color. Another option is to purchase lard at a Mexican grocery store. It will be called *manteca* and have a slightly stronger flavor because it's rendered with higher heat. *Manteca* works great for frying, but it's not as good for pie dough. One other thing to know: The majority of lard is fat trimmed from the body and back of the animal. But there is a special type of lard that comes from the fat surrounding the animal's kidneys. Called leaf lard, this type is very dense and produces the finest pastry crust you can imagine. Crisco shortening was actually developed as a substitute for leaf lard.

HAM HOCKS AND SHANKS: This is the shin of the animal. The meat has a concentrated flavor, lots of connective tissue, and surrounds one or two central bones, depending on how far down the shin the piece is cut. When smoked with the skin on, it's called a ham hock, and it's used mostly for flavor in a pot of beans or greens, or for making stock. With the skin off and left raw, it's called a pork shank. You can buy pork shanks whole for dishes like German-Style Whole Roasted Pork Shank (page 215) or you can buy them crosscut for Pork Osso Buco (page 213). Either way, pig shins have a ton of flavor and a fair amount of gelatin, which is why I use them to make Ham Broth (page 27), a staple ingredient in my kitchen.

PIGSKIN: Pork rinds, cracklings, and fried pork skin are all pigskin cooked in one form or another. The differences come down primarily to method. Cracklings are pork skins that have simply been fried. The fat is scraped off the skin, maybe the skin is salted, and then it's cut into pieces and fried. Cracklings are dense and, for some people, too rich and crunchy. To make pork rinds, the skin is cooked first, which helps it puff up. This precooking step could entail boiling the skin in lard, baking it, smoking it, or drying it with low heat in a dehydrator. Each method works, but the softer the skin gets during this precooking step, the puffier it becomes once it's fried. Generally speaking, most people like their pork rinds puffy but not too airy so there's still some crunch. To get that texture, you need to dehydrate the skin like beef jerky before frying it. Then when you fry the skin, the speck of liquid left inside instantly steams and puffs up the pork rind. How much fat should be left intact on the skin? Some people say none. Some say a little. There's no right answer. To see the difference side by side, go to the meat department of a Mexican market; they sell all sorts of pork rinds and you can see the kind with some fat on the skin, the kind with a little fat, and the kind with all the fat removed. My recipe for Homemade Pork Rinds (page 224) takes the middle ground and produces what most people want—a moderately puffy, moderately crunchy pork rind.

JOWLS: Here's a widely underutilized cut. The beauty of it is how unbelievably tender it gets. The downside is that it requires lots of trimming to get to the usable part. One-third to one-half of the jowl (the side of the pig's face) consists of glands, which must be removed because they are highly perishable. But once you trim those away, hog jowls are like jewels that can be transformed into rich and creamy-tasting meat. Jowls are the basis of *guanciale*, a richer, creamier sort of pancetta. I also use jowls to make smoked Jowl Bacon (page 133), a softer, richer kind of bacon than pork belly makes. Look for hog jowls at your farmers' market. You may need to request them one Saturday and pick them up the next, but that's your best avenue for procuring this cut. Oh, and technically, the jowl is the whole side of a pig's face, while pork "cheeks" are a specific muscle cut from behind the jaw.

SAVE YOUR TRIM: I encourage you to go in with some friends or family on a whole hog from a local farmer. The meat will be fresher and tastier than anything you can buy in a store. And anytime you work with whole animals, you will get some trim. When you cut a pork chop or pork loin, there will be a piece of meat or fat that's too small here or too big there. Save all those pieces of trim. Separate them into lean meat pieces and fat pieces and then freeze them in separate zip-top bags. After a while, you'll have enough lean and fat to make sausages, burgers, or Brunswick Stew (page 218). It's just another way of using the whole animal.

PORK OSSO BUCO

FEEDS 4

I have to admit, I'm not a huge braised-meat guy. I like braises, but braised meat alone often tastes oversaturated with fat and caramelized sugar. The dark, monotone richness just kills my palate. But not this braise. Other than using pork instead of veal, this recipe is a dead-on traditional osso buco. The classic accompaniments help set the dish apart from other braises. The first is a light, fresh saffron risotto on the side and the second is a generous garnish of chopped parsley and lemon zest, known as *gremolata*. Add those two elements to these shanks, and you'll taste what I'm talking about. It's so good you might even wonder why the original version wasn't made with pork in the first place.

4 crosscut pork shanks, each about 1½ inches thick

Kosher salt and ground black pepper

⅓ cup grapeseed oil or canola oil

1 small white onion, root and stem ends trimmed, cut into eighths, about 1 cup

2 stalks celery, cut into 1½-inch pieces, about ¾ cup

1 carrot, peeled, cut into 1-inch pieces, about ¾ cup

1 cup dry red wine

3 cups Chicken Stock (page 26)

1 cup canned crushed tomatoes

8 sprigs thyme

2-inch piece cinnamon stick

⅛ teaspoon finely grated lemon zest

Preheat the oven to 350°F.

Pat the shanks dry and season both sides with salt and pepper. Heat a Dutch oven over high heat and add the oil (it should generously cover the bottom). Heat until shimmering. Add the shanks and cook until deep golden brown, about 4 minutes, then flip and cook until deep golden brown, another 2 minutes or so. Transfer the shanks to a plate, and pour off the excess fat and discard.

Add the onion, celery, and carrots to the pan, occasionally stirring to turn and cook until the vegetables are nicely caramelized on the edges, about 2 minutes. This is a hot, quick caramelization; your vegetables will get color but stay a little crunchy. Deglaze the pan with the red wine, scraping all the browned bits into the sauce. Continue to boil until the wine is reduced to a glaze, 2 to 3 minutes. Add the chicken stock, tomatoes, thyme, and cinnamon stick and stir to combine. Bring to a boil, add the shanks back to the pan in a single layer, and cover. Transfer the pan to the oven and braise for 1½ hours.

Transfer the shanks to a plate. Strain the sauce through a medium-mesh strainer into a bowl and discard the solids. Return the sauce to the pan, add the shanks, and cool to room temperature. Cover and refrigerate overnight (yeah, I know; but, honestly, the meat has to sit in the sauce overnight to develop a full flavor).

Return the shanks and sauce to the stove and heat over medium heat just to a low simmer. Stir in the lemon zest and season to taste with salt and pepper; you'll need about ½ teaspoon salt.

Continued

Good to know

Most butcher shops don't cut pork shanks across the bone. You'll have to ask them to, but they'll be impressed. You want 1-inch disks of crosscut pork shank; it's the same area as the hock. Leave the skin on for flavor, and then remove it after cooking.

When you heat any piece of meat at high temperatures, the muscle fibers constrict, squeezing out their moisture. At the same time, the connective tissues break down and dissolve in the released moisture. Allowing the meat to cool in the sauce allows the muscle fibers to reabsorb the juices they lost, so your end result will be a tender, flavorful, and juicy piece of meat. That's why resting meat—even in a braise—is so important. The ideal scenario here is to cool the meat in liquid overnight so it can rehydrate. Or cook this in the morning, let it cool, then reheat it in the evening. This is probably the way your granny cooked: Just after fixing breakfast, she'd start getting supper ready, and then let it cool all day. That way, when it's time for dinner, the food really just needs to be reheated.

GERMAN-STYLE WHOLE ROASTED PORK SHANK

FEEDS 4

I first traveled to Austria in 2003 for a culinary school "immersion experience." We visited pastry shops, cooked in restaurants, and practiced making strudel. During my free time one night, I stopped in a local bar. When I looked down the communal table, these two guys were gnawing on some kind of a giant ham hock. It looked like an entire pig's leg from the knee to the trotter. That's exactly what it was, and they called it *schweinshaxe*. Of course I ordered it. That shank was super-porky, with crunchy skin, melty fat, and soft meat underneath. The choice of side dishes was either pickles and mustard, or boiled potatoes and gravy. You couldn't order both. Being the bastard American that I am, I wanted both. This recipe satisfies that craving with a pan gravy that has some mustard swirled in. It's bar food on steroids. Invite some friends over, crack open some beers, and four grown men could eat on this for the better part of an hour.

1 cup caraway seeds

1 whole pork shank, skin on

6 bay leaves

¼ cup kosher salt

2 parsnips, cut into 2-inch chunks

4 shallots, peeled

6 cloves garlic, peeled

1 (12-ounce) bottle German-style lager

Reserve 1 tablespoon of the caraway seeds and set aside for later use. Place the whole shank, trotter end up (large or meat end down), in a large, heavy-bottomed stockpot and add enough water to cover the shank. Add the remaining caraway seeds, the bay leaves, and salt to the pot. Cover and bring to a boil over high heat. Lower the heat and simmer until the meat starts pulling away from the bone and the skin starts shrinking down and exposing the meat, about 45 minutes. This step helps tenderize the skin and loosen the connective tissues in the meat while infusing the pork with the caraway flavor.

Continued

Preheat the oven to 325°F. Using tongs, remove the shank from the pot and discard the cooking liquid. Use a towel to securely hold on to the trotter end of the bone. Starting 1 inch from the top end of the bone, slice around the shank, all the way to the bone, and remove the top 1 inch of skin and fat and discard. Move 1 inch down and score the skin all the way around, cutting through the skin and fat just to the meat. Continue to score the skin around the shank in 1-inch intervals all the way to the bottom. The skin at the large/meat end will not go all the way around the shank; that's fine, just score 1-inch slices at that point. Run your fingers through the scores, making sure you've cut all the way through the skin and fat to the meat, moving all the way around and down the shank, separating the slices accordion style. Scoring the meat will help will make the fat render properly as the skin shrinks during cooking.

Spray a roasting pan and V-rack with nonstick spray. Sprinkle the parsnips and shallots in the bottom center of the pan and fit the rack into the pan. Stand the shank up in the rack, meat end down. Slice the garlic lengthwise and wedge into the scored skin, all around and down the shank. Stuff the reserved 1 tablespoon caraway seeds between the garlic slices and sprinkle the shank lightly with salt. Add the beer to the pan and roast until the shank is deep golden brown and skin is very crispy, at least 2 hours.

Pan Gravy MAKES ABOUT 1 CUP

⅓ cup all-purpose flour

1 cup dry white wine

1 cup Ham Broth (page 27)
or beef broth

1 teaspoon kosher salt

1 tablespoon whole-grain mustard

Ground black pepper

Transfer the shank from the pan to a plate, tent with aluminum foil, and set aside. Remove the roasting rack and, using a spoon, remove and discard the roasted vegetables. Place the roasting pan over medium-high heat and, using a wooden spoon, stir the flour into the fat in the pan. Stirring constantly, cook for 1 minute over low heat to remove the raw flour taste. Stir in the wine, pork stock, and salt and bring to a boil to cook for 3 minutes, or until reduced by half. Remove from the heat and stir in the mustard. Adjust the seasoning with salt and pepper as needed. Slice the meat and serve with the pan gravy.

BLACK-EYED PEAS WITH JOWL BACON

MAKES 6 CUPS

This dish is a tribute to New Year's Day in the South. Its three main ingredients—black-eyed peas, greens, and some kind of pork—symbolize your intentions. The idea is to eat like a poor man on New Year's Day, then be rich for the rest of the year. Peas are coins, greens are dollars, and the pig is a good luck symbol. I like to use cured and smoked Jowl Bacon (page 133) because it adds more richness than Belly Bacon (page 132). The peas and bacon need to cool after stewing them, so you could do that part the day before. Then add the collards and cook the whole thing for 30 minutes before serving. Serve this alongside pan-roasted fish, or if you cook up a skillet of corn bread, you could eat this humble dish by itself as a meal.

4 cups fresh or frozen black-eyed peas

4 ounces Jowl Bacon (page 133) or other jowl bacon, cut into ¼-inch dice

2 stalks celery, cut into 3-inch chunks

1 onion, peeled, stem and root ends trimmed, quartered

1 carrot, peeled, cut into 2-inch chunks

1 dried bay leaf

4 cups packed collard greens cut into 2-inch pieces, about 6 ounces

1 cup Ham Broth (page 27), Chicken Stock (page 26), or chicken broth

2 tablespoons Pepper Vinegar (page 24)

1 tablespoon Frank's RedHot sauce

1 tablespoon butter

2 teaspoons kosher salt

In a Dutch oven, combine the peas, bacon, celery, onion, carrot, and bay leaf and add just enough water to cover the peas. Bring to a boil over high heat and, using a slotted spoon, skim and discard the scum. Cover, lower the heat so that the liquid simmers, and cook until the peas are tender, about 1½ hours. Check about 1 hour into cooking to make sure there's plenty of liquid; sometimes the peas will soak it right up, so add water as needed.

Remove the Dutch oven from the heat, and using tongs, remove the bacon and reserve. Remove the carrot, celery, and bay leaf and discard. Gently stir the peas to break up the onions into the liquid. Add the collards and broth and return to a simmer. Cover and cook for another 30 minutes. Remove the lid and cook just to evaporate some excess liquid, another 4 minutes.

Aggressively stir in the vinegar, hot sauce, butter, and salt. This will break up the peas a little, releasing some starch to make the mixture even creamier.

Good to know

You could substitute slab bacon here, but you really want the soft texture and creaminess of jowl bacon. If you use slab bacon, the end result will be more meaty and less creamy. You could also substitute fatback for the sake of creaminess, but then you'll lose the smoky flavor of the bacon. If you must, try a combo of slab bacon and fatback.

BRUNSWICK STEW

MAKES ABOUT 9 QUARTS (THAT'S A LOT, BUT IT FREEZES WELL)

Where I grew up, barbecue was always served with Brunswick stew. In Georgia, it's a side-dish stew of finely chopped meat, tomatoes, and corn. Squirrel is the traditional meat, but I like to use beef and pork or even scraps of barbecued pork such as Slow-Cooked Pork Barbacoa (page 50). I simmer the meat in a pot with water and beef bouillon cubes. I know I'll catch hell for this, but it has to be bouillon because of the MSG, which amplifies the flavors of everything else. Once the meat is falling apart, I use a potato masher to shred the meat right in the pot. Then I add tomatoes, onions, and garlic and freshly grated corn, which helps thicken the stew. A shot of spicy vinegar at the end livens everything up.

2 pounds boneless Boston butt, trimmed, cut into 1½-inch cubes (see Worth Knowing)

1½ pounds beef chuck/stew meat, cut into 1½-inch cubes

1 cup apple cider vinegar

4 beef bouillon cubes

2 tablespoons kosher salt

1 tablespoon ground black pepper

6 ears corn

2 (28-ounce) cans petite diced tomatoes

1 large Vidalia onion, finely diced, about 2 cups

5 cloves garlic, finely minced

⅓ cup Pepper Vinegar (page 24)

In a 12-quart (or larger) Dutch oven, combine the pork, beef, vinegar, bouillon, 1 tablespoon of the salt, and the pepper with 2 quarts water and bring to a boil over high heat. Decrease the heat to low, cover, and simmer until the meat is fall-apart tender, 2½ to 3 hours.

Using a small, handheld strainer or ladle, skim the scum from the top of the stew and discard. Using a potato masher, mash the meat until all the meat is shredded into the stew.

Remove the husks and silks from the corn and discard. Grate the corn on the largest holes of a box grater. You'll end up with about 3 cups corn. Add the corn, tomatoes, onion, and garlic to the stew and return to a boil. Simmer, uncovered, for 20 minutes. Remove the pot from the heat and cool to room temperature. Refrigerate, covered, overnight.

Return the pot to the stove and heat over medium-high heat to a simmer. Stir in the remaining 1 tablespoon salt and the pepper vinegar.

Worth Knowing

You can replace the raw pork with leftover pulled pork or Slow-Cooked Pork Barbacoa (page 50). Just cook the beef as above and add the cooked pork to the mixture when you add the corn.

If there's a prepared pepper vinegar that you like, you can use that instead.

Yeah, yeah, I know, another recipe that has to sit overnight. Again, this resting process is vital to a good result. It ensures the meat has an opportunity to "rehydrate." You'll notice the next morning when you pull it out of the fridge that the mixture has thickened and soaked up a lot of the juice, and it will taste better.

FATBACK FRIED CORN
FEEDS 4

Most Americans call this creamed corn. In the South, it's called fried corn, which is a better term because there's barely any cream in it. The creaminess comes from the corn itself, not the cream. I ate this dish every summer. My granny cut fresh corn from the cob with a knife. I like to grate the corn on a box grater—just like cheddar cheese—to make sure I get all the creamy corn milk from the cob. That grating method also breaks the corn into smaller pieces and releases some of its sugar and starch, which helps to sweeten and thicken the dish. Fatback is critical for flavor. It provides a savory juxtaposition to the sweetness. You could use bacon grease instead of fatback but not butter. You need some kind of pork fat for savoriness here. And the tiny amount of cream? That's only emulsifying the corn milk and corn starches so the whole mix holds together.

5 ears corn

3 ounces fatback, cut into strips

¼ cup finely minced onion

2 tablespoons heavy cream

2 teaspoons kosher salt

½ teaspoon ground black pepper

½ teaspoon freshly squeezed lemon juice

Remove the husks and silks from the corn and discard. Grate the corn on the largest holes of a box grater. You'll end up with about 2 cups corn.

Heat a large skillet over medium heat, add the fatback, and cook to render the fat. Using tongs, transfer the fried fatback to a plate and set aside. Pour the fat from the skillet into a small metal bowl. Put 2 tablespoons of the rendered fat back into the skillet and heat over medium-high heat. Add the onions and corn and cook for 30 seconds, tossing so they won't stick. Add the cream, salt, and pepper and cook, using the washing machine method (see page 21), until the corn releases its starch and thickens the mixture. When the corn basically binds into a blob, remove from the heat and stir until the bubbles subside. Stir in the lemon juice and serve immediately. For a guilty pleasure, mince the fried fatback and use as a garnish.

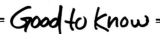

===================== Good to know =====================

This rudimentary dish only works with fresh summer corn on the cob. Frozen kernels won't cut it here because you need the corn milk from the cobs.

Get all your equipment and ingredients ready, and the actual cooking time here is less than a minute.

PORK FAT POMMES FRITES

FEEDS 6 TO 8

Some folks like skinny fries, but I prefer thick fries—with the skins on. The trick is to get those thick potato pieces fluffy on the inside and crunchy on the outside. For years, I did that by twice-frying the spuds in oil—first to fluff up the interior and the second time to crisp the exterior. Then a friend of mine turned me on to a technique used by Heston Blumenthal, a brilliant British chef. Blumenthal blanches the potatoes in salted water for the first cooking. It works great and is a far superior seasoning method than just sprinkling salt on at the end. I discovered that the seasoning is even better when you use Ham Broth (page 27) instead of salted water. For the second cooking, I like to fry the potatoes in lard. It doesn't impart much flavor, but lard does create a super-crunchy exterior.

1 quart Ham Broth (page 27)

¾ cup kosher salt

2 teaspoons Accent seasoning

4 large russet potatoes, peel on, cut into planks 1 inch wide by ½ inch thick

Lard for frying, about 2 quarts

Fine sea salt

In a large pot, bring the broth and 3 quarts water (or 1 gallon water) to a rolling boil, and add the kosher salt and Accent seasoning. Add the potatoes and cook for 5 minutes, just until tender but not fully cooked through. Using a spider or slotted spoon, transfer the potatoes to a baking sheet, cool, and refrigerate, uncovered. This step can be done a day ahead.

Line a baking sheet with paper towels and a cooling rack.

Heat the lard to 350°F in a deep fryer, or heat 2 inches of lard in a large Dutch oven. Pat the fries dry and, working in batches, fry until browned, 5 to 6 minutes. Do not overcrowd the fryer. Using a spider, transfer the fries to the prepared cooling rack and immediately sprinkle with fine sea salt.

Worth Knowing

If you have the time, do the blanching the day before and set the fries on a rack on a baking sheet in the fridge overnight, uncovered. They will dry out some and produce a crispier French fry when you drop them in the oil the next day.

I use Accent seasoning here to amplify the savory flavor of the pork. Yes, it has MSG in it, but that's what enhances the taste. If salt enhances flavors like a small guitar amp, MSG is a giant Marshall stack. Just the right amount creates the best-tasting fry you'll ever have.

HOMEMADE PORK RINDS

FEEDS 6 TO 8

When people go in on half a hog or buy skin-on pork from a farmers' market, most folks throw away the skin. That's tragic. If you know what to do with it, pork skin is absolutely delicious. This simplest way to make pork rinds is to cut the skin into 2-inch squares and then simmer them in salt water until they're soft enough to pierce with a knife. Different pig breeds have thinner or thicker skins, so the simmering time can vary from 1 to 3 hours. Then you scrape off the excess fat and dry out the skins in a dehydrator. The cooking and drying break down the cells so that when you fry the skins, the little bit of moisture left in them makes them puff up like Cheez Doodles.

2 pounds pork skin

3 tablespoons kosher salt

½ teaspoon Accent seasoning (see Good to Know)

Lard for frying

Lay the pork on your work surface, skin side down, and cut away enough of the fat so you can grasp the skin. Using a paper towel, grasp the skin and with a very sharp knife and long slicing motions, slice the fat from the skin. You can render the fat into lard and save it for another purpose.

Place the cleaned pork skins in a large pot and fill with water. Stir in the salt and Accent seasoning. Bring to a rolling boil, lower to a strong simmer, and cook until fork-tender, about 1½ hours.

Remove the rinds and pat dry; discard the cooking liquid. Cut the rinds into 2- or 3-inch pieces, depending on the final size rinds you want.

Spread in a single layer with plenty of room between the pieces on a screen mat in a dehydrator and dehydrate at 150°F until light brown, dried, and crispy, about 20 hours.

Heat lard in a deep fryer to 375°F. You need at least a 4½-inch depth of fat, as the rinds really puff up and expand; the more fat you have, the more evenly they will cook and the crispier the rinds will be. Drop a couple of rinds in at a time and fry until airy and puffy, about 45 seconds. When you drop them in, the rinds will sink and just sit there, but . . . wait for it . . . like magic, they puff and puff and puff and when they stop puffing, transfer them to a paper towel–lined baking sheet. The salt used during the boiling stage seasons these just enough. Store in an airtight container for up to 1 week.

Good to Know

You can find Accent seasoning in the salt aisle of the grocery store. It adds a delicious savory component here that you can't get with anything else except pure monosodium glutamate.

To make Pork Rind Cracker Jacks, cut the rind pieces small and then mix the fried rinds with Bacon Popcorn (page 117), Virginia peanuts, and freshly made butterscotch, which is simply brown sugar cooked in butter and mixed with cream and vanilla extract.

ACKNOWLEDGMENTS

VALERIE COMBS

My confidant and biggest fan. My better half and more than half of my brain. The voice of reason and encouragement. My wife and best friend. I find it hard to put into words how much of my success she has made possible. Simply put, I would be a fraction of the man I am today without her. I love you, Val.

THE GUNSHOW CREW

Joey Ward, Andreas Muller, Blake Morley, and every single guy and gal whom I have the pleasure of working beside each day. They have been there to help create many of the recipes in this book as well as to give honest criticism when I am not at my best. More important, they keep the dream alive each and every day while I am both home and away. Thank you.

CATHY AND KEVIN GILLESPIE

My parents have always been my biggest advocates, and without them I doubt I would have been able to dream so big. They helped from a young age to solidify my love of pork and exposed me to food from all over the world. They have suffered through several bad dishes of mine and I hope some good ones too, all with a smile. I love you both.

GENA BERRY AND CREW

Along with Gena, Crystal Leach, Rebecca Cochran, and Braden Rolland were tasked with the seemingly impossible job of translating my kitchen euphemisms and peculiar techniques into recipes that would actually come out right. They are magicians—and patient ones at that. We spent quite a few early mornings together, and yet we have still not killed one another. That has to be an accomplishment unto itself. Thank you for making this book work.

DAVE JOACHIM

The man with the not-so-easy job of listening to me talk for hours—often with too little or too much caffeine in my system—and then putting onto paper my voice and vision. He is clearly the brains behind this operation and certainly deserves a round of applause. Thanks, Dave.

ANGIE MOSIER

The only person I know with a more hectic schedule than my own. Angie is a great friend and a wonderfully talented photographer. The beautiful and striking images that grace these pages are her handiwork. I have worked with many photographers and stylists over the years, but no one captures the truth behind the food we make quite like Angie. Go Team Ginger!

ANDREWS MCMEEL TEAM

For letting me write another book and giving me so much freedom to shape it into a very personal expression. From the start, the team has been a real pleasure to work with and has helped keep this ship on course time and again. Your support has been very much appreciated.

LISA EKUS GROUP

Everyone at the Lisa Ekus Group has championed my ideas and goals from the moment we met each other. They helped bring this book to life, and if we are lucky will be able to see that happen many more times in the years to come. Great job.

MELISSA LIBBY TEAM

My friend and publicist, Melissa Libby, has been with me through thick and thin and kept me alive as the years have gone by. She and her team always do a great job supporting my crew in every endeavor. This book could not have come to life without that support. Thank you.

METRIC CONVERSIONS AND EQUIVALENTS

APPROXIMATE METRIC EQUIVALENTS

VOLUME

¼ teaspoon	1 milliliter
½ teaspoon	2.5 milliliters
¾ teaspoon	4 milliliters
1 teaspoon	5 milliliters
1¼ teaspoons	6 milliliters
1½ teaspoons	7.5 milliliters
1¾ teaspoons	8.5 milliliters
2 teaspoons	10 milliliters
1 tablespoon (½ fluid ounce)	15 milliliters
2 tablespoons (1 fluid ounce)	30 milliliters
¼ cup	60 milliliters
⅓ cup	80 milliliters
½ cup (4 fluid ounces)	120 milliliters
⅔ cup	160 milliliters
¾ cup	180 milliliters
1 cup (8 fluid ounces)	240 milliliters
1¼ cups	300 milliliters
1½ cups (12 fluid ounces)	360 milliliters
1⅔ cups	400 milliliters
2 cups (1 pint)	460 milliliters
3 cups	700 milliliters
4 cups (1 quart)	0.95 liter
1 quart plus ¼ cup	1 liter
4 quarts (1 gallon)	3.8 liters

WEIGHT

¼ ounce	7 grams
½ ounce	14 grams
¾ ounce	21 grams
1 ounce	28 grams
1¼ ounces	35 grams
1½ ounces	42.5 grams
1⅔ ounces	45 grams
2 ounces	57 grams
3 ounces	85 grams
4 ounces (¼ pound)	113 grams
5 ounces	142 grams
6 ounces	170 grams
7 ounces	198 grams
8 ounces (½ pound)	227 grams
16 ounces (1 pound)	454 grams
35.25 ounces (2.2 pounds)	1 kilogram

LENGTH

⅛ inch	3 millimeters
¼ inch	6 millimeters
½ inch	1¼ centimeters
1 inch	2½ centimeters
2 inches	5 centimeters
2½ inches	6 centimeters
4 inches	10 centimeters
5 inches	13 centimeters
6 inches	15¼ centimeters
12 inches (1 foot)	30 centimeters

METRIC CONVERSION FORMULAS

TO CONVERT	MULTIPLY
Ounces to grams	Ounces by 28.35
Pounds to kilograms	Pounds by .454
Teaspoons to milliliters	Teaspoons by 4.93
Tablespoons to milliliters	Tablespoons by 14.79
Fluid ounces to milliliters	Fluid ounces by 29.57
Cups to milliliters	Cups by 236.59
Cups to liters	Cups by .236
Pints to liters	Pints by .473
Quarts to liters	Quarts by .946
Gallons to liters	Gallons by 3.785
Inches to centimeters	Inches by 2.54

OVEN TEMPERATURES

To convert Fahrenheit to Celsius, subtract 32 from Fahrenheit, multiply the result by 5, then divide by 9.

Description	Fahrenheit	Celsius	British Gas Mark
Very cool	200°	95°	0
Very cool	225°	110°	¼
Very cool	250°	120°	½
Cool	275°	135°	1
Cool	300°	150°	2
Warm	325°	165°	3
Moderate	350°	175°	4
Moderately hot	375°	190°	5
Fairly hot	400°	200°	6
Hot	425°	220°	7
Very hot	450°	230°	8
Very hot	475°	245°	9

COMMON INGREDIENTS AND THEIR APPROXIMATE EQUIVALENTS

1 cup uncooked white rice = 185 grams
1 cup all-purpose flour = 140 grams
1 stick butter (4 ounces • ½ cup • 8 tablespoons) = 110 grams
1 cup butter (8 ounces • 2 sticks • 16 tablespoons) = 220 grams
1 cup brown sugar, firmly packed = 225 grams
1 cup granulated sugar = 200 grams

Information compiled from a variety of sources, including *Recipes into Type* by Joan Whitman and Dolores Simon (Newton, MA: Biscuit Books, 2000); *The New Food Lover's Companion* by Sharon Tyler Herbst (Hauppauge, NY: Barron's, 2013); and *Rosemary Brown's Big Kitchen Instruction Book* (Kansas City, MO: Andrews McMeel, 1998).

INDEX

PURE PORK AWESOMENESS

Andrews McMeel Publishing, LLC
an Andrews McMeel Universal company
1130 Walnut Street, Kansas City, Missouri 64106

www.andrewsmcmeel.com

15 16 17 18 19 SDB 10 9 8 7 6 5 4 3 2 1

ISBN: 978-1-4494-4707-6

Library of Congress Control Number: 2014950712

www.chefkevingillespie.com

Photography: Angie Mosier
Editor: Jean Lucas
Cover design: Brian Manley
Interior design: Holly Ogden
Art director: Tim Lynch
Production manager: Carol Coe
Production editor: Maureen Sullivan
Demand planner: Sue Eikos

Photography on pages 7, 76, and 105 by Valerie Combs.

At the time of printing, we have made every effort to contact original sources for publication permissions. If notified that an oversight has occurred, the publisher will gladly correct any omissions in future editions.

Pages vi, vii, and 13, lyrics from "Kiss a Pig" by Ray Stevens reprinted with permission from the author.

Page 146, excerpt from the poem "Hymn to Ham" by Roy Blount, Jr., reprinted with permission from the author.